101 TAX SECRETS FOR CANADIANS

Smart Strategies That Can Save You Thousands!

Also by Tim Cestnick

A Declaration of Taxpayer Rights

Your Family's Money

Death & Taxes

Winning the Education Savings Game

Winning the Estate Planning Game

The Tax Freedom Zone

Winning the Tax Game

101 TAX SECRETS FOR CANADIANS

Smart Strategies That Can Save You Thousands!

TIM CESTNICK

WILEY

John Wiley & Sons Canada, Ltd.

Library and Archives Canada Cataloguing in Publication Data

Cestnick, Timothy J., 1966-

    101 tax secrets for Canadians : smart strategies that can save you thousands.

Annual.

2007-

ISBN: 978-0-470-15978-1 (2009 edition)

    1. Tax planning—Canada—Popular works. 2. Income tax—Law and legislation—Canada—Popular works. I. Title. II. Title: One hundred and one tax secrets for Canadians.

KE5682.C47   343.7105'205   C2007-906441-5

Production Credits
Cover design: Ian Koo, Mike Chan
Interior design: Pat Loi
Typesetting: Natalia Burobina
Back cover photo: Lorella Zanetti
Printer: Tri-Graphic Printing Ltd.

John Wiley & Sons Canada, Ltd.
6045 Freemont Blvd.
Mississauga, Ontario
L5R 4J3

Printed in Canada
1 2 3 4 5 TRI 13 12 11 10 09

For tax updates, visit **www.timcestnick.com**

Contents

Dedication

I dedicate this book to my wife, Carolyn, my son Winston (my Big Guy), my daughter Sarah (my Sweet Pea), my son Michael (my Little Guy), and Ginger, our dog.

Acknowledgements

Well, here we are. Year eleven. The eleventh edition of this book, like the editions before it, is chock full of changes. It seems that the only thing certain in tax is that things will always change. The year 2008 was no exception, and this book reflects those changes.

As always, I have several colleagues to thank for making this book better than I alone could have made it over the years. I'm thinking particularly of my partner, Randy McLachlan, and some of our staff at the WaterStreet Group Inc.—a group of CAs, lawyers, CFAs, MBAs, and CFPs who all "know their stuff." Specifically, I'd like to thank Leigh Vyn, Cathy Wild, Michael White, Audrey Robinson, Jacob Kim, Jeremy Nicholls, Mike Stulp, and Shannon Cox. It's a pretty high-octane group of professionals I can turn to for assistance. I must also thank my assistant, Kathy Stradwick, for being so organized that I can't possibly miss a deadline.

I would also like to thank the staff at John Wiley and Sons Canada, Ltd. who have shown confidence in me as a tax specialist and author. In particular, I want to thank Karen Milner and Robert Harris for their enthusiasm and support in this work.

Finally, I want to thank my wife, Carolyn, for her continued willingness to not only see me locked away to work on this and other books, but to be the brunt of many embarrassing—but mostly true—stories that I write in my regular column in the *Globe and Mail*.

Tax Planning Tip Sheet

This Tax Planning Tip Sheet has been designed to simplify your tax planning. It lists all the tax-saving tips that I discuss throughout the book. Start by reading a chapter, then come back here to review the tips for that chapter. For each tip, simply answer the question: Can this apply to me? That is, even though a strategy may not currently apply to your situation, can you make changes to your life to permit you to apply the strategy? Check *Yes* next to those strategies that either apply or could apply if you were to make certain changes to your life—your Fact Situation. If you're not sure about a strategy, check *Not Sure*. Once you're done, take a closer look at the *Yes* and *Not Sure* answers. These strategies will form the foundation of your tax plan.

Don't worry about putting all the ideas into practice in a single year. It's not going to happen. Choose up to four to implement this year. Keep the other ideas on file and think about setting them in motion next year or the year after. And by the way, I highly recommend that you visit a tax pro with your Tax Planning Tip Sheet, just to make sure you're on the right track. A tax professional will help you to do things right.

Tim's Tips	Strategy	Can This Apply to Me?		
		Yes	No	Not Sure
Chapter 1.	Pre-Game Warm-Up: The Basics of Tax Planning			
1.	Avoid taxes like the plague, but don't evade them.	○	○	○
2.	Understand this thing called your marginal tax rate.	○	○	○
3.	Know the difference between a deduction and a credit.	○	○	○
4.	Always wait to trigger a tax hit.	○	○	○
5.	Pay your taxes on time, but not ahead of time.	○	○	○
6.	Think of taxes when big things happen in life.	○	○	○
7.	Dispute your assessment when you think you're right.	○	○	○
8.	Consider requesting relief when circumstances were beyond your control.	○	○	○

Tim's Tips	Strategy	Can This Apply to Me?		
		Yes	No	Not Sure
9.	Structure your affairs to avoid application of the General Anti-Avoidance Rule.	○	○	○
Chapter 2.	**Home Team Advantage: Tax Planning for the Family**			
10.	Split income for hefty tax savings, with smart strategies from A to Z.	○	○	○
11.	Consider family trusts for income splitting.	○	○	○
12.	Use an RESP to save for your child's education.	○	○	○
13.	Set up in-trust accounts properly; otherwise stick to an RESP.	○	○	○
14.	Change the ownership of a second property to multiply tax savings.	○	○	○
15.	Plan the family's move carefully to maximize tax benefits.	○	○	○
16.	Maximize the base for your childcare expenses.	○	○	○
17.	Challenge the tax collector if a disability credit is disallowed.	○	○	○
18.	Choose carefully whether to claim disability support costs as a deduction or a credit.	○	○	○
19.	Count the tax cost when splitting family assets.	○	○	○
20.	Claim the eligible dependant tax credit, if applicable.	○	○	○
21.	Avoid a tax hit when splitting retirement plan assets.	○	○	○
22.	Maximize Child Tax Benefits by applying for one-income status.	○	○	○
23.	Consider splitting real estate when dividing up assets.	○	○	○
24.	Deduct legal costs incurred to collect support payments.	○	○	○
25.	Consider preserving pre–May 1997 support agreements.	○	○	○
Chapter 3.	**Signing with the Team: Strategies for Employees**			
26.	Take non-taxable benefits as part of your compensation, with smart strategies from A to Z.	○	○	○

Tim's Tips	Strategy	Can This Apply to Me?		
		Yes	No	Not Sure
44.	Maximize your eligibility to claim capital cost allowance.	○	○	○
45.	Pay salaries to family members for a number of tax benefits.	○	○	○
46.	Recognize the special tax treatment for certain expenses.	○	○	○
47.	Deal properly with losses from your business.	○	○	○
48.	Avoid tax on loans from your company through a strategy involving your spouse and the bank.	○	○	○
49.	Understand the various "taxes" affecting your business.	○	○	○
Chapter 5.	**Bulls, Bears, and Baseball: Strategies for Investors**			
50.	Consider the impact that taxes can have on a non-registered portfolio.	○	○	○
51.	Call your profits *capital gains* and your losses *business losses*.	○	○	○
52.	Claim a capital gains reserve to spread your tax bill over time.	○	○	○
53.	Consider investing to earn eligible dividends for big tax savings.	○	○	○
54.	Think about reporting your spouse's dividends on your own tax return where possible.	○	○	○
55.	Use a tax-free savings account for a number of benefits.	○	○	○
56.	Understand the advantages and drawbacks of income trusts.	○	○	○
57.	Look at flow-through shares for a tax deduction and diversification.	○	○	○
58.	Utilize an equity monetization strategy to diversify without triggering tax.	○	○	○
59.	Consider an investment in a private company in certain situations.	○	○	○
60.	Consider an exempt life insurance policy for tax-sheltered growth.	○	○	○
61.	Learn how to use cascading life insurance to shelter investment growth from tax for years.	○	○	○

Tim's Tips	Strategy	Can This Apply to Me?		
		Yes	No	Not Sure
78.	Contribute to your RRSP instead of paying down your mortgage.	○	○	○
79.	Contribute to a spousal RRSP to equalize incomes in retirement.	○	○	○
80.	Make RRSP withdrawals during periods of no or low income.	○	○	○
81.	Consider the impact of using RRSP assets to buy a home.	○	○	○
82.	Consider the impact of using RRSP money for full-time education for you or your spouse.	○	○	○
83.	Take three steps to minimize the tax hit on RRSP withdrawals if you're planning to leave the country.	○	○	○
84.	Roll your RRSP to a RRIF or annuity to defer tax well beyond age 69.	○	○	○
85.	Defer tax on your RRIF withdrawals as long as possible.	○	○	○
86.	Split eligible pension income for tax savings as a family.	○	○	○
87.	Consider opting out of your company pension plan if you have the choice.	○	○	○
88.	Look into an Individual Pension Plan (IPP) to avoid a big tax hit when leaving your company pension plan.	○	○	○
Chapter 7.	**American League Rules: United States' Connections**			
89.	Claim a foreign tax credit when you've paid withholding taxes to Uncle Sam.	○	○	○
90.	Use the net rental income method on your U.S. rental property in most cases.	○	○	○
91.	Take two steps to minimize the tax hit on the sale of your U.S. real estate.	○	○	○
92.	Register at a casino or hotel to track gambling losses for tax savings.	○	○	○

FOREWORD:
STEPPING UP TO
THE PLATE

If you want to win the game, you've got to step up to the plate.

L et me tell you about Renee. She visited my office for the first time not long ago. And from the moment she sat in the chair across from me, even before she said a word, I assumed two things. First, I assumed that she was feeling the weight of a tax burden that only Canadians can truly understand. Second, I assumed that she was in my office to learn what she could do to fix the problem. I was only half right.

While it was true that Renee was discouraged about the level of taxes she had come to expect as a Canadian taxpayer, she wasn't in my office to learn how to lighten the load. The fact is, Renee and her husband Gerrald had already decided to leave Canada, and they were looking for me to explain the tax implications of making the move.

I couldn't resist asking the question: "Renee, before we talk about leaving the country, what is it that you and your husband have done in the last couple of years to save income taxes?" Her response didn't surprise me.

"Tim, there's really nothing we can do. We're claiming the $2,000 pension credit and a deduction for our safety deposit box fees. But big deal—these things save us next to nothing each year."

You see, this couple had come to the conclusion that their only hope for a prosperous retirement was to get up and leave Canada. Given their net worth, level of income, and our Canadian tax burden, Renee and Gerrald were convinced that they were bound to run out of retirement savings before running out of retirement.

Here was a woman who was truly discouraged. You could see it in her eyes. It was as though someone had left her a hundred kilometres from shore in a canoe without a paddle. If you had checked the dictionary on that day under the word "discouragement," you might have found the family's name with a picture of Renee and Gerrald.

Discouraged? Why Be Discouraged?

It was the day after my meeting with Renee that I learned a lesson about discouragement—and from an unlikely source, I might add. I was driving down Lakeshore Road in Oakville, Ontario, where I grew up, and I saw some kids playing baseball at Bronte Park. I grew up playing baseball at that same park, and I was reminiscing a little, so I got out of my car and walked over to the baseball diamond.

The kids were having a great time. They were laughing and cheering. They were even shouting the same insults that we used to shout as kids. You know, things like: "Batter needs a beach ball" and "Pitcher has a rubber nose, wiggles every time he throws." The point is, you couldn't find a glum face at that park.

I leaned over and asked one of the kids what the score was. A little boy smiled up at me and said, "Fourteen–nothing!" Impressed, I replied, "Fourteen–nothing, that's great, you're killing them!" "Nope," the boy corrected me. "We're losing fourteen–nothing!" Surprised me for sure. From the way the kids were laughing, you'd never know they were down for the count. I had to ask the question: "If you're losing fourteen–nothing, how come you're so happy? Why aren't you discouraged?"

I'll never forget what that little boy said next: "Discouraged? Why should we be discouraged? We haven't even been up to bat yet."

Good point. There's no use being discouraged if you haven't been up to bat.

Renee and Gerrald are like many Canadians: They had not yet stepped up to the plate.

If you want to save significant tax dollars, you've got to step up to the plate.

Get in the Game

It's frightening to think of how many Canadians have done little or nothing to reduce their income taxes. Here's what I mean: According to Statistics Canada, just 34.5 percent of taxpayers who were eligible to contribute to RRSPs in 2006 (the most recent year for which data is available) actually contributed. This means that almost two-thirds of Canadians who could have contributed did not bother. These stats don't faze you? Try this on for size: There was $330 billion in available RRSP contribution room in 2006, and Canadians contributed just $28.8 billion to RRSPs in that year. Yikes! Do you think that Canadians who are not even putting money into their RRSPs are likely to implement other, more intricate, tax planning strategies? Don't count on it.

You should realize that the odds are against you. Seventy percent of the people who read this book cover to cover will simply file the information in a drawer at the back of their mind labelled "interesting tax stuff." Thirty percent will actually use the information to create tax savings. If you've read this far, then you've shown up at the ball park. The question is, will you choose to be part of that 30 percent who actually get into the game?

Making It Easy

I've made it very easy to get into this game we call tax planning. Throughout this book, you're going to find tip after tip of good tax ideas. I want to encourage you to make note of more than simply the strategies that apply to you today. While you'll certainly want to implement those strategies, I'd like you to also consider those strategies that could apply if you were to make certain changes to your life. For example, you may otherwise choose to ignore Chapter 4 since you're not currently self-employed. But rather than bypassing the tips in that chapter, I'd like you to consider making certain changes to your life—your Fact Situation—to allow you to implement some of those strategies. Perhaps part-time self-employment makes sense for you.

This approach is the result of my belief that you can save much more tax over the long run if you're willing to make certain changes to your life. This is really the theme of my book *The Tax Freedom Zone*, which explains how to go beyond paying the least amount of tax you're currently required to pay and shows you how to pay even less. I call this moving into the Tax Freedom Zone.

At the front of this book, you'll find your own Tax Planning Tip Sheet, listing all the tax-saving tips from each chapter. As soon as you've read a chapter, flip to the front of the book and review the tips for that chapter. Ask yourself, "Can this tip apply to me?" Then check ○ *Yes*, ○ *No*, or ○ *Not Sure* for each tip. Follow me? When you've finished this book, all those *Yes* and *Not Sure* answers on your Tip Sheet will form a complete list of tax-saving measures, ready for your use or further research. A visit to a tax pro will often make sense once you've finalized your list.

There's one more thing to keep in mind: Tax rules are always changing. The advice I offer here is current as of August 31, 2008. A good tax pro will be able to bring you up to date on late-breaking developments from the Department of Finance or the Canada Revenue Agency (CRA).

Calling All Hitters

Have you heard of Charlie Grimm? Charlie was a baseball manager—he used to manage the Chicago Cubs. There's a story about a scout who called Charlie up one day. The scout was so excited he could hardly utter the words. "Charlie! I've just discovered the greatest young pitcher I have ever seen! I watched him pitch a perfect game. He struck out every man who came to bat. Twenty-seven stepped up to the plate, and twenty-seven struck out! Nobody even hit a foul ball until the ninth inning. I've got the kid right here with me. Do you want me to sign him?"

"No," replied Charlie. "Find the kid who hit the foul ball in the ninth inning and sign *him*. I'm looking for hitters."

Charlie Grimm was looking for hitters. And so am I. With these pages, I'm going to get you off the bench and put a bat in your hands.

But remember: If you want to win the tax game, you've got to step up to the plate.

CHANGES MAKING THE HEADLINES

In the world of tax, change is the only constant.

I f you're looking for a quick summary of what's changed in Canadian tax rules in the past year, you've come to the right place. Here's a summary of key changes and proposed changes up to August 31, 2008. Some of these were introduced in the federal budget of February 26, 2008, but some changes relate to press releases, government pronouncements, or court cases. Keep in mind that proposed measures are generally enforced by the Canada Revenue Agency (CRA) even before they're passed into law.

Topic	What's New
Tax Calculations	
Federal tax rates	Federal tax brackets for 2008 were adjusted upward by 1.9 percent as the result of indexing to inflation. The brackets for 2008 are: $37,885 ($37,178 in 2007), $75,769 ($74,357 in 2007), and $123,184 ($120,887 in 2007). In addition, the lowest tax rate decreased from 15.5 percent to 15 percent for 2008.
Basic personal credit	The basic personal amount for 2008 remained at $9,600 (the same as 2007). This amount is to be increased in 2009 to $10,100. The basic personal credit is 15 percent of this amount for 2008.

Canada Employment Credit	The 2006 federal budget introduced the Canada Employment Credit—a non-refundable tax credit—in recognition of work-related expenses incurred by employees. The maximum amount on which the credit is calculated remains at $1,000 for 2008, to a maximum of the amount of employment income for the year. Think of this credit as a boost to the basic personal amount for those who are employed.
Other personal credits	The following personal credits for 2008 were indexed to inflation and are based on the following amounts: Spouse and eligible dependant amounts—$9,600 ($8,929 for 2007), child tax credit—$2,038 ($2,000 for 2007), age amount—$5,276 ($5,177 for 2007), disability amount—$7,021 ($6,890 in 2007), supplement to disability amount—$4,095 ($4,019 in 2007), and caregiver and infirm dependants amounts—$4,095 ($4,019 in 2007). The actual credit in each case is 15 percent of the respective amount for 2008. Also new for 2007 and later years: The threshold above which a dependant's income will cause a clawback of the spousal and eligible dependant amounts has been eliminated so that the clawback applies from the first dollar of the dependant's net income.

Family Care

Canada Child Tax Benefit	The amount of the Canada Child Tax Benefit (CCTB), National Child Benefit (NCB) Supplement, and the income threshold at which these benefits are clawed back was increased effective July 1, 2008. The basic CCTB base amount has been increased to $1,307 ($1,283 in 2007) for the first child, and the NCB Supplement has been increased to $2,025 ($1,988 in 2007) for the first child. See Tip 22 for more.
Medical Expense Tax Credit	As a matter of policy, the federal government regularly reviews the list of expenses that are eligible for the medical expense tax credit (METC). The 2008 federal budget expanded the list of eligible medical expenses to include:

- altered auditory feedback devices for the treatment of a speech disorder;

- electrotherapy devices for the treatment of a medical condition or a severe mobility impairment;

- standing devices for standing therapy in the treatment of a severe mobility impairment;

- pressure pulse therapy devices for the treatment of a balance disorder;

- expenses related to the training and care of a service animal to assist individuals with autism or epilepsy.

Our tax law will also be revised to clarify that drugs, medications, vitamins, etc., that are purchased without a prescription will not be eligible for the METC. Some recent court decisions had sided in favour of the taxpayer, contrary to the intention of the Department of Finance.

Disability Measures

Child Disability Benefit

The Canada Child Tax Benefit has three components: the CCTB base benefit, the National Child Benefit (NCB) supplement, and the Child Disability Benefit (CDB). The CDB is payable in respect of children in low- and modest-income families who meet the eligibility criteria for the disability tax credit. The maximum annual CDB is increased to $2,395 ($2,351 in 2007). The phase-out of CDB benefits will begin at $37,885 in 2007 ($37,178 in 2007), at the rate of two percent of income over that amount, for one eligible child.

Registered Disability Savings Plan

The 2008 federal budget amended the Registered Disability Savings Plan (RDSP) rule that provides for a mandatory collapse of the plan if the beneficiary ceases to be eligible for the disability tax credit (DTC). Previously, the rule would have required a collapse of the RDSP where the beneficiary rescinds his or her DTC certification (even though he/she may still suffer an impairment that would make him/her eligible to claim the DTC). The new rule provides instead for a mandatory collapse of the plan only where the beneficiary's condition has factually improved to the extent that the beneficiary no longer qualifies for the

DTC. This change will not affect a plan holder's ability to voluntarily collapse the plan. The measure will be effective for 2008 and subsequent taxation years.

Employment Measures

Automobile limits

The ceiling on the cost of a vehicle for purposes of capital cost allowance remains at $30,000 plus federal and provincial taxes for 2008; the limit on deductible lease costs remains at $800 per month plus taxes, and the limit on interest deductions on amounts borrowed to buy a vehicle remain at $300 per month. The limit for deductibility of tax-exempt allowances paid by employers to employees is increased to $0.52 ($0.50 in 2007) per kilometre for the first 5,000 kilometres, and $0.46 ($0.44 in 2007) per kilometre thereafter ($0.56 and $0.50 respectively for the Yukon, Northwest Territories, and Nunavut). Finally, the general prescribed rate to determine the taxable benefit relating to the personal portion of vehicle operating expenses paid by employers is increased to $0.24 ($0.22 in 2007) per kilometre for 2008. See Tips 31 and 32 for more.

Northern Residents Deduction

For those individuals that find themselves living in pre-scribed areas of northern Canada for at least 6 months each year there was good news from the government contained in the 2008 federal budget. As a resident of one of these prescribed areas, the amount that you are permitted to claim as a deduction has been increased by 10 per cent. Previously, each member of a household could claim up to $7.50 per day as a deduction. As of 2008, this amount has been increased to $8.25. This could mean a deduction of just over $3,000 for the year. This applies to 2008 and subsequent tax years.

Retirement Issues

RRSP and pension limits

The 2005 federal budget introduced changes that increased contribution limits to registered pension plans (RPPs), registered retirement savings plans (RRSPs), and deferred profit sharing plans (DPSPs). For money purchase RPPs, the annual contribution limit for 2008 through 2010 respectively is as follows: $21,000, $22,000, and indexed to inflation thereafter. For defined benefit RPPs, the maximum pension benefit per year of service for 2008 is $2,333, $2,444 for 2009, and indexed thereafter. RRSP annual contribution limits for 2008 through 2011 respectively are: $20,000, $21,000, $22,000, indexed thereafter.

RRSP Maturity Age   For the last several years, Registered Retirement Savings Plans (RRSPs), Registered Pension Plans (RPPs), and Deferred Profit Sharing Plans (DPSPs) had been scheduled to mature by the end of the year in which the RRSP annuitant, or RPP or DPSP member, turns 69 years of age. The 2007 federal budget increased this age to 71 for the 2007 and subsequent calendar years. As a transitional measure, the government will waive the minimum registered retirement income fund (RRIF) withdrawal rules in 2007 and 2008 for RRIF owners turning 70 or 71 in 2007, or 71 in 2008.

Life Income Funds   The 2008 Federal Budget proposed adding more flexibility for withdrawals from life income funds (LIFs), which was implemented by amending the Pension Benefits Standards Regulations, 1985. A Department of Finance News Release, dated May 8, 2008, stated that the amendments provide for the following changes for the withdrawal of funds from LIFs:

• Individuals 55 or older with total holdings in federally regulated locked-in funds of up to $22,450 will be able to wind up their accounts or convert to a tax-deferred savings vehicle with no maximum withdrawal limit, such as a Registered Retirement Income Fund or a Registered Retirement Savings Plan. The threshold for small holdings will increase with the average industrial wage.

• Individuals 55 or older will be entitled to a one-time conversion of up to 50 per cent of LIF holdings into a tax-deferred savings vehicle with no maximum withdrawal limit.

• All individuals facing financial hardship (e.g. low income, high disability or medical-related costs) will be entitled to withdraw up to $22,450 a year. This maximum will also increase with the average industrial wage.

Investment Measures

Tax-Free Savings Account (TFSA)

The 2008 federal budget introduced a new Tax-Free Savings Account (TFSA). Starting in 2009, Canadian residents age 18 or older will be entitled to contribute up to $5,000 annually (indexed after 2009) to a TFSA. The contributions will not be deductible (as with an RRSP), but income earned in the TFSA will be tax free. In addition, there will be no tax on any amounts withdrawn from a TFSA. The contribution room will be cumulative and can be carried forward indefinitely. Any amounts withdrawn can be added to the contribution room available, so that you can "re-contribute" at a later date those amounts withdrawn. See Tip 55 for more on TFSAs.

Taxation of Dividends

In the fall of 2007, the Department of Finance announced reductions to general corporate taxes payable, to 15 per cent through 2012. As a result, the 2008 federal budget proposed to bring the dividend gross-up and dividend tax credit (DTC) in line with the reduced level of general corporate income tax payable. On an "eligible divided," the gross-up amount will be as follows: 2008 and 2009—18.9655%, 2010—17.9739%, 2011—16.4354%, later years—15.0198%. And, on an "eligible dividend," the DTC will be as follows: 2008 and 2009—45%, 2010—44%, 2011—41%, and later years—38%.

Mineral Exploration Tax Credit

The 2006 federal budget re-introduced the mineral exploration tax credit for flow-through share agreements entered into on or after May 2, 2006 and before April 1, 2007. This credit has been extended to flow-through share agreements entered into before April 1, 2009.

Foreign Investment Entities and Non-Resident Trusts

It has been a few years since the first introduction of new rules around Foreign Investment Entities and Non-Resident Trusts. Those proposed rules have been revised a few times. The rules are intended to ensure that Canadian residents do not defer tax on investment income earned outside of Canada through foreign entities and trusts. The draft rules are now effective for tax years after 2006. The details of these proposed rules are beyond the scope of this book, but you'll find a good summary of them at PricewaterhouseCoopers' website: www.pwc.com/ca/taxmemo. Look for the tax memos: "New Rules for Foreign Investment Entities" and "New Rules for Non-Resident Trusts" (February 2007). The government reconfirmed, in the 2008 federal budget, its intention to enact the changes introduced in the past.

Specified Investment Flow-Through Entities

"Specified Investment Flow-Through" trusts and partnerships (SIFTs)—publicly traded income trusts (including business and energy trusts) and partnerships—are subject to a tax (SIFT Tax) on their distributions of what are termed "non-portfolio earnings". (For SIFTs that existed on October 31, 2006, the SIFT Tax will not apply until 2011, as long as their growth does not exceed certain limits.) The rate of the SIFT Tax is made up of two components. The first is equal to the federal general corporate tax rate, and will be reduced in step with the reduction of that federal corporate tax rate to 15 per cent by 2012. The second component is an additional tax in lieu of provincial tax: its rate is currently 13 per cent, which approximates the average provincial corporate income tax rate. Revenues from the additional rate are to be distributed to provincial governments. The 2008 federal budget proposed that for a SIFT's 2009 and subsequent taxation years the provincial component of the SIFT Tax (and thus the provincial share of the resulting revenue) be based instead on the general provincial corporate income tax rate in each province in which the SIFT has a permanent establishment. This will ensure that the rate of the SIFT Tax is the same as the federal-provincial tax rate for large public corporations with the same activities.

Charitable Issues

Donation of Exchangeable Securities

In recent federal budgets, measures were introduced that eliminate the capital gains tax liability that could arise upon the donation of certain publicly traded securities to a registered charity or other qualified donee. There has been a problem, however, for those who have wanted to donate securities that are not publicly traded, but are exchangeable into securities that would qualify for the special capital gains treatment. Individuals in this situation would not, in the past, receive the preferential capital gains treatment when exchanging their units into the publicly traded security, even if those securities were then donated to charity. The 2008 federal budget fixed this inequity for owners of exchangeable securities. Starting February 26, 2008, the existing capital gains exemption on the donation of publicly traded securities was extended to also include the capital gain realized on the exchange of unlisted securities (that are shares or partnership interests) for publicly traded securities. This exemption will apply where: (1) The unlisted securities included, at the time of issue, a condition allowing the holder to exchange them for the publicly traded securities, (2) the publicly traded securities are the only consideration received on the exchange, and (3) the publicly traded securities are donated to a registered charity or other qualified donee within 30 days of the exchange.

Private Foundations: Excess Corporate Holdings

In order to limit the potential for an individual who is connected to a private foundation to use the foundation's shareholdings for his own benefit, the 2007 federal budget introduced an "excess corporate holdings" regime which can require a foundation to divest itself of a certain number of the shares in question. Specifically, where a foundation and certain relevant persons together own more than 20 per cent of a class of shares (other than "entrusted shares"), the foundation is required to divest itself of enough shares to bring the total owned by the foundation and relevant persons to 20 per cent or less. The 2008 budget proposed to exempt from this regime certain holdings of shares that are not listed on a designated stock exchange and that were held on March 18, 2007. The 2008 budget also introduced certain other technical amendments related to entrusted shares.

Student Issues

RESP Changes

The 2007 federal budget removed some of the limits and restrictions surrounding Registered Education Savings Plans (RESPs). For instance, the lifetime funding limit amount has been increased to $50,000 with the annual contribution limits being removed. In Budget 2008 the government is going a step further and has increased the length of time that contributions can take place, the age of the beneficiaries and the longevity of the plan itself by 10 years. RESPs can now be held open for a maximum of 35 years (up from 25 years). Plans will terminate in the year that includes the 35th anniversary of the plan. Currently, contributions are not permitted for beneficiaries who are 21 years or older, but the 2008 federal budget increased this to age 31. Finally, the budget provided more flexibility for beneficiaries to receive Educational Assistance Payments (EAPs) from an RESP by proposing a six-month grace period during which EAPs can be received after ceasing to be enrolled in a qualifying program, provided the payment would have qualified under the rules for EAPs if it had been made prior to enrollment ceasing.

Administrative Issues

Tracking vehicle use

The 2008 federal budget announced that, starting in 2009, a logbook that is maintained for a sample period during the year will be sufficient evidence to support motor vehicle expenses and taxable benefit calculations.

Sale of Property by Non-Residents

The rules surrounding the sale of "taxable Canadian property" (TCP) by non-residents have been amended for years after 2008. TCP includes Canadian real estate among other assets that our government reserves the right to tax when sold by non-residents. The changes to the rules will: (1) exempt certain dispositions from the withholding tax and clearance certificate requirements if the gain on the sale will not be taxable in Canada due to a tax treaty, (2) expand the circumstances in which purchasers are exempt from the withholding requirements, and (3) eliminate the need for non-residents to file a Canadian tax return in certain situations when no tax is payable to the Canada Revenue Agency.

Withholding tax on interest

Bill C-28 which received royal assent on December 14, 2007 eliminates withholding tax on interest paid or credited to a non-resident lender with whom the taxpayer deals at arm's length (i.e. a foreign financial institution), except on "participating debt interest" as defined in the Income Tax Act. And so, withholding tax still applies to interest payments made to non-resident lenders who deal non-arm's-length to the Canadian taxpayer borrowing the money, regardless of the terms of the loan.

Business Measures

General Corporate Tax Rate and Surtaxes

Previous announcements by the government will reduce the general corporate income tax rate (after the 10 percent provincial abatement) to 18.5 percent from 21 percent, by 2011. Specifically, the rate will be reduced to the following rates on January 1st of the following years: 20.5 percent (2008), 20 percent (2009), 19 percent (2010), 18.5 percent (2011). This reduction does not apply to income already eligible for the small business tax rate. Also, the elimination of the 1.12 percent corporate surtax took place January 1, 2008 for all corporations (as announced in the 2006 federal budget).

Small Business Limit and Tax Rate

The 2006 federal budget did two things to help small businesses: (1) it increased the amount of income eligible for the small business tax rate from $300,000 to $400,000 effective January 1, 2007, and (2) the 12 percent federal tax rate that applies to that income will be reduced by one percent (to 11.5 percent for calendar 2008, and 11 percent effective January 1, 2009).

Enhanced Capital Cost Allowance

In Budget 2007 the federal government provided some assistance to the manufacturing sector by making changes to the way that certain machinery and equipment is depreciated through capital cost allowance (CCA). Previously this machinery was only eligible for a 30 per cent declining balance CCA rate (Class 43). The 2007 budget changed this to a 50-per cent straight-line CCA rate effective through the end of 2009. The 2008 federal budget proposed a transition period that will allow favourable CCA rates to be in place for an additional three years. This will include a one-year extension of the 50% straight line rate followed by a two-year period where the accelerated CCA will be applied at a 40 per cent rate followed by a 30 per cent rate, both on a declining basis. As an example, machinery purchased in 2009 will be subject to the 50 per cent straight-line CCA treatment. Machinery purchased in 2010 will be eligible for a 50-per cent declining balance rate in the first year, 40 per cent in the second year and 30 per cent in the third. Budget 2008 also proposed changes to the CCA rates for "green" technologies and the further alignment of rates for the "useful life" of some classes of equipment such as railway locomotives and carbon dioxide pipelines.

Remittance of Source Deductions

In 2003 Canada Revenue Agency (CRA) launched a "pilot project" in an attempt to deal more fairly with late remittances from employers. Instead of levying a straight 10 per cent penalty on all late filing, that project introduced a graduated program where penalties ranged between 3 and 10 per cent depending on the length of time that the remittance was late. The "pilot project" has been successful and has achieved the goal of a more fair treatment of these penalties. The 2008 federal budget proposed that the graduated penalty program be enacted permanently. The changes will be in effect for remittances on or after February 26, 2008. Finally, the budget proposed that remittances which are required to be deposited directly with a financial institution will be considered remitted to a financial institution if received by CRA at least one full day prior to the due date (this was not the case in the past; CRA insisted that remittances be made to the financial institution).

Business Number Initiative

The business number or "BN" is used as a main identifier by CRA to track information relating to a business or organization. It is also used to determine the eligibility for government programs. As part of the government's initiatives to reduce the paper burden on business, budget 2008 proposed to broaden the scope of what BN related information can be shared with BN partners in an attempt make government interaction at different levels more streamlined and efficient.

Scientific Research and Experimental Development

The 2008 budget proposed to help small and medium-sized businesses by enhancing some aspects of the SR&ED program. The following changes will be made:

- The expenditure limit on which enhanced 35 per cent investment tax credits (ITCs) can be claimed will be increased from $2 million to $3 million;

- The upper limit of the phase-out range for prior-year taxable income will be increased to $700,000 from $600,000;

- The upper limit of the phase-out range for prior-year taxable capital will be increased to $50 million from $15 million;

- Certain salaries or wages incurred by the taxpayer in respect of SR&ED carried on outside Canada will now be recognized for ITC purposes. This will apply to SR&ED carried on outside Canada after February 25, 2008.

Court Decisions

General Anti-Avoidance Rule

In the case *MacKay* et al. (2008 FCA 105) the Federal Court of Appeal (FCA) overturned the decision of the Tax Court of Canada (TCC) and found that the General Anti-Avoidance Rule (GAAR) denied the taxpayers' deductions for a partnership's $6 million loss. In *MacKay*, the transactions were part of a real-estate purchase where a partnership was created and used to transfer losses to its partners. The TCC agreed with the taxpayers' position that the primary purpose of each transaction was to enable the taxpayers to complete the acquisition of a shopping centre, and not to obtain tax losses. Therefore, the transactions were not "avoidance transactions" under the Income Tax Act, and GAAR did not apply. In reaching this conclusion, the TCC said that the avoidance transaction analysis is not a results-based one that focuses on the tax benefit, but rather focuses on the primary purpose of each individual transaction. The FCA disagreed and suggested that the existence of a *bona fide* non-tax purpose for a series of transactions does not preclude the possibility that the primary purpose of one or more transactions within the series is to obtain a tax benefit. The FCA found that the primary purpose of the subset of the series of transactions in *MacKay* was to obtain a tax benefit, being the transfer of tax losses to the partners. And so, the FCA seems to have adopted a results-oriented approach in its analysis of GAAR, in contrast to the approach that the Supreme Court of Canada has established. The FCA's conclusion that GAAR applied in *MacKay* creates uncertainty for taxpayers. The decision implies that whenever a taxpayer carries out tax planning in a bona fide commercial transaction (which the SCC in *Canada Trustco* (2005 SCC 54) said a taxpayer is entitled to do), the only defence against GAAR may be to show that "no abuse" took place.

Compensation Related to a Non-Compete Provision

In *RCI Environnement Inc.* (2007 CCI 647), the Tax Court of Canada (TCC) recently held that compensation for the termination of a non-compete agreement was taxable as the disposition of eligible capital property (under section 14 of the Income Tax Act). RCI had purchased certain waste management assets from a seller, who agreed not to compete with RCI in the greater Montreal area. Later, the seller (who had been acquired by a U.S. company) made a $12 million payment to RCI to get out of the non-compete provision. RCI argued that the amount was a windfall, and was not taxable since the provision had never intended to bind the U.S. company. The TCC decided that the amount was paid to RCI not for the termination of a contract entered into in the normal course of business, but for relinquishing the protection of goodwill, a capital asset, and it was capital in nature. The TCC concluded that the taxpayers' rights under the non-compete agreement were property, although it said that section 14 only required a disposition, not property. At any rate, the amount was taxable to the taxpayer.

Payments to a Non-Resident Holding Company

In the case *Prévost Car* (2008 TCC 231), the Tax Court of Canada held that a Dutch holding company (Holdco) was the beneficial owner of dividends paid by a Canadian operating company (Opco) and thus was entitled to the benefits of the Canada–Netherlands tax treaty—and more specifically, a reduced withholding tax rate of just 5 per cent on dividends paid to the Dutch Holdco. The ultimate corporate shareholders were UK and Swedish residents, and the Canada Revenue Agency tried to argue that the UK and Swedish residents were the true beneficial owners of the dividends, and therefore the Netherlands treaty and the reduced withholding tax rate should not apply. The CRA lost this battle. But it is worth remembering that CRA's current attack on royalties and interest payments received by non-resident holding companies will test *Prévost's* breadth of application.

Denial of Deductions in the United States

The Third Circuit of the US Court of Appeals in *Swallows Holding, Ltd.* (no. 06-3388, February 15, 2008) recently affirmed the denial of deductions to a foreign corporation for years for which the corporation failed to timely file US income tax returns. This newly added support by a Court of Appeals decision will reinforce the IRS's practice of denying US tax deductions and credits otherwise allowable to a Canadian corporation that fails to file its US return on time.

Promises of the Canada Revenue Agency

In the case *Liddar* (2007 FCA 323), the CRA first agreed and then refused to waive interest and penalties owing on a tax assessment. The Federal Court of Appeal (FCA) ordered that the taxpayer's request for a waiver of interest and penalties be sent back to the CRA for reconsideration. That is, the taxpayer won this case. *Liddar* is very favourable to taxpayers because it limits the circumstances in which the CRA can successfully refuse to act on a promise to or an agreement with a taxpayer. If the CRA makes a deal with respect to collections and promises or agrees to waive interest or penalties (or to refund them once paid), it appears that the courts are prepared to effectively enforce those promises and agreements. Liddar also highlights the importance of documenting any such agreement with the CRA.

Scholarships to the Children of Employees

In the case *DiMaria* (2008 TCC 114), the Tax Court of Canada (TCC) held that a $3,000 scholarship paid by an employer under its higher education award program to an employee's child was not a taxable benefit to the employee, but rather should be included in the income of the student (to take this a step further, the student may have to report the income, but scholarships are no longer taxable to students, and therefore an offsetting deduction would end up causing the scholarship to be tax-free). The case appears to be the first to come before the court in which the employee and the student were different taxpayers. The CRA did admit (in an advance tax ruling) that a payment may be taxable as a scholarship or bursary to the student if the CRA is satisfied that objective selection criteria focused on the student's scholastic achievement. The CRA said that the selection criteria must exceed the minimum entrance requirements for most post-secondary institutions; otherwise, any dependant could qualify. The CRA also said that an employer must limit the number of scholarships. The CRA said that the presence of these factors ensures that the student's merit, not the employee's relationship with the employer, is the overriding criterion for the scholarship award. The CRA ultimately said that the scholarship arrangement offered by Dow Chemical Canada Inc. (DiMaria's employer) did not meet these tests. The TCC disagreed. The TCC concluded that the award was a scholarship and should have been included in the son's income. The court said that the criteria for granting a scholarship should be determined by its donor, and the CRA should not impose its view of eligibility. Furthermore, the Act does not require that any particular academic threshold be met (the CRA suggested otherwise).

Contingent Liabilities on Marriage Breakdown

A recent non-tax court decision, *Stein* (2008 SCC 35) will have an impact on the division of assets and liabilities when a marriage breaks down. In this case, the Supreme Court of Canada (SCC) ruled 6 to 1 that dividing a tax-shelter-related contingent liability equally between ex-spouses was fair. Mr. and Mrs. Stein separated in 2003 after a 12-year marriage, during which Mrs. Stein cared for their two children and the home and Mr. Stein was the sole income earner. The divorce settlement equally divided family assets worth $1.7 million; Mrs. Stein was awarded support based on Mr. Stein's annual income of $200,000. Mrs. Stein was granted ownership of the family home, and Mr. Stein kept his interest in the family business, worth $650,000. The SCC stated that it seemed self-evident that both assets and debts must be considered to ensure fairness on the marriage breakdown. The SCC noted that the term "family debt" evolved in jurisprudence in recognition that spouses jointly contribute to the accumulation of assets and debt, and therefore debts (even those that are contingent or uncertain at the time of separation) should be shared.

Losses Treated as Capital Losses

In the case *Joseph Azrak v. The Queen* (2008 DTC 4581) the taxpayer attempted to claim losses from trading in stocks as business losses rather than capital losses. The taxpayer's appeal was dismissed. Although the taxpayer, like millions of Canadians, purchased shares with a view to making a profit, there was no evidence to show that his buying and selling of shares was a business or commercial venture or that it was speculative in nature. The short period of time during which the taxpayer's shares were held was not, by itself, the determining factor in this case. The court sided with CRA on this one. This serves as a reminder that capital or income treatment of transactions is a tricky matter. See Tip 51 for more.

PRE-GAME WARM-UP:
THE BASICS OF TAX PLANNING

Only fools come to bat without first tying their shoes.

1

To this day, I can still remember my first season—in fact, my first game—in the Oakville Minor Baseball Association. I was six years old, a pretty good hitter for a rookie, and knew next to nothing about running the bases. My first time at bat, I belted a line drive into left field, then proceeded to run as fast as I could directly to third base. I can still remember the umpire showing me which way to run after hitting the ball.

Eventually, I became a pretty good base stealer—but only after I learned the basics. Once I had the basics down, my playing improved to a whole new level. And so will yours.

In this chapter, we're going to look at the basics of the tax game.

Playing by the Rules

Tim's Tip 1: **Avoid taxes like the plague, but don't evade them.**

There's a big difference between avoiding taxes and evading them: One's okay; the other's a definite no-no.

Tax avoidance simply involves structuring your affairs legally so that you're paying less tax than you might otherwise pay. You do, after all, have the right to pay the least amount of tax the law will allow. Avoiding tax could involve using loopholes, which are inadvertent errors in the *Income Tax Act*, but more commonly will involve using provisions of the law to your advantage.

Tax evasion, on the other hand, is an attempt to reduce your taxes owing or increase refundable credits by illegal means, such as making false statements about your income or deductions, or destroying records. Trust me, if the Special Investigations Unit of the Canada Revenue Agency (CRA) catches you in the act of evasion, you're in for a rough ride. Here's what happens: You'll not only have to make good on the taxes you've evaded, but you'll face penalties equal to 50 percent of those taxes. In addition, you'll face interest charges from the year of the crime until the day you pay those taxes and penalties owing. To top it off, you could face criminal charges filed by CRA that may result in additional criminal penalties of 50 to 200 percent of the taxes evaded and up to five years in prison. Yikes!

If you've been evading taxes and haven't yet been caught in the act, there's some good news for you. The tax collector has said, in Information Circular 00-1R, that if you come forward and correct deficiencies in your past tax affairs—through what's called a voluntary disclosure—you'll be given a break. No penalties will be levied, and no prosecution will be undertaken. Folks, this is not such a bad deal. And by the way, once CRA has begun an audit or enforcement procedure, you can forget about making a voluntary disclosure—it's too late at that stage.

TO MAKE A LONG STORY SHORT:

- Tax avoidance involves legally structuring your affairs to take advantage of provisions or loopholes in our tax law.

- Tax evasion is a no-no. It can bring civil and criminal penalties, and can mean up to five years in prison.

- A voluntary disclosure may be your best option to come clean if you've been evading taxes.

Knowing the Numbers Game

Tim's Tip 2: Understand this thing called your marginal tax rate.

You're going to hear a lot about marginal tax rates as you browse the pages of this book—and for good reason. Your marginal tax rate is used to calculate all kinds of things. In particular, if you want to know how much tax a deduction is going to save you, or what the after-tax rate of return on your investments happens to be, you'll need to know your marginal tax rate.

Quite simply, your marginal tax rate is the amount of tax that you'll pay on your last dollar of income. Suppose, for example, you're living in Ontario and you earned $65,000 in 2008. How much more tax do you suppose you'd pay if you earned one more dollar of income? The answer is 32.98 cents. You'd keep just 67.02 cents for yourself. In other words, your marginal tax rate is 32.98 percent. Similarly, if your marginal tax rate happens to be 26 percent, then 26 percent of the last dollar you earn will disappear in taxes. For a list of marginal tax rates by province, check out the tables starting on page 296.

You're going to discover that marginal tax rates really depend on three things: your province of residence, your level of income, and the type of income earned.

> **Caution!**
>
> A voluntary disclosure (VD) will allow you to come clean if you haven't exactly been honest, but it may open a can of worms, too. You see, a VD could lead CRA to take a hard look at your financial affairs, including bank and brokerage account transactions. Sure, a VD may be your best bet if you're talking about significant tax dollars, but a simple adjustment request (using Form T1-ADJ) to your prior years' tax returns may be a better option if the dollars are minimal. Talk to a tax pro before deciding which way to go!

Basically, the higher your level of income, the higher the percentage of that income the tax collector is going to take. Further, Canadian dividends and capital gains are taxed at lower marginal rates than interest, salaries, and other types of income.

*J*udi and Ned are shareholders in a small business, Money Inc., located in Manitoba. In 2008, Judi received a salary of $75,000, while Ned earned $40,000. In addition, each received ineligible dividends of $5,000 from the company. Who do you think had the higher marginal tax rate on the salary? Good guess. Judi did. In fact, Judi's marginal tax rate on her salary in 2008 is 43.40 percent in Manitoba, while Ned's marginal rate is just 34.75 percent. As for the dividend income, Judi will face a marginal tax rate of 33.64 percent, and Ned will pay 22.83 percent (see the tables starting on page 294).

TO MAKE A LONG STORY SHORT:

- Your marginal tax rate is generally the most important tax figure for you to know.

- Simply put, it's the amount of tax you'll pay on your last dollar of income.

- Your marginal tax rate depends on three things: your province of residence, your level of income, and the type of income earned. To determine your marginal tax rate for 2008, see the tables starting on page 294.

Tim's Tip 3: **Know the difference between a deduction and a credit.**

No doubt about it, you've heard of them before. Deductions and credits are the friends of every taxpayer. The question is, do you know the difference between the two? Most Canadians don't. Let me explain.

A *deduction* is claimed to reduce your taxable income. Once you've calculated your taxable income, it's multiplied by current federal and provincial tax rates to arrive at your tax bill both federally and provincially. Make sense? But we're not done yet. Once your federal and provincial taxes are determined, those amounts are reduced dollar for dollar by any *credits* that you claim in each jurisdiction, to arrive at your basic federal and provincial tax bills. Finally, you'll have to add provincial surtaxes where they apply to arrive at your total tax bill.

DEDUCTIONS AND CREDITS: WHAT'S THE DIFFERENCE?

	Federal	Provincial	Total
	Net Income		
Subtract	**Deductions**		
	Taxable Income	Taxable Income	
Multiply	Federal Tax Rate	Provincial Tax Rate	
	Federal Tax	Provincial Tax	
Subtract	**Federal Credits**	**Provincial Credits**	
	Basic Federal Tax	Basic Provincial Tax	
Add		Provincial Surtaxes	
	Total Federal Tax	Total Provincial Tax	Total Combined Tax

Notes
- The provinces (except Quebec) and territories currently use the federal definition of "Taxable Income" when applying tax rates.
- No surtaxes are levied federally any more.
- Surtaxes are levied in 2008 by Ontario, Nova Scotia, PEI, and Yukon.
- The federal government still collects taxes for the provinces (except Quebec).

What's the bottom line? A deduction will reduce your total tax bill by an amount equal to your marginal tax rate. Consider Roshaan's story.

*R*oshaan had income of $48,000 in 2008, which put her marginal tax rate at about 35 percent. She claimed a deduction of $10,000 for childcare expenses in 2008, which brought her taxable income down to $38,000. How much tax do you think Roshaan saved in 2008 because of her $10,000 deduction? The answer is about $3,500 (35 percent of $10,000).

Some tax credits can be claimed on the tax return of either spouse. Where this is the case, you'll generally be better off claiming the credits on the higher-income earner's tax return. The reason? The higher-income earner is likely to pay more in provincial surtaxes where those taxes apply. The medical expense credit is an exception to this rule. Generally, medical expenses should be claimed on the lower-income earner's return since the lower the income, the greater the credits for medical expenses.

Since a deduction saves you tax at your marginal tax rate, you can expect to save about 25 percent if your income is under $37,885, 35 percent on income between $37,885 and $75,769, 42 percent on income between $75,769 and $123,184, and 46 percent on income over $123,184. These figures are Canada-wide averages for 2008.

A tax credit, on the other hand, will save you federal or provincial tax, dollar for dollar. That is, a $100 tax credit will actually save you $100 in taxes. And there's more. Those credits may also save you provincial surtaxes (where your province still levies a surtax—see Chapter 8). By 2001, all provinces and territories had moved to a tax-on-income system (TONI), where they used to levy a tax simply as a percentage of your basic federal tax (see Chapter 8 for more).

Here's one last word on credits. There are two types: *non-refundable* credits can be used to bring your total tax bill down to zero, but don't offer any relief beyond that point, and *refundable* credits, as the name implies, can result in a cash refund once your total tax bill reaches zero.

TO MAKE A LONG STORY SHORT:

- A deduction reduces your taxable income and offers tax savings equal to your marginal tax rate.

- A credit reduces your basic federal or provincial tax bill, dollar for dollar, and results in savings on provincial surtaxes where they apply.

- There are two types of credits: non-refundable and refundable.

Timing Your Taxes

Tim's Tip 4: Always wait to trigger a tax hit.

You know, there are lots of events in life that can lead to a tax bill. And most of the time, there are things that you can do to delay the tax collector's knock at your door. Here's an example: Every time you switch from one mutual fund to the next outside a Registered Retirement Savings Plan (RRSP) or Registered Retirement Income Fund (RRIF), you could be triggering a taxable event and could have some tax to pay. If you're intent on switching those funds, why not wait until January of the next year to make that switch? This will push the tax bill one year into the future.

Want another very common example? Kathie has a story to tell.

Kathie: *Last year, I wanted to help my daughter, Laurie, who has been struggling to save the down payment for a home. Since I had some stocks that I had inherited a few years ago, I decided to give them to Laurie.*

Tim: *You were in for a nasty surprise, weren't you?*

Kathie: *That's for sure. I didn't realize that simply giving something to my daughter could lead to a tax bill.*

Tim: *Yup. Any time you give an asset away, you are deemed to have sold it at fair market value. So if the property has gone up in value since you acquired it, you could have a tax bill to pay. A common exception is when you give the property to your spouse.* In this case, your spouse acquires it at your original cost, so there won't be a tax bill to face until your spouse disposes of the property.*

Kathie: *I wish I'd known that earlier.*

After speaking with Kathie, it became obvious to me that, despite the tax bill, Kathie is still glad she gave the stocks to Laurie. It was the only way she could help her daughter. The question is this: Could Kathie have waited to trigger the tax hit?

---

* For brevity I will use the term "spouse" to refer to both spouses and common-law partners (same sex or not). All are afforded the same tax treatment under our tax law.

For guaranteed tax savings, do all that you can to push a tax bill to a future year. The amount you save will depend on your rate of return on the money between now and the time you have to pay your tax bill. If you owe $100 in taxes but can push the tax bill off for five years and can earn 15 percent on your money between now and then, you'll cut the real cost of your tax bill in half! Consider the following numbers:

Rate of Return	True Cost of $100 Tax Bill Paid in the Future		
	1 Year	5 Years	10 Years
5 percent	$95	$78	$61
10 percent	91	62	39
15 percent	87	50	25
20 percent	83	40	16

Sure, she could have waited to give Laurie those stocks until Laurie was ready to buy the home that she is still saving for today. This way, Kathie's tax hit could have been put off for a year or two.

I can understand that there might be good reasons for switching your mutual funds, giving assets away, or involving yourself in other taxable events, but my point here is simple: Be sure to understand what kind of events can lead to a tax hit, and then wait to trigger that tax bill if you can.

TO MAKE A LONG STORY SHORT:

- Educate yourself about what kinds of events can lead to a tax bill.

- There may be good reasons for involving yourself in some of these taxable events, but wait until a future year to trigger the tax hit if you can.

Tim's Tip 5: **Pay your taxes on time, but not ahead of time.**

Wouldn't it be nice if you could simply wait until April 30 each year to pay your entire tax bill for the previous year? Sure it would. But forget it—the tax collector has other ideas. You see, the government figures that if you're earning income in a particular year you should make your tax payments throughout that year. I'm referring, of course, to source withholdings and installments.

Source Withholdings

I can still remember the feeling of receiving my first real paycheque after graduating from university. I was broke, so any amount of money seemed like a windfall. But still, my reaction was mixed. I was thrilled to have some cash to throw around, and shocked that the tax collector would have the nerve to take such a hefty portion for the government to throw around. That year, I claimed a number of deductions that saved me $3,000 in taxes, which came back to me as a refund when I filed my tax return. I was not amused: The last thing I wanted was a refund!

You see, most Canadians are of the opinion that, next to being shot at and missed, there's nothing more satisfying than a big tax refund each year. The problem with a refund is that it means just one thing: You have effectively made an interest-free loan to the tax collector during the year. Rather than allowing this to happen, why not request permission from CRA to reduce the taxes that are deducted at source? Use Form T1213 to make this request, and file it with your local CRA tax services office. Your employer will gladly go along with the idea as long as CRA has given the green light. All that's necessary is to provide CRA with proof that you're expecting a refund due to any number of deductions, such as RRSP contributions, charitable donations, medical expenses, alimony and maintenance payments, and so on. I suggest you file Form T1213 in early November each year for the upcoming calendar year to make sure you will get CRA's approval before January 1st.

Your aim should actually be to pay a small balance each year when you file your tax return; then you know you haven't made your tax payments ahead of time.

Installments

If you happen to be self-employed or you receive a decent income from your investments each year, you're an obvious candidate for making quarterly installments, since folks in these situations are not often subject to source withholdings. This leaves installments as the only other option to ensure the tax collector gets paid throughout the year. Installments are due on the 15th of the month in March, June, September, and December.

In a nutshell, you'll be required to make installments if the difference between your total tax payable (federal and provincial) and any amounts withheld at source is more than $3,000 (starting in 2008) in the current year and either of the two preceding years. If you live in Quebec, the threshold is $1,800 of federal tax, since provincial tax is not collected by CRA in Quebec.

You've got three options for calculating your installments:

Second Prior Year Method. For each of your March and June installments, calculate one-quarter of your total tax liability from two years ago. For each of your September and December installments, start with your tax liability from last year, then subtract your March and June installments and divide the balance by two. This means that in 2009, your March and June installments would each be one-quarter of your total 2007 tax. The September and December installments would each be equal to your 2008 tax bill, less your March and June installments, divided by two.

Prior Year Method. Calculate each quarterly installment as one-quarter of your total tax liability from last year (2008 for the 2009 tax year).

Current Year Method. Estimate your tax liability for the current year (2009) and pay one-quarter of that amount each quarter.

You may want to choose the option that provides the lowest quarterly payments. Keep in mind that as long as your payments are made on time and in accordance with the Second Prior Year Method, you'll escape interest and penalties. If, however, you choose the Current or Prior Year Method, deficient installments could lead to interest and penalties.

TO MAKE A LONG STORY SHORT:

- Don't hope for a refund when you file your return. Aim for a small balance owing instead.

- Request to have source withholdings reduced when you expect a refund due to certain deductions (file Form T1213 with CRA in November each year).

- You may have to make quarterly installments when your income is not subject to source withholdings.

- Consider the installment method that results in the lowest quarterly payments.

Tim's Tip 6: **Think of taxes when big things happen in life.**

Matthew paid me a visit not long ago. He wasn't sure if there were any tax issues to worry about in his situation, so he thought he'd play it safe and visit me to find out. When I asked him to tell me what's been happening, he replied in a single breath:

"Tim, my wife and I aren't getting along so well so we decided to separate earlier this year and my son is away at school for the first time and has been withdrawing funds from the Registered Education Savings Plan we set up for him 10 years ago and my California condominium was sold in the year because we haven't been using it very much and my wife and I are going to split the money from that sale then I became concerned about my personal liability in my business so I set up a corporation but only after I gave my brother some money to help him buy a farm. Is any of this going to affect my taxes?"

"Yes, Matthew, I would say so," I said.

Folks, any time a big event happens in life, ask yourself the question, "Will this affect my taxes?" While I couldn't possibly list every event to watch for, here are some of the most common that cross my desk:

- getting a separation or divorce
- negotiating salary or other compensation
- moving to another province or country
- setting up a business in another country
- investing offshore
- buying or selling a vacation or rental property
- starting, incorporating, or selling a business
- investing in someone else's small business
- inheriting assets
- creating or revising a will
- giving assets away during your lifetime

Whom should you visit when it's time to see a tax pro? Many people out there call themselves tax experts. Some are really just tax preparers. If in doubt, your best bet is to visit a tax professional who has completed the Canadian Institute of Chartered Accountants' In-depth Tax Course. This is a three-year comprehensive course that only those specializing in tax full-time are permitted to take. Most students of the course are chartered accountants, but you'll also find a handful of lawyers and certified general or certified management accountants as well.

If these or other big events appear on your horizon, visit a tax professional—sooner rather than later. You'd hate to find out after the fact that the tax collector wants more than you bargained for.

TO MAKE A LONG STORY SHORT:

- Think of taxes any time big events happen in life.

- Visit a tax professional before the events take place, if possible.

Fighting When You're Right

Tim's Tip 7: Dispute your assessment when you think you're right.

If one thing can be said about Canadian taxpayers, it's that we're a passive bunch. By this I mean that many Canadians are content to accept any assessment issued by CRA, under the assumption that CRA must be right. I admit, when the government receives your tax return, takes a look at it, and then issues you an assessment notice making changes to the return you've filed, it's easy to assume that you—or your tax preparer—probably made a mistake when filling out the forms. Bad assumption. The folks at CRA are prone to making mistakes as often as anyone else.

Notice of Objection

After filing your tax return, you can expect to receive a Notice of Assessment from CRA within 8 to 12 weeks. If you disagree with CRA's assessment of your tax return, don't let it go. Your first line of attack is to call your local CRA taxation office to talk over your concerns. You might just resolve the whole issue at that time.

If that call doesn't resolve the problem to your satisfaction, then you should consider filing a Notice of Objection.

A Notice of Objection can be filed on Form T400A, but doesn't have to be. You can also file an objection by detailing the facts and your reasons for objecting in a letter addressed to the Chief of Appeals at your local tax services office or taxation centre. Remember, you've got to file your objection on time—otherwise CRA is not obligated to hear you out. For individuals and testamentary trusts, the deadline for any Notice of Objection is 90 days after the mailing date noted on your assessment, or one year after the due date of the tax return you're fighting, whichever is later. If, for example, your 2008 assessment notice is dated May 15, 2009, you'd have until April 30, 2010 (one year after the due date of your 2008 return) to file an objection. The same deadlines apply in Quebec.

Take 'em to Court

What happens if you file a Notice of Objection and the tax collector still refuses to assess your return the way you think it should be assessed? Your next option is to take CRA to court—to the Tax Court of Canada (or the Court of Quebec for Quebec tax issues).

At the Tax Court of Canada, you've got two options: the *informal* or the *general* procedure. With the informal procedure, you can represent yourself, or have anyone else (your accountant, lawyer, another advisor, or your brother's friend's cousin, for example) lend a hand in the appeal, and you can expect to have a judgment on your case in 6 to 12 months. To be eligible for the informal procedure, the amount of federal tax in dispute has to be less than $12,000 (about $19,000 including provincial taxes, excluding Quebec tax) for each year in question, or less than $24,000 in disputed losses where disallowed losses are the issue. If you don't qualify for the informal procedure, the Court's general procedure is your other option.

The general procedure is going to mean a visit to a lawyer who will represent you in court. Don't get me wrong: You can represent yourself in court under the general procedure as well, but I wouldn't recommend it. Formal rules of evidence and other legal procedures will apply, and unless you're completely familiar with these, you won't stand a chance on your own.

If the Tax Court of Canada judgment doesn't work out in your favour, you can usually appeal to the Federal Court of Appeal. The final step is to request an appeal to the Supreme Court of Canada, although very few cases (fewer than five or so) make it that far each year.

TO MAKE A LONG STORY SHORT:

- If you disagree with your Notice of Assessment, call CRA to straighten things out.

- If a phone call doesn't help, consider filing a Notice of Objection within the required time limits.

- Your last line of attack is to take CRA to court, starting with the Tax Court of Canada's informal or general procedure, and potentially ending at the Supreme Court of Canada.

Tim's Tip 8: Consider requesting relief when circumstances were beyond your control.

Have you ever been subject to interest, penalties, or other tax treatment that you thought was unfair? There may be relief today. You see, our tax law contains fairness rules that give CRA the ability to waive interest and penalties and perform other acts to help you out in certain situations—particularly when circumstances were beyond your control. For example, a serious illness, an accident, or a natural or human-made disaster might cause you to file your tax return late, or to make payments late. Specifically, CRA may be able to provide you with some relief under the fairness rules, including:

- forgiving interest and penalties on overdue tax filings and payments
- issuing tax refunds after the late-filing deadline (typically three years after the original due date)
- accepting certain tax elections that are filed late

Keep in mind that the tax collector is not obligated to give you relief under the fairness rules—but there's nothing shameful in begging for it (I'll do anything for $5). You should be aware that CRA will take a look at your history when assessing whether they'll grant you relief. So, if you've filed your tax return late every year for the last 10 years, you're not as likely to find relief when you really need it. CRA will also look at the promptness with which you've made your request. And if you're asking for relief in a situation where you were simply negligent or didn't understand the rules—forget it, the tax collector isn't that merciful.

Finally, while the provinces and territories don't have similar fairness legislation, they often will offer the same type of relief that the feds offer. So don't forget to ask.

TO MAKE A LONG STORY SHORT:

- If you have faced circumstances beyond your control that led to interest, penalties, or other unfair tax treatment, don't be afraid to ask for relief under our tax law's fairness rules.

- CRA is not obligated to provide relief, and they will look at your history when making a decision.

- Your province or territory may also offer similar relief if you ask.

Tim's Tip 9: Structure your affairs to avoid application of the General Anti-Avoidance Rule.

I can recall one situation where a man had been accused by the CRA of tax evasion. "I know the evidence is strongly against me, but I have $250,000 to fight the case," the man said to his lawyer, as I recall. The lawyer replied: "As your attorney, I assure you that you'll never go to prison with that amount of money." And he didn't. He went to prison broke. Tax evasion and some legal fees will do that to you.

Now, there's a big difference between tax evasion and tax avoidance. Still, CRA doesn't always appreciate tax avoidance either, and it sometimes attempts to apply the General Anti-Avoidance Rule (GAAR) found in subsection 245(2) of the Income Tax Act (the Act). GAAR is a provision of last resort used by CRA to address what it views as abusive tax avoidance. Two recent decisions of the

Supreme Court of Canada (SCC) dealt with the GAAR issue and set guidelines for all future GAAR cases.

If you're thinking of any aggressive tax planning, it's worthwhile knowing the ground rules to avoid a CRA reassessment.

The Cases

On October 19, 2005, the SCC handed down decisions in two landmark GAAR cases: *Canada Trustco Mortgage Co. v. Canada* (2005 SCC 54) and *Mathew v. Canada* (2005 SCC 55). The difference between these cases is that, in the Mathew case, the Minister was able to show that allowing the tax benefit obtained by the taxpayer in his situation would be inconsistent with the object, spirit, or purpose of the provisions of the Act that the taxpayer relied upon. In the Canada Trustco case, the Minister failed to show this.

The Ground Rules

The SCC cases were important because they established three general principles, or tests, that must be met for you to be caught under GAAR. Here they are:

1. There must be a tax benefit resulting from a transaction (or part of a series of transactions). No tax benefit to you? Then GAAR shouldn't apply.
2. The transaction must be an "avoidance" transaction in the sense that it was not arranged primarily for bona fide purposes, other than to obtain a tax benefit. This doesn't mean that there must necessarily be a business purpose for the trans-action(s), but there should be some purpose beyond gaining a tax benefit for the transaction to avoid the label "avoidance transaction."
3. The avoidance transaction must be abusive. That is, allowing the tax benefit would be inconsistent with the object, spirit, or purpose of the provisions of the Act relied upon by the taxpayer.

Now, the burden is on the taxpayer to refute the first two principles in each case. The onus, however, is on the CRA to establish the third principle—that the avoidance transaction was abusive. By the way, if it's unclear that a transaction was abusive, the benefit of the doubt is supposed to go to the taxpayer.

What does all of this mean for you? Unless it's clear, based on the known purpose and wording of the specific provisions in the Act, that a tax strategy is abusive, you should be given the benefit of the doubt. Also, while a transaction may be tax-motivated, this isn't enough to apply GAAR and deny you the tax benefit. The transaction must also be abusive.

Lord Tomlin would be pleased. He expressed it best in the well-known case, *I.R.C. v. Duke of Westminster* (1936), when he said: "Every man is entitled, if he can, to order his affairs so that the tax attaching under the appropriate Acts is less than it otherwise would be."

The bottom line is this: If you are going to engage in any type of aggressive tax planning, be sure to work with a tax professional to structure your affairs so that you avoid meeting the three tests I've talked about here.

TO MAKE A LONG STORY SHORT:

- Two landmark decisions by the Supreme Court of Canada have clarified the criteria that CRA must follow if it hopes to prevent a tax strategy under the General Anti-Avoidance Rule (GAAR).

- There are three tests that must be met for GAAR to apply: (1) there must be a tax benefit from the transaction(s), (2) the transaction(s) must be an "avoidance" transaction, and (3) the avoidance transaction(s) must be abusive.

- Try to structure your affairs to avoid meeting all three of these tests for any particular tax strategy; a tax pro can help here.

Getting into the Game

Okay, you've taken the first step: You know the tax basics. It's time to turn to the Tax Planning Tip Sheet at the front of the book and review the strategies introduced in Chapter 1. Ask yourself, "Can this tip apply to me?" Each *Yes* or *Not Sure* could bring you one step closer to winning the tax game.

HOME TEAM ADVANTAGE: TAX PLANNING FOR THE FAMILY

The thing that a parent will never understand is why all bachelors aren't rich.

2

It seems like only yesterday that Carolyn and I got married. In fact, we tied the knot on August 3, 1997. I have to admit, one of Carolyn's virtues—and she has many—is that she can cook like no one else I know. I can't even make my way around in the kitchen except to raid the fridge. In fact, some people accuse me of getting married solely for the culinary benefits. That's ridiculous. After all, there are countless income tax benefits as well.

Here's some advice for you: When you think of tax planning, think of it as a family affair. Just think of the fun it could be—you, your spouse, and your kids if you have any, sitting around the table sharing tax strategies. It's not something my family did when I was young. Too bad. I think my sisters would have enjoyed it. So, next time you're tempted to pull out the Monopoly board, think twice, and pull out this book instead.

You need to realize that any effective tax plan will involve your family members. And I realize that families come in all shapes and sizes. Some involve single parents, adoptive parents, or common-law partners,* including same-sex relationships. The strategies in this chapter apply, for the most part, to all families. I should mention that 2001 represented the first year that same-sex couples were given the same tax treatment as opposite-sex couples—for better or worse!

Let's take a look at some of the best ideas available to make tax planning a family affair.

Splitting Family Income

Tim's Tip 10: Split income for hefty tax savings, with smart strategies from A to Z.

Maybe you've heard the term *income splitting* before. It's not a complicated tactic, but it's certainly one of the pillars of tax planning. Income splitting involves moving income from the hands of one family member, who is going to pay tax at a higher rate, into the hands of another, who will pay tax at a lower rate. The savings can be substantial. Check out Ron and Becky's situation.

*I*f Becky earned $60,000 in 2008 in Ontario and was the only spouse earning income, the family's tax bill would amount to $11,070. But things change dramatically if both Becky and Ron each bring home $30,000. With two income earners in this case, the family's total income remains at $60,000, but the family's tax bill drops to just $8,700, for savings of $2,370 each year. Why the tax savings? Simple. Think back to our talk about marginal tax rates in Chapter 1, Tip 2. With each spouse earning just $30,000, nearly every dollar

---

* For brevity I will use the term "spouse" to refer to both spouses and common-law partners (same sex or not). All are afforded the same tax treatment under our tax law.

Did You Know?

You could be liable to pay another's tax bill in certain situations. If the other person owes taxes at a time when he or she gives any type of asset to you at all, you could be jointly liable for that tax owing to the extent you didn't pay for the asset transferred to you. Section 160 of the *Income Tax Act* says so.

earned by the family is taxed at the lowest marginal tax rate possible for employment income—about 25 percent. When Becky earned all the money herself, every dollar over $37,885 was taxed at a higher marginal rate—about 35 percent—giving rise to a higher tax bill.

Not impressed so far? The truth is, your tax savings from splitting income can be as high as $15,990 (Canada-wide average) annually! The actual savings from splitting income depend on your province of residence and the difference between your marginal tax rate and that of your family member.

THE VALUE OF SPLITTING INCOME

	Becky's Income	Ron's Income	Total
One Income Earner			
Employment income	$60,000	$ –	$60,000
Tax to pay	$11,070	$ –	$11,070
Two Income Earners			
Employment income	$30,000	$30,000	$60,000
Tax to pay	$ 4,350	$ 4,350	$ 8,700
Tax saved annually			**$ 2,370**

The Attribution Rules

The problem is this: The tax collector will not allow you to simply hand a portion of your income to your spouse or child to be taxed in their hands. If you try this, you'll be caught under the *attribution rules* found in our tax law. These rules say that when you try to pass income to your spouse or common-law partner, children, in-laws, nieces or nephews by transferring income-producing property to them, *you* will be taxed on the income, and not the person whom you intended to pay the tax.

By the way, a common-law partner is someone, same sex or not, with whom you've been living in a conjugal relationship for 12 months or more, or one you're living with who is also a parent of a child of yours.

THE ATTRIBUTION RULES IN A NUTSHELL

	Type of Transfer		
Transfer To	**Gift**	**Loan With No Interest**	**Loan at Interest***
Spouse**	Attribute all investment income and capital gains back to transferor	Attribute all investment income and capital gains back to transferor	No attribution
Minor Child	Attribute all investment income, but not capital gains, to transferor	Attribute all investment income, but not capital gains, to transferor	No attribution
Adult Child	No attribution	Attribute all investment income and capital gains if loan made specifically to avoid tax	No attribution

* Interest charged must be the prescribed rate, or commercial rates if these are less.
** Transfers to a spouse or common-law partner are treated the same.

Never fear. There are ways to sidestep the attribution rules. What follows is the A to Z of income-splitting strategies.

a. Lend money and charge fair interest.

Set up a loan between you and the family member you'd like to split income with. As long as you charge interest on the loan at the rate prescribed by our tax law or at current commercial rates (you should choose whichever rate is lower), then you'll avoid attribution back to you of any income earned on the money you've lent. The interest must be paid to you by January 30 following any year the loan is outstanding, and will be taxable to you. Your family member can deduct the interest paid on the loan. One last thing: You're required to set the rate on the loan permanently at the time the loan is set up—which can be great news if interest rates happen to be low at that time.

b. Lend money, then take repayment.

This idea works well if you'd rather not charge interest on money lent to family members. It works this way: Lend money to a family member for investment purposes—say $15,000—then take back those funds after five years. Those funds will earn, say, $1,000 each year, which, in most cases, will be taxed in your hands because of the attribution rules. Here's the kicker: That $1,000 can be reinvested each year, and any second-generation income—in other words, income on income—will not be attributed back to you. By lending money to a family member for five years or more, there will be enough time for the second-generation income to grow and take on a life of its own. Soon, your family member will have a sizeable portfolio growing and facing tax in his or her hands—not yours. You'd be wise to transfer the income earned each year to a separate account to keep the second-generation income segregated.

c. Transfer money for business purposes.

You'll manage to avoid the attribution rules if you lend or give money to family members for use in a business. If it's a loan, there's no need to charge interest to avoid the dreaded attribution rules, but there are right ways and wrong ways to invest in a small business. I'll talk more about this issue in Chapter 5, Tip 59.

d. Transfer money to cover interest on investment loans.

The fact is, when you've transferred money to a lower-income family member, and those funds are used to pay for expenses and not to invest, the attribution rules won't apply. So, why not give cash to your family member in order to pay the interest on any investment loans? Giving that family member the cash to make those interest payments will make it much easier for that lower-income family member to borrow for investing. The result? Investment income is taxed at a lower marginal tax rate in the hands of your family member. Be careful that you do not provide collateral, guarantee the loan, or make principal repayments— otherwise you'll wind up with the tax bill, not your lower-income family member.

> **Caution!**
> When a family member borrows money to invest, make sure that a higher-income family member does not guarantee the loan or give the borrower funds to repay the loan principal. The problem? Quite simply, the attribution rules. These rules will cause any income earned on the borrowed funds to be taxed in the hands of the person guaranteeing or effectively making payments on the loan.

e. Swap assets with another family member.

We've been talking, so far, about splitting income by passing investment assets to other family members who are going to face a lower marginal tax rate than you are. Why not swap assets to make this happen? Here's how: "Sell" some of your investments to your spouse or child in exchange for another asset you take back in return. The asset you take back should be worth at least as much as the investments you're handing over, and should not produce an income of any kind. I'm talking about things like jewellery, artwork, a coin or other collection, or even your spouse's half of the family home—provided your spouse actually contributed to its purchase. If the house was purchased with your money alone, the attribution rules will catch up to you. Keep in mind that, for tax purposes, any swap is considered to be a sale at fair market value, so there could be tax to pay on any accrued gains when you make the swap.

f. Generate capital gains in the hands of your kids.

One of the most common ways to split income with the kids is to give or lend them cash to invest. Regardless of the age of your kids, there will not generally be attribution of capital gains on the invested money back to you. That is, your kids will pay the tax on any capital gains generated. The best part, of course, is that your kids can earn up to $19,200 in capital gains in 2008 without paying much tax, if any, if they have no other source of income. Besides cash, you could also transfer existing investments to your kids. But beware: When you give assets away, you are deemed to have sold those assets at fair market value. So, if those assets have appreciated in value, there could be some tax to pay on the gains. This tax cost, however, could pale in comparison to the taxes you'll save by splitting income with the kids.

g. Transfer any investment income to your adult child.

While you'll generally be able to move capital gains to the hands of your children and avoid attribution, it's a whole new ball game when we talk about interest, dividends, rents, royalties, and other *income from property*. If you transfer money to your minor children for investment, you're going to pay the tax on any income from property. But there's good news. Any income generated on assets given to an adult child (18 years or older at the end of the year) will avoid attribution, no matter what the type of income. The only catch is that your child now owns and controls the assets. To avoid having your child spend your hard-earned money on the finer things in life, consider setting up a formal trust to maintain control over the assets. One last point to note: If you transferred the money to your adult child as a loan rather than a gift, and the tax collector decides that your primary motive was to avoid tax, you're going to face the attribution rules.

h. Give funds to your adult child, then charge room and board.

When you give money to a child who has reached age 18 by December 31, you'll avoid attribution on any income earned. Of course, you may not want to give up the income you were enjoying on those investments, so here's a plan: Charge your child room and board for living at home. This will enable you to recover the income that you've given up by giving away your money. If you're not thrilled with the idea of handing over a sum of money to your semi-responsible 18-year-old, consider transferring the assets to a trust. This will allow you to accomplish the same thing, but will give you control over the money as long as you're a trustee and the trust is set up properly.

i. Make a corporate loan to a related student.

If you're a shareholder of a corporation, consider setting up a loan from the corporation to a student who is not dealing at arm's length with you and who will be 18 or older in the year. If the loan is not repaid within one year of your company's year-end, the loan is going to be taxed in the hands of the student. That's no big deal: The student will likely pay little or no tax on the amount if he or she has very little other income. But there's more. Once that student graduates and is earning a regular income, the loan can be repaid, and the student will be allowed a deduction for the amount of the repayment. Not a bad deal! Little or no tax to pay when the loan is included in income, but a healthy deduction when it's repaid later. This idea is great where the student doesn't work in the business and it would be tough to justify paying salary or wages. Keep in mind that the company won't be entitled to a deduction for the cash paid to the student. After all, it's a loan.

j. Pay an allowance to your working child.

I know, I know, you've been looking forward to the day when your children are out working, earning their own spending money, if only because it will teach them responsibility. What if I were to tell you that paying your children an allowance makes sense once they're earning their own money? Here's why: Giving your children an allowance will free up their earnings for investment. When they invest their own income, the attribution rules won't apply and you will have effectively split income. By the way, a child who has earned income will be entitled to RRSP contribution room, which will save tax down the road when the child starts contributing to that RRSP.

k. Pay an adult child to babysit the younger kids.

If you haven't got investments or cash simply to hand over to the kids to split income, try this idea on for size: Pay your adult child who was 18 or older in the year to babysit your younger kids who were 16 or under in the year. Babysitting fees, like other childcare expenses, may be deductible if they were paid out to allow you to earn income. Follow me now: You may be entitled to a deduction for the payments to your adult child, and that child will report the payments as income. There's a very good chance, however, that your child will face little or no tax on those payments. In this case, you've managed to split income by moving income directly from your tax return to your kid's return. Oh, and there's another big benefit: This *earned income* will entitle your child to RRSP contribution room.

l. Pay an adult child to help in a move.

Where you're entitled to claim moving expenses, why not pay your adult child to help you with the move? Let's face it, someone's got to drive the truck or lift the furniture. It might as well be a family member. You'll not only keep the money in the family, but you'll be entitled to a deduction for the payment made—subject, of course, to the usual moving expense rules (see Tip 15). Your child will have to report the income, but may not pay much tax, if any, when his or her income is low. The payment will also entitle your child to RRSP contributions, since it's earned income. There's nothing quite like moving income directly from your tax return to your child's—and this is what you're accomplishing here.

m. Transfer assets before leaving the country.

Suppose that you and your spouse have decided to leave Canada. Did you realize that you could face an ugly tax hit when you leave? Here's why: When you leave, you are deemed to have "sold" everything you own at fair market value, with some exceptions, and so you could face tax on certain property that has appreciated in value. You could minimize this tax hit with a clever tactic used by Burt and Margaret.

After spending several winters in the sunny south, Burt and Margaret decided to retire to California in January 2009. At the time the couple decided to move, Burt owned stocks worth $20,000 that he had paid $5,000 for. Burt was due to face a tax bill on the $15,000 ($20,000 minus $5,000) *accrued capital gain when leaving Canada, thanks to the rule that deems him to have sold these stocks. In December 2008, just before leaving, Burt gave the stocks to his wife Margaret (with no tax effect to himself since assets transferred to a spouse generally transfer at original cost). On January 5, 2009, Burt left for California and became a resident of the U.S. Margaret left one month later to join Burt and became a resident of the U.S. in February 2009. When Margaret left, she owned the stocks with the $15,000 gain, and had to pay tax on that gain when leaving. Normally, the attribution rules would require the gain to be taxed in Burt's hands, but not in this case, since Burt is no longer a resident of Canada. Instead, Margaret paid the tax on the $15,000 gain at her lower marginal tax rate. The couple successfully split income.*

By the way, normally the tax collector will consider two spouses to have given up residency on the same day. In Burt and Margaret's case, Margaret had business reasons to stay behind. I should also mention that there is a court case, *Min Shan Shih v. The Queen* (2000), which supports the notion that a spouse can, in some cases, be a non-resident of Canada at the same time that the other spouse is resident here. Make sure you visit a tax professional to talk over the residency issue before trying this idea.

n. Transfer capital losses to your spouse.

When I met Paul a couple of years ago, he had a common problem: unrealized capital losses. You see, Paul paid $20,000 for shares in XYZ Corp. that today are worth just $5,000, so Paul has an unrealized capital loss of $15,000. While Paul does not have any capital gains against which to deduct this loss, his wife Esther does. Esther has about $15,000 of realized capital gains this year. Wouldn't it be nice if we could transfer Paul's $15,000 unrealized capital loss to Esther? She could then shelter her capital gains from tax. The good news is, we can. There are three steps to take.

If you're leaving Canada, be sure to visit a tax professional who can help you to determine, in advance, whether or not you are properly giving up residency for tax purposes. CRA will make this determination for you if you complete Form NR73, but I rarely recommend sending a completed Form NR73 to the tax collector! You see, if there's any way to call you a resident of Canada—the tax collector will. In most cases, there's no need to send anything to the tax collector before giving up residency.

Caution!

Step 1 Paul will sell his XYZ shares on the open market and trigger the $15,000 capital loss. As you'll see in a second, Paul won't actually be able to claim the loss. Not to worry—this is precisely what we want!

Step 2 Esther will then acquire the same number and type of XYZ shares on the open market immediately (or within 30 days) after Paul sells his. This step has two results: First, Paul's $15,000 capital loss is denied. You see, the *superficial loss rules* in our tax law will not allow you to claim a capital loss if you or a person affiliated with you (your spouse, for example) acquires identical property within a certain time frame (30 days prior to and 30 days after your sale of the property, a 61-day window). The second result is that Esther will pay just $5,000 for her XYZ shares, but the $15,000 loss denied to Paul will be added to her cost, providing her with an adjusted cost base (ACB) of $20,000. That's right, the taxman won't deny Paul's loss forever. It's handed to Esther in the form of a higher ACB so that when she ultimately sells the shares, she'll have a lower capital gain or greater capital loss at that time.

Step 3 Esther will wait until that 61-day superficial loss time window is over (this is necessary to ensure the loss is denied to Paul), and then will sell the XYZ shares on the open market. Don't forget, Esther's ACB is $20,000, but the shares are worth just $5,000—so she'll realize a $15,000 capital loss. Esther can then use this capital loss to offset the capital gains that she has already realized this year.

By the way, it's not critical that Esther have capital gains in the same year that Paul has capital losses. Why? Because capital losses can be carried back up to three years, or forward indefinitely, to offset gains in those other years. So, if Esther reported gains in a prior year, it may be possible for her to take that $15,000 capital loss and carry it back to recover taxes paid in a prior year. Form T1A is used to carry losses back, and must be filed with your tax return in the year the losses are realized.

Here's the bottom line: Don't try this stunt at home. Visit a tax professional for help. You'll want to do it right since the superficial loss rules can be complex.

o. Transfer personal tax credits.

There are a few non-refundable personal tax credits that can be transferred from one spouse to the other. The idea here is to transfer these credits to the higher-income spouse when possible. Overall, this could save the family taxes—largely due to the provincial surtax savings you'll enjoy where your province levies a surtax (see Chapter 8). Which credits can be passed by your spouse to you? Eight in particular: the age credit (if your spouse was 65 years or older in the year); disability credit (where your spouse had a severe mental or physical impairment, supported by a signed Form T2201—see Tip 17); pension credit (where your spouse had pension income); tuition, education, and textbook credits (where your spouse attended a qualifying post-secondary school); public transit tax credit; and donation tax credits.

p. Pay household expenses through the higher-income spouse.

This is, perhaps, the simplest technique for splitting income. Let's suppose that you have a higher income and marginal tax rate than your spouse. If you pay for all or most of the household expenses, this will free up your spouse's income for investment. You can even pay your spouse's income taxes. There won't be any attribution of income in this case, since you are not giving money to your spouse to earn income. The result? This will free up some of your spouse's income to invest, and your spouse will face the tax on those investment earnings at his or her lower marginal tax rate.

q. Invest inheritances in the right name.

Make sure that any inheritance received by the lower-income spouse is kept separate and apart from any joint accounts you might have as a couple. As long as the inherited money is invested solely in the name of the lower-income spouse, the investment income will be taxed in the hands of that spouse alone, which will spell tax savings for the family. Likewise, where money has been left to both of you, be sure to invest the lower-income spouse's half separately rather than keeping the money in a joint account. The tax savings on an inheritance properly invested could be enough to pay for a family vacation each year!

When investing Canada Child Tax Benefits in the name of your child, your best bet is to open an investment account in the name of the child alone. Many financial institutions will do this for you. Obtain a Social Insurance Number (SIN) for your child and visit your financial institution armed with that SIN to open the account properly. This will avoid any confusion with the tax collector when it comes time to report the income on the child's tax return.

r. Invest Child Tax Benefits in the child's name.

It was in January 1993 that the tax collector replaced the old Family Allowance system with the Child Tax Benefit system. You know what I'm talking about. Canada Child Tax Benefits are those payments that many Canadian families are entitled to receive on a monthly basis until the children reach age 18. Did you realize that benefit payments can be invested in your child's name without the attribution rules kicking in? You better believe it. And it makes good sense. Ensure that the payments are deposited directly into an investment account for the child, and not commingled with funds you might have given the child. Then consider investing those funds for the long term—perhaps to help with your child's education. Be aware that, at the time of writing, CRA's position is that the new Universal Child Care Benefit is not available for similar income-splitting treatment.

s. Transfer pension income to your spouse.

On October 31, 2006, the federal government introduced changes that will alter how Canadians save for retirement. You're now able to transfer up to 50 percent of eligible pension income to your spouse. You'll claim a deduction for this transferred amount, while your spouse will report the income instead. Eligible pension income is that which qualifies for the pension tax credit. For those 65 years of age or older, this includes lifetime annuity payments under a registered pension plan (RPP), registered retirement savings plan (RRSP), deferred profit-sharing plan (DPSP), or registered retirement income fund (RRIF). If you're under 65, eligible pension income includes lifetime annuity payments under an RPP and certain other payments received as a result of the death of your spouse or common-law partner.

t. Consider an RESP for a child's education.

Registered Education Savings Plans (RESPs) are special plans registered with the government to help save for post-secondary education. Here's the deal: You won't be allowed to deduct your contribution to an RESP, but the funds will grow tax-deferred in the plan over the years. When the money is withdrawn from the RESP for education purposes, the income that had accumulated in the RESP will be taxed in the hands of the student. I like it—a perfect splitting of income. By the way, RESPs are also attractive because the government will pay grant money into the plan with your own dollars for eligible kids. I'll be talking more about RESPs in Tip 12.

u. Split the tax bill on your CPP benefits.

Here's an income splitting idea that the tax collector openly endorses. You're entitled to take up to one-half of your Canada Pension Plan (CPP) benefits and report the amount on your spouse's tax return provided you're both over age 60. The arrangement is actually reciprocal so that the same proportion of your spouse's CPP benefits will have to be reported on your tax return. As long as your benefits are higher than your spouse's, and you have a higher marginal tax rate, you're going to save some tax. Be sure to contact Human Resources Development Canada to arrange for this splitting of benefits.

v. Report your spouse's dividends on your tax return.

What if I told you that reporting someone else's income on your tax return could actually save you tax? You'd probably have me committed. The truth is, the idea can work. You see, you can elect to report all of your spouse's Canadian dividends on your own tax return. It can make sense if your spouse's income is quite low. By putting your spouse's dividends on your return, you'll reduce your spouse's income, which may, in turn, increase the spousal tax credit you're entitled to claim. In fact, you'll only be allowed to make this election if it increases your spousal tax credit. Since you'll also be entitled to claim a dividend tax credit on the dividends reported, your family could save hundreds of dollars in tax by making this swap (see Tip 54 for more).

The tax rules say that when you transfer dividends from one spouse to the next, you'll have to transfer all the dividends. You can't simply pick and choose which dividends to transfer. Watch out! Transferring all the dividends to the higher-income spouse's tax return might increase that spouse's income enough to cause a clawback of Old Age Security benefits. In this case, you might want to avoid this type of transfer.

Caution!

w. Pay family members a salary.

If you happen to run a business of any kind, you'll be able to pay your family members a salary or wage to work in that business. The only catch is that the amount you pay must be reasonable for the services provided. What's reasonable? Consider what you would pay an unrelated third party and this should give you a pretty good idea. Your business will claim a deduction, and your family member will report the income. More on this in Tip 45.

x. Become a partner with family members.

Did you know that a partnership does not pay taxes itself? Rather, the income or loss of the partnership is passed along to each of the partners, who are then responsible for reporting the income or loss to the tax collector. If you become a partner with your spouse or children, you'll split income by having some of your profits taxed in their hands, in accordance with your partnership agreement. By the way, a written partnership agreement is critical, both to avoid misunderstandings with family and to satisfy CRA of the partnership allocations.

y. Own a corporation with family members.

If you're a co-shareholder with your spouse or kids, you can split income with them in a number of ways. As shareholders, your family members are entitled to dividends from the corporation. In addition, they may be entitled to directors' fees if they are directors of the company, or salary if they are actively employed by the company. It's also common to see family trusts set up where the trust owns shares in the corporation, and the kids are beneficiaries of the trust. Dividends can be paid to the trust and allocated out to the children to be taxed in their hands, although the 1999 federal budget made this tactic unattractive for minor children as of January 1, 2000. (I'll talk more about this in Tip 11.) Adult family members can receive up to about $37,000 in ineligible dividends from a Canadian corporation in a year and pay little or no tax (varies by province) if they have no other income, thanks to the dividend tax credit.

z. Use two corporations to transfer money.

The ugly attribution rules we've been talking about apply to transfers of assets between two individuals or between an individual and a corporation—but not between two corporations. If, for example, you and your spouse own separate corporations, funds can be lent from your corporation to your spouse's without attribution. If those funds were used in a business or invested inside your spouse's corporation, your spouse could access the funds by taking dividends. Your spouse will be able to take up to about $37,000 in ineligible dividends from his or her corporation and pay little or no tax (varies by province), thanks to the dividend tax credit, provided those dividends are your spouse's only source of income. Be sure to visit a tax pro before trying this idea. You'll have to set things up properly to satisfy the anti-avoidance provisions in the *Income Tax Act*.

TO MAKE A LONG STORY SHORT:

- Splitting income involves moving income from the hands of one family member, who will be taxed at a higher rate, to the hands of another, who will face tax at a lower rate.

- The attribution rules prevent many attempts at passing income to other family members.

- Splitting income most commonly entails investing money in lower-income hands, making deductible payments to lower-income family members, and claiming deductions and credits on the most appropriate tax return.

Tim's Tip 11: Consider family trusts for income splitting.

Trusts can offer a ton of flexibility in managing your affairs and controlling the use of your property. And a trust can be as simple to set up as a visit to your lawyer. Sure, it's going to take some legal fees up front and some accounting fees each year to file the appropriate T3 income tax and information return for your trust, but the costs could be well worth it.

How a Trust Works

A trust is not a legal entity itself. It's a *relationship* between three parties: the settlor, the trustee, and the beneficiary. The settlor creates the trust by transferring property to the trustee. The trustee holds legal title to the trust property for the benefit of the beneficiary, rather than for the trustee's own benefit. Of course, it's possible to have more than one beneficiary. In fact, it's possible to have more than one settlor and trustee, too.

William is elderly and has two sons, Scott and Jason. Jason is mentally impaired. William wants to ensure that Jason will always be provided for, so he gave $300,000 to Scott to hold in trust for Jason. A trust agreement was drawn up so that Scott is able to use the funds to provide for Jason's needs. Scott is responsible for investing the funds until they are paid out for Jason's benefit. Scott is legally bound to use the funds for Jason's benefit alone. In this case, the trust agreement provides that an annual fee is paid to Scott for his services. William is the settlor of the trust, Scott is the trustee, and Jason is the beneficiary.

> **Caution!**
>
> You should remember that whenever you transfer any property to another individual or to most trusts, you're deemed to have sold that property at its fair market value at the time of the transfer. What does this mean for you? It means that, if the property has appreciated in value, you could end up with some tax to pay on the capital gain. You won't have to worry about this with cash and near-cash investments, like Guaranteed Investment Certificates and Canada Savings Bonds, because these don't appreciate in value.

How is a trust taxed? Just like any other individual. That's right, the trust will have to file a tax and information return each year (called a T3 return) and will have to report any income earned in the trust. There's a way for the trust to avoid tax on its income, and that is to pay out to the beneficiary, or make payable to the beneficiary, any income earned in the trust each year. This way, the beneficiary will pay tax on the income instead.

Here's an important point: A trust that is set up while the settlor is alive is called an *inter vivos* trust and will face tax at the highest marginal tax rates going! All this means is that you'll generally want to ensure that any income in an inter vivos trust is taxed in the beneficiaries' hands, and not in the trust. A *testamentary* trust, on the other hand, is created through the will of a deceased individual. This type of trust is taxed just as you and I are, at graduated tax rates.

A family trust can be set up for lots of reasons—including some not related to income tax, such as:

- protecting assets from creditors or ex-spouses
- protecting the privacy of asset owners
- providing for the needs of disabled children
- avoiding probate fees

Of course, trusts are also useful for splitting income to reduce income tax.

Trusts for Income Splitting

Let's talk about inter vivos trusts now. Testamentary trusts can also be an effective income splitting tool, but these relate more to estate planning, so I'll cover them in Tip 101.

Before we jump to it, let me just say that splitting income using inter vivos trusts has some advantages over other income-splitting strategies. For example:

- Parents or grandparents can retain control over the property even after transferring beneficial ownership to the kids to split income.
- The assets in a trust are generally protected from the creditors of the settlor, trustee, or beneficiaries, provided the trust terms are drafted properly.
- It's possible to transfer ownership to the beneficiaries of the trust without having to decide yet which specific child or children will ultimately end up owning the properties or assets held in the trust.

The two most common uses of inter vivos family trusts for income splitting are to hold portfolio investments and to hold shares in a private corporation.

Portfolio Investments

The name of the game here is splitting income from investments. Most commonly, parents or grandparents "settle" a trust by transferring assets (usually cash) to the trustee for the benefit of minor children, who are usually the beneficiaries.

While the trustee and the settlor can be the same person, this isn't ideal from a tax point of view. You see, where the settlor is also the sole trustee, Subsection 75(2) of our tax law will kick in and cause the settlor rather than the beneficiaries to pay all the tax on income that is earned in the trust. The bottom line? If you're the settlor, you'd be wise to name your spouse, other family members, or an advisor to be trustees (perhaps in addition to yourself).

You should visit a tax pro with experience in trusts to make sure the trust is settled properly and to give proper consideration to tax and other legislation before naming the trustees.

Once the trust has been created, the funds must be invested carefully. The reason? If you're not careful, the ugly attribution rules I spoke about in Tip 10 could cause the income to be taxed in the hands of the settlor rather than the minor beneficiaries. Simply inserting a trust into the tax plan doesn't allow you to escape the attribution rules. Those rules look right through a trust. As a result, it's common to see trust funds invested to generate capital gains rather than interest or dividends. After all, capital gains escape the attribution rules and will be taxed in the hands of the minor beneficiaries (refer to Tip 10*f*). Once the beneficiaries reach 18 years of age you've got no problem: The attribution rules are generally shut down at that point (refer to Tip 10*g*). To generate capital gains rather than current income, consider investing in equity mutual funds, stocks, or other equity investments. A financial advisor can help you to choose the right investments.

From a practical point of view, any income in the trust that is *paid* or *made payable* to the beneficiary is deducted from the income of the trust on its tax return. The beneficiary gets a T3 slip for the same amount, and must report the income on his or her own tax return. If there's more than one beneficiary, the deducted amount will be split between the beneficiaries in whatever manner the trust agreement specifies.

Private Corporation Shares

If you're a shareholder in a private company, you may be able to split income with family members through a family trust. In the past, the structure has looked something like this: a grandparent transfers a gold coin to the trustee; the trustee then borrows a few dollars on behalf of the trust to buy shares in the family corporation for a nominal amount. The trust now owns shares in the family company. The minor children or grandchildren are typically the beneficiaries.

There's a clear reason why Grandma or Grandpa settles the trust with a gold coin, rather than with enough cash to buy the shares in the family corporation. You see, the gold coin is not an income-producing asset, and so the income from the trust will not be attributed back to the settlor (the grandparent).

Once the trust owns shares in the family corporation, the corporation can pay dividends to the trust. Who do you suppose is going to pay the tax on these dividends? You got it—the beneficiaries. In the past, the dividend tax credit made it possible to pay up to about $24,000 in dividends to the trust for each beneficiary, with little or no tax to pay if the beneficiary had no other source of income.

Changes introduced in the 1999 federal budget put a stop to this for minor beneficiaries through something tax pros call the "kiddie tax," as I discuss below. But the trust structure I've been talking about here will still work to pass along ineligible dividends of about $37,000 annually to adult children or to a spouse or common-law partner. And adult beneficiaries with little or no other income will pay little or no tax on the dividends.

The Kiddie Tax

There's no question that family trusts holding shares of family corporations have, in the past, meant big tax savings for some. Through a tactic known as "dividend sprinkling," it was possible for a private company to pay dividends to a trust for the benefit of minor children. The kids would typically pay no tax on those dividends, with the result that money could be extracted from the private company on a very tax-efficient basis.

The tax collector wasn't thrilled with this set-up and took steps in 1999 to minimize dividend sprinkling. So the 1999 federal budget took a shot at dividends

> **Did You Know?**
>
> Any income earned in a trust can be taxed in the hands of the beneficiaries rather than the trust if the income is paid out or made payable to the beneficiaries. "Paid out" does not just include direct payments to the beneficiaries alone. In fact, the tax collector has said that payments to third parties (for example, summer camps or private schools) or to parents to reimburse them for costs incurred on behalf of a child beneficiary also qualify. Be sure to keep all receipts to show that the payments were for the child's benefit.

paid directly or indirectly to minors. Minor beneficiaries will now pay a tax at the highest rate—about 32 percent on ineligible dividends. This is called the "kiddie tax." Here's a closer look at the rules:

- A special tax, at the top marginal rate, will be imposed on certain income (called "split income") received by individuals under age 18 throughout the year. This special tax will apply to taxable dividends and other shareholder benefits from private companies (both Canadian and foreign), including dividends received indirectly through a trust.

- The tax will also apply to income from a partnership or trust that supplies property or services to, or in support of, a business carried on by a relative of the child or in which the relative participates. Rental income will generally be caught under these rules (as of December 20, 2002).

- Income subject to this tax will not be eligible for any deductions or credits, except the dividend tax credit and the foreign tax credit where they apply.

- The measures do not apply to payments to or for adults (those 18 or older in the year).

- The measures do not apply to dividends from publicly traded shares.

- The measures apply to transactions in 2000 and future years.

Trusts Still Make Sense

If you've already set up a family trust or are wondering whether or not it still makes sense to create a family trust to hold shares of your private company, you'll be glad to know that tax savings can still be had.

Here's what I mean: Any dividends that are paid from your private company to your family trust will face tax at the highest rate going due to the kiddie tax rules. The good news, however, is that the money remaining, after taxes, can then be invested in the trust with no concern whatsoever about the kiddie tax or attribution rules.

*P*eter and Janice are married and have four minor kids: Tori, Lincoln, Virginia, and Lewis. Peter is a shareholder in his own corporation specializing in landscaping and lawn care in B.C. A family trust was set up a few years ago to *hold shares of the corporation, and the kids are beneficiaries. In 2008, the corporation will pay $20,000 in ineligible dividends to the trust for each child. Each child will face taxes of $6,316 on those dividends, but a total of $54,736 will remain in the trust, after taxes, and will be invested in publicly traded securities and mutual funds. It doesn't matter what type of investment portfolio income is earned in the trust; all the income earned will be taxed in the hands of the children at their graduated tax rates, with no more application of the kiddie tax or the attribution rules.*

Why is it that the kiddie tax and attribution rules won't apply anymore to the portfolio income in the story above? The kiddie tax won't apply since this investment income is not derived from a private company, and the attribution rules won't apply because this is all second-generation income. Further, it's quite likely that when the trust in the above example was set up, it was settled by a gold or silver coin provided by the grandparents of the beneficiaries, and a coin is not an income-producing asset. This alone allows avoidance of the attribution rules.

In closing, let me say that there is no shortage of tax laws dealing with trusts. I've only touched on the basics here. In addition, I have dealt with the issue of alter ego trusts (a type of inter vivos trust for seniors) in Tip 103. Alter ego trusts are really an estate-planning tool. If you're considering a family trust, be sure to visit a tax pro. You've heard it before: Don't try this by yourself at home.

TO MAKE A LONG STORY SHORT:

- Every trust has at least one settlor, one trustee, and one beneficiary, along with trust property.

- A trust is commonly used to split income by holding investment portfolios or private company shares.

- When setting up a trust, be sure to visit a tax pro to ensure that the trust is settled, the trustees are named, and the trust documentation is prepared properly.

- The "kiddie tax" is legislation introduced in the 1999 federal budget that will cause tax to be paid at the highest rate by minor beneficiaries who receive certain types of income from a private company or business—even through a trust.

- There are still opportunities to use these family trusts to split second-generation income.

- Alter ego trusts are an estate-planning tool that seniors may want to consider. I'll talk about these trusts in Tip 103 in Chapter 9.

Educating the Family

When it comes to saving for education, there are a number of tax-smart strategies you can consider. I want to focus here on the two most common: Registered Education Savings Plans and in-trust accounts. I also cover the subject of education briefly in other parts of the book. Refer back to Tip *9i* if you're a shareholder in a closely held corporation, or check out Tip 82 in Chapter 6 if you're wondering about using RRSP savings for education. Now let's talk about those two most common strategies I was referring to.

Tim's Tip 12: Use an RESP to save for your child's education.

Do you have any idea what it's going to cost to send that special child in your life to post-secondary school? Plenty. In my book, *Winning the Education Savings Game*, I spell out the expected costs of an education down the road. If your child or grandchild enrolls at a college or university away from home in, say, 15 years, you can expect the cost to be approximately $130,000 for a four-year program. Even if your child lives at home, the four years will still cost about $97,000. And this is the cost for just *one* child. What if you have three or more kids at school? All of a sudden, your savings goals look like a huge challenge.

    The bottom line is that saving for your child's education should not be left to the last minute. It's going to take some careful planning. In my book *Winning the*

Education Savings Game, I walk through the five strategies to pay for your child's education: begging, borrowing, stealing, sweating, and saving. At this point, I want to talk about the fifth strategy: saving for education.

Choosing an RESP

There's no doubt in my mind that a Registered Education Savings Plan should form the cornerstone of any planned savings program. Here's why:

- The Canada Education Savings Grant (CESG) and the Canada Learning Bond (CLB), available from Ottawa, can boost your RESP savings.
- An RESP offers 100-percent-guaranteed tax-free compounding inside the plan.
- The plan is simple to administer once you set it up. No annual tax filings are required.
- RESPs can provide all the investment choices you'll ever really need to save effectively for an education.
- It's possible to claim a refund of your contributions to the plan if you want.
- RESPs are quite flexible, allowing some practical alternatives if your child doesn't enroll in a qualifying educational program.
- RESPs let you split income, since the income that accumulates in the plan will be taxed in the beneficiary's hands when it's paid out as educational assistance payments.
- There's a psychological advantage to an RESP: The deadline each December 31 provides a sense of urgency about contributing, and the plan's specific purpose discourages you from using the funds for other things.

RESP Rules

I couldn't possibly cover all the rules around RESPs in one tip, which is why I wrote *Winning the Education Savings Game*. But let me share with you the most important rules:

- The RESP subscriber can contribute an unlimited amount (new in 2007) each year for each beneficiary, with a lifetime maximum of $50,000 per beneficiary.
- Contributions are not tax deductible, but the assets in the plan can compound tax-free over the years.

- The student beneficiary will be taxed on the accumulated income when educational assistance payments are made from the plan.
- At any time, the subscriber may withdraw any contributions made to the plan (although a particular RESP promoter may place restrictions on withdrawals even though our tax law does not).
- If a child does not enroll in a qualifying educational program, the subscriber can do one of six things: (1) name a new beneficiary under the plan; (2) allocate the accumulated income to other beneficiaries already on the plan (this is possible under "family plans" where each beneficiary is connected to the subscriber by blood or adoption); (3) transfer the assets to another RESP for other beneficiaries; (4) roll up to $50,000 of RESP assets into an RRSP, provided the subscriber has sufficient RRSP contribution room; (5) donate the accumulated income in the plan to a college or university; or (6) withdraw the contributions (called a "refund of payments") and accumulated income (called "accumulated income payments") from the plan for the subscriber's own use. The accumulated income payments in this last option are fully taxable to the subscriber, and a 20-percent penalty tax will also apply.

Canada Education Savings Grants

Back in 1998 the government introduced the Canada Education Savings Grant (CESG). The CESG works alongside any RESP. Any contributions made to an RESP for a child who is 17 or under in the year will net you a grant from the federal government, paid directly to the RESP. The grant is generally equal to 20 percent of contributions made to the RESP, to the extent the child has CESG contribution room (more on CESG room in a minute).

Beginning in 2005, the CESG rate was increased from 20 to 40 percent on the first $500 of contributions to an RESP for the child of a family with income of $37,885 (for 2008) or less in the year. If the family's income is between $37,885 and $75,769, the CESG rate will be increased to 30 percent on the first $500 of contributions to an RESP. If the family's income is over $ 75,769, the usual 20 percent CESG rate applies to all RESP contributions.

Now, let's talk about CESG room. The CESG is a distant cousin to your RRSP. Each child 17 or under in the year is entitled to CESG contribution room of $2,500 per year (new in 2007; it used to be $2,000 per year). If no contributions are made to an RESP in a given year, that contribution room is carried forward to a future year. When you contribute to the RESP, you use up that amount of contribution room, and the RESP receives a grant equal to 20 percent (or higher, as discussed above) of the contribution room used. The most in CESGs that can be received per beneficiary in a lifetime is $7,200. I should mention that any contributions over and above the CESG contribution room cannot be carried forward to attract a CESG payment in a future year. Confused? Consider Jake's story.

Jake is four years old and his CESG contribution room for 2008 is $2,500. In February 2008, Jake's father (who earns over $75,000 annually) contributed $800 to Jake's RESP. A CESG payment of $160 (20 percent of $800) is paid directly to the RESP in the following month. A few days later, Jake's grandmother made a $3,000 contribution to another RESP on behalf of Jake. Since only $1,700 of Jake's CESG contribution room is available at the time of Grandma's contribution (his dad used up $800 of it), only $1,700 of her contribution qualifies for a CESG payment. The remaining $1,300 of her contribution will not qualify for a CESG payment in the following year. By the way, if no contributions other than Dad's had been made, the remaining $1,700 of Jake's CESG contribution room would have been carried forward for use in a future year.

> **Action Step**
>
> If you're going to make use of an RESP, be sure to contribute enough to take maximum advantage of the CESG payments the government is offering. This will mean contributing at least $2,500 each year or $5,000 every two years. The truth is, the more you can sock away the better, because post-secondary school is not going to be cheap.

To ensure that Canadians are making use of RESPs on a regular basis, there's another catch to be aware of. If you're hoping to put money into an RESP for a child who is 16 or 17 in the year, you're going to receive CESG payments only where one of two conditions are met:

- a minimum of $2,000 in RESP contributions must have been made on behalf of the child before the year he or she turns 16, *or*
- a minimum of $100 in annual RESP contributions must have been made on behalf of that child in any four years before the year the child turns 16.

A child who turned 16 or 17 in 1998 will be eligible for CESG room for 1998 if he or she was a beneficiary of an RESP during any four years before 1998.

Get the drift? Make an RESP a regular habit if you want the benefits of the CESG.

The Canada Learning Bond

The 2004 federal budget introduced the Canada Learning Bond (CLB) to help kick-start education savings for children of low-income families. The CLB is similar to the CESG in that it's a grant from the government that will be paid into an RESP for an eligible child.

Under this program, eligible children who were born after December 31, 2003 will receive annual payments of $100 paid into an RESP. The payment is increased to $500 in the first year the CLB is paid on behalf of a child. Further, an additional $25 will be paid into the RESP in the first year the child receives the CLB, to help the family cover the costs of setting up an RESP. A maximum of $2,000 in CLB payments will be made on behalf of a child in his lifetime.

Which children are eligible for the CLB? Any child in a family that is entitled to receive the National Child Benefit Supplement (NCBS—see Tip 22)—generally, those families with incomes under $37,885. A child will qualify for the CLB payment in each year (until age 15) that the family is entitled to the NCBS.

TO MAKE A LONG STORY SHORT:

- RESPs should form the cornerstone of any planned education savings.

- The Canada Education Savings Grant (CESG) and the Canada Learning Bond (CLB) mean a direct contribution by the government to a child's RESP, making these plans hard to resist.

- Read my book, *Winning the Education Savings Game*, for some bright ideas on education planning, or go to **www.timcestnick.com**.

Tim's Tip 13: **Set up in-trust accounts properly; otherwise stick to an RESP.**

In-trust accounts are more common than ever and are often used by parents, grand-parents, or others to save for a child's education. The account is used to invest funds for a minor and, typically, an adult looks after the investment decisions on behalf of the child. These accounts are *informal* or *bare* trusts.

Normally, in-trust accounts are set up with the intention that the child, and not the adult, should pay the tax on any capital gains on the investment (see Tip 10*f*). After all, the child's income is usually so low that reporting the gains in the child's hands won't trigger a tax hit at all. Of course, any interest or dividends earned by the investment will be taxed in the hands of the adult under the attribution rules, so it's typical to invest in mutual funds or securities that will generate primarily capital gains.

Doing it Properly

Here's the problem: If the in-trust account is not set up properly, you could be in for a nasty tax surprise. In a nutshell, our tax law says that there must be a real and irrevocable transfer of property to the child. That's right; if you've set up the in-trust account with the belief that you can simply access that money down the road for your own benefit—maybe to buy a new car or a set of golf clubs—you're mistaken. In the words of CRA, you have to "divest, deprive, or dispossess" yourself of title over the money you've transferred to the account.

If you fail to make this type of transfer, then you're still considered to effectively own the assets. And if you're still the owner, guess who pays tax on every cent of income from the investment, including capital gains? Right. You do. That will defeat the purpose of setting up the account in the first place!

*R*andy wanted to ensure that he wasn't offside with the tax collector, so he took two steps to make sure the in-trust account for his daughter, Chloe, passed the smell test.

Step 1   When Randy set up the in-trust account for Chloe, he ensured that the contributor (known as the settlor) of the account was not also the trustee. Since Randy contributed the money to Chloe's account, he ensured that someone else—his wife Skye—was named trustee. Naming the account "Skye Doe, in trust for Chloe Doe" provides some assurance to the tax collector that Randy has made a true transfer of assets when he set up the account.

Step 2   Randy signed an agreement providing that: (1) the property cannot revert back to Randy; (2) Randy will not require that the property be passed to persons to be named by him after setting up the account; and (3) Randy will not require that his consent or direction be obtained before the assets in the account are disposed of. Signing this agreement is not absolutely necessary to satisfy the tax collector, but it's going to help. The agreement should simply be kept by the trustee in a safe place.

By the way, what you actually do with money in an in-trust account will speak volumes to CRA about whether there was a true transfer of property. Be sure that the funds in the account are reserved only for the beneficiary child. Let's take it a step further. You should realize that the in-trust account arrangement is really a bare trust: The trustee's authority is limited to holding those funds until the child reaches the age of majority, then passing those funds to the child at that time.

Hmm. Food for thought.

In-Trust Accounts versus RESPs

There's only one question more perplexing than "Which came first, the chicken or the egg?" and that would be "Which is better for a child's education savings, an in-trust account or an RESP?" Both are good questions. Neither has an easy answer. In my opinion, both can have a place in any education savings program. The RESP is extremely valuable because of the free money available through the CESGs and CLBs, and in-trust accounts can be useful when the RESP lifetime contribution limits make it difficult to save enough for your child's education through an RESP alone (which should be a rare situation). See the table on pages 47–48 to compare the two.

TO MAKE A LONG STORY SHORT:

- In-trust accounts are a popular method of saving for a child's education but are often set up improperly. There are two steps involved in setting up an in-trust account properly.

- Once the money is in the in-trust account, forget about getting it back—it belongs to the child and he or she has a right to it at age of majority to use for education or otherwise.

- Both RESPs and in-trust accounts can play a significant role in paying for a child's education.

REGISTERED EDUCATION SAVINGS PLANS AND IN-TRUST ACCOUNTS		
	Registered Education Savings Plans	In-Trust Accounts
Contribution limits	Lifetime maximum of $50,000 per beneficiary. No annual limit.	No limit.
Investment options	All investments eligible for RRSPs also qualify for RESPs. There are no foreign content restrictions.	Generally no restrictions, although some have expressed concern due to provincial trustee legislation. These concerns will likely be put to rest over time.
Government assistance	Canada Education Savings Grant and Canada Learning Bond.	None.
Control over assets	The subscriber controls the investments and decides when to pay the assets to the beneficiary.	The trustee of the account controls where the money is invested. The assets, however, must be held for the child until age of majority, when the assets revert to the child.

continued

continued

	Registered Education Savings Plans	In-Trust Accounts
Use of assets	A beneficiary must use the plan assets for post-secondary education; otherwise, assets revert to the subscriber. If assets revert to subscriber, income tax plus a 20-percent penalty will be due on the accumulated income in the plan, unless the assets are transferred to the subscriber's RRSP.	Child may use the assets for any purpose once reaching age of majority. Contributor may not use the assets in any way, since the assets belong to the child.
Recovery of capital	Subscribers may receive a tax-free return of original capital at any time. Certain trustee or administration fees may apply.	Contributor has no right to recover the assets in the account since the assets belong to the child.
Taxation of assets	Assets grow tax-deferred over the years. When the student withdraws this money to attend a qualifying educational program, the student will pay tax on accumulated income in the plan.	Interest and dividends are taxed in the hands of the contributor annually. Realized capital gains and second-generation income are taxed in the hands of the child annually.
Tax filings	No annual filings are required until the student makes withdrawals from the RESP. Then the student must file returns to report the taxable income.	Technically, you must file a tax return for the child to report capital gains. A trust tax return should also be filed annually, but CRA has not, to date, enforced these filings for in-trust accounts.

Heading for Home

When Dorothy returned from Oz, she declared, "There's no place like home." I'd have to agree and not simply because home is a place to hang your hat. Your home can also provide tax savings. I want to focus here on the two most common tax matters related to the family home: the principal residence exemption and moving expenses. Virtually every Canadian homeowner will face these at some point. I cover some other home-related issues elsewhere in the book. See home office expenses in Chapter 4, Tip 41; the "mortgage versus RRSP" debate in Chapter 6, Tip 78; and the Home Buyers' Plan in Chapter 6, Tip 81.

Tim's Tip 14: Change the ownership of a second property to multiply tax savings.

My guess is that unless you've been living under a rock for the last few years you're probably already aware that when you sell your home at a profit it's going to be tax-free. You see, every family unit (which includes you, your spouse or common-law partner, and any unmarried kids under age 18) is entitled to one principal residence exemption. The exemption will shelter any gains on your home from tax. By the way, your home can include a house, condominium, cottage, mobile home, trailer, live-aboard boat, or a foreign property. Sorry, but vacant land or a rental property that you've never lived in won't qualify as your principal residence.

Sheltering Pre-1982 Gains

As I've already mentioned, your family is entitled to only one principal residence exemption. This simply means that, if you own more than one property that has appreciated in value, you may have to pay some tax at some point. There may be some good news for you, however, if you and your family have owned two properties since before 1982. You see, before 1982 your family was entitled to an exemption for each individual. As a result, it may be possible for you to change the ownership of one of those properties today to shelter capital gains that had accrued up to 1982. That's right, our tax law will allow a current change in ownership to retro-actively shelter pre-1982 gains from tax.

*J*im and Angela are married and own two properties: a home in Fredericton, New Brunswick, and a cottage in Gaspé, Quebec. Both properties were purchased back in 1975, and both properties have been jointly owned by the couple since that time. The home is worth $300,000 more today than when the couple bought it in 1975, and the cottage is worth $200,000 more than what they paid. They are selling the cottage this year. Although they'd like to shelter the $200,000 gain on the cottage from tax, they would rather save their principal residence exemption for the home—which they plan on selling in a couple of years. They can, however, take advantage of two principal residence exemptions for years prior to 1982. This means that they'll be able to shelter the pre-1982 gains on the cottage from tax. To do this, however, they'll have to separate their joint ownership of the cottage. They first paid a visit to a tax professional before arranging for the ownership transfer with their lawyer.

Folks, this is not something to try in the comfort of your living room. The rules surrounding the principal residence exemption are complex! Be sure to visit a tax pro before getting yourself knee-deep into this tax strategy.

Multiplying the Exemption

Don't forget the tax collector's definition of a family unit for purposes of the principal residence exemption: you, your spouse or common-law partner, and any unmarried kids under 18. This means that any children who have reached 18, or are married, will be entitled to their own exemptions. This can be great news for the family!

Consider transferring the ownership of a cottage or other property to a child who is eligible for his or her own exemption. This way, the property can be sold at some point in the future, and any gains after the date of transfer can be sheltered by your child's principal residence exemption.

Of course, there could be some unwanted side effects here. First, when you give the property to your adult child, you will be deemed to have sold it at its fair market value at that time. The result? You could end up paying some tax on the gains to date if the property is worth more than your adjusted cost base. This might not be so bad if the gain is small and if you expect the tax savings down the road to be that much greater when your child sells the property. Further, you may be able to use your principal residence exemption here to shelter the gain on the transfer from tax.

Second, keep in mind that when you give your property away to your adult child, the property then legally belongs to your child. The question is, can you trust your child to do with the property as you wish? Maybe. But if you're not comfortable with the idea of handing ownership over, you should consider the use of a family trust. (See Tip 11.) The trust will allow you to maintain control over the property while still effectively passing it to your child for purposes of multiplying the principal residence exemption.

In any event, it's going to be important to do things right, so be sure to visit a tax professional before taking your first step to transfer ownership.

TO MAKE A LONG STORY SHORT:

- Every family is entitled, for 1982 and later years, to one principal residence exemption to shelter from tax the profits on the sale of a home.

- A child who is 18 years or older in the year, or who is married, is entitled to his or her own principal residence exemption.

- Ownership of a second property can be transferred to multiply the available exemptions, but professional tax advice is going to be important here!

Many Canadians make the mistake of assuming that, just because they are able to sell a principal residence without paying tax on the capital gains, they should pour more and more money into that residence with the intention of enjoying tax-free returns. Folks, think of your home as an investment. If too much of your money is tied up in your home, are you well diversified? Maybe not. Let's face it, while real estate can provide decent returns on investment, it can also provide big losses too. There may be better places to invest your hard-earned money. Be sure to talk to a trusted advisor about what investments make the most sense for you.

Caution!

Tim's Tip 15: **Plan the family's move carefully to maximize tax benefits.**

If you're going to pack up your bags and move, you might as well do it properly— from a tax point of view.

Why Are You Moving, and How Far?

The rules dealing with moving expenses are pretty clear. They say that you're entitled to deduct costs for making a move to start a business, begin working at a new location, or go to school. To boot, you're only entitled to claim expenses when your new residence is at least 40 kilometres closer to your new work location or school than your old residence. By the way, that's 40 kilometres taking the shortest normal route of travel—not as the crow flies, which used to be the test.

Most importantly, you're only entitled to deduct costs up to the amount of income you've earned in the new location. Not to worry, if you can't claim all your moving costs in the year of your move because your income from the new location is too low, you'll be able to carry those expenses forward to claim them in the next year, subject to the same restrictions. The types of expenses you can deduct include:

- travelling costs, including meals and lodging
- moving and storage costs for your household effects
- lease cancellation costs
- selling costs for your old home, including real estate commissions
- legal costs on a new home purchase
- land transfer tax payable on the new home, if you've sold your old one
- costs of maintaining a vacant former residence (including mortgage interest and property taxes to a maximum of $5,000)
- cost of revising legal documents to reflect your new address, replacing driver's licences, auto permits, and utility connections and disconnections

Want to maximize your claim? Here's my advice: Plan your move so that it coincides with a new work or school location, and make sure you meet the 40-kilometre test. If you're a student, don't forget that research grants qualify as income in your new location, provided the amounts are taxable. Scholarships, fellowships, and bursaries are no longer taxable (for 2006 and later years), so you won't be able to claim moving expenses if these are your only sources of income.

Moving to a New Province?

If you're going to be moving to a new province, keep in mind that, in most cases, you're considered to be a resident of the province where you lived on December 31.

Why is this so important? Simple. You're going to pay tax to the province in which you're a resident on December 31. So here's your game plan: If you're moving to a province with lower tax rates, make the move before the end of the year if you can. This way, you'll take advantage of those lower rates sooner. If your new province has higher tax rates, consider waiting until the new year to make the move. You'll enjoy your current lower tax rates for an extra year.

TO MAKE A LONG STORY SHORT:

- You can deduct costs for moving as long as you're moving to a new work location or to school, and your new home is at least 40 kilometres closer than your old home.

- Plan your move so that it coincides with a new work or school location and meets the distance test.

- If you're moving to a new province, time your move to take advantage of lower tax rates.

- Remember that you can pay an adult child to help in the move and then deduct this as an expense. (See Tip 10*l.*)

Action Step

There are two court cases that support the notion that you may be able to move from one residence to the next and claim moving expenses even when you are not moving to take on new employment or to start a new business. Rather, you may be simply maintaining your existing employment or business but are moving because you need additional office space in your home or for other reasons. See *Gary Adamson v. The Queen* (2001) and *Templeton v. The Queen* (1997).

Claiming Family Care Costs

Tim's Tip 16: Maximize the base for your childcare expenses.

Even though Carolyn has decided to stay at home with our kids, I do happen to know a thing or two about childcare expenses—from a tax angle. Let me tell you about them.

Caution!

There has been talk that it's possible to deduct childcare costs as a business expense. Sorry, but this simply won't work. A 1993 Supreme Court decision (*Symes v. Canada*) made it clear that you won't be able to deduct these costs as a business expense. Too bad, really. Nevertheless, if you've claimed childcare as a business expense in the past, you can expect a reassessment if the tax collector catches the write-off.

Gimme the Facts

Childcare expenses can be claimed when you've incurred them to enable you or your spouse (or common-law partner) to earn an income. In a two-parent family, the lower-income spouse has to claim the expenses in all but a few situations. If you're a single parent, you'll be allowed to make a claim as well. By the way, the tax collector changed the rules in the 1998 federal budget to allow childcare expenses to be deducted where a single parent is in school full- or part-time or where both parents in a two-parent family are in full- or part-time study at a post-secondary school.

You're not necessarily going to be able to deduct every dime of your childcare expenses. There are some restrictions here. In a nutshell, you'll be able to deduct up to $7,000 of costs for each child under seven on December 31 or who suffers from a less-than-severe physical or mental infirmity. The amount is reduced to $4,000 for kids age 7 to 16 in the year or for those over 16 suffering from a less severe infirmity who are still dependent on you. Costs of up to $10,000 annually to have someone care for a child, of any age, with a severe and prolonged physical or mental infirmity can be deducted. I should mention that the tax collector might further restrict your child-care deductions. The tax collector will calculate two-thirds of your *earned income* for childcare purposes (basically your employment and self-employment income) and, where this figure is less than the limits I've already mentioned, you'll be limited to two-thirds of your earned income.

Childcare expenses include payments for babysitters, day nursery services, boarding schools, and camps. You should know that deductions for payments to a boarding school or camp are limited to $175 per week of attendance for kids under 7 years of age and $100 per week for kids 7 to 16. This same dollar restriction applies to parents in full-time attendance at school. (Parents in part-time attendance are limited to $175 per month for kids under 7 and $100 per month for kids 7 to 16.)

So when, exactly, is the higher-income spouse allowed to claim the childcare expenses? When the lower-income spouse was at school full- or part-time, in a prison or similar institution for at least two weeks in the year, certified to be incapable of caring for children, confined to a wheelchair or bed for at least two weeks, or separated due to a marriage breakdown. If you're the higher-income spouse claiming the childcare expenses, you'll be limited to $175 per week for each child under 7 or infirm, and $100 for kids 7 to 16.

CHILDCARE DEDUCTIONS: MAXIMUM CLAIM*			
		Child Is Infirm	
Age of Child on December 31	No Infirmity	Less than Severe	Severe and Prolonged
Under 7	$7,000	$7,000	$10,000
7 to 16	$4,000	$4,000	$10,000
Over 16	None	$4,000	$10,000

* The maximum deduction is two-thirds of earned income, or the amount in the table, whichever is less.

Increasing the Base for Your Claim

The tax collector does not attach specific childcare expenses to specific children. All that matters is that your total expenses deducted for all the kids not exceed the number of kids multiplied by the maximum expenses allowed for each child. Confused? Lindsay, Logan, and Jamie will help to make things clear.

*L*indsay *is 12 years old. Her brother Logan is 9, and her sister Jamie is 6. Their parents spent $13,000 on childcare this year ($8,000 for Jamie, $5,000 for Logan, and none for Lindsay). Their parents figure they can deduct a maximum of $7,000 out of $8,000 spent for Jamie, plus another $4,000 out of $5,000 spent for Logan, for a total of $11,000. They were mistaken. The tax collector* *doesn't attach costs to specific children. Their parents were actually entitled to claim up to $15,000 ($4,000 for Lindsay, $4,000 for Logan, and $7,000 for Jamie). Since their total costs are just $13,000, they'll be entitled to deduct the full costs incurred in the year!*

Here's the moral of the story: Remember to report all your children aged 16 or under in the year, or those with infirmities, on your tax return—even if you didn't incur expenses for some of them. This will maximize the base for your childcare deduction.

I should mention that the court decision in *Stewart A. Bell v. The Queen* (2000) established that payments for recreational and educational activities may not be deducted as childcare expenses. So, those skating or music lessons won't generally be considered deductible. Unless the primary objective of the expense is to provide for the protection and security of the kids, the expense will be denied, even if the activity takes place while you're at work.

TO MAKE A LONG STORY SHORT:

• Claim childcare expenses where they were incurred to allow you or your spouse to earn income.

• The deductible amount will be based on the age of your child and whether or not he or she has any infirmities.

• Maximize the base for your claim by reporting all your kids 16 or under on your tax return, even if you didn't incur childcare expenses for some of them.

Tim's Tip 17: Challenge the tax collector if a disability credit is disallowed.

You know, there are certain tax breaks available to those who have disabilities. The problem is, it can be like pulling teeth to convince the tax collector that the disability is severe enough to warrant tax help. You're entitled to a federal disability tax credit worth $1,053 in 2008, plus a federal supplement of up to $614 for children who qualify for the disability tax credit. So who qualifies for the disability tax credit? In 2003 a Technical Advisory Committee was established to address issues and concerns related to tax measures for people with disabilities. In response to this committee's recommendations, the 2005 Federal Budget included changes that clarified and broadened eligibility for the disability tax credit. Under the new rules you can claim the credit where you have a severe and prolonged impairment in physical or mental functions. The term "mental function" used to be defined as "perceiving, thinking or remembering," but has now been broadened to include all mental functions necessary for everyday life, which includes memory, problem-solving, goal setting and judgment, and adaptive functioning.

In the past, to be eligible for the disability tax credit, a person had to be markedly restricted in at least one basic activity of daily living. Thanks to changes made in the budget, starting in 2005, eligibility is extended to include individuals with multiple restrictions where the cumulative effect of those restrictions is equivalent to a marked restriction in one basic activity of daily living. Your province will also offer a tax credit for a disability, but the amount of the credit will vary by province. By the way, the impairment must have lasted or be expected to last for one year or more, and your disability will have to be verified by a medical doctor, optometrist, audiologist, occupational therapist, psychologist, or speech pathologist, on Form T2201, which should be filed in the first year you make a claim for the credit.

You might be surprised at what will not qualify. In one case, a gentleman was unable to visit the washroom on his own because of a disability. His disability was viewed by the tax collector as being less than severe, however, and no disability credit was allowed. Fair? Probably not. Especially when you consider that the government already admitted to the severity of his disability by qualifying him for Canada Pension Plan disability payments.

A whole slew of court cases have dealt with the issue of whether or not certain disabilities will qualify for the tax credit. And you'll be glad to know that the courts have found CRA to be wrong in disallowing the credit in some instances. So, if your claim for a disability credit has been disallowed and you believe you meet the criteria set out in the *Income Tax Act*, then consider filing a Notice of Objection or appealing to the Tax Court of Canada (see Chapter 1, Tip 7).

Now picture this: Your child is eligible to claim the disability credit but doesn't have enough income to take advantage of it. Not to worry, the disability credit can be claimed by you—the supporting person. And there's more. If you support a dependent child who is over age 18 and suffers from a physical or mental infirmity, you'll be entitled to an additional federal tax credit of $614, which will be reduced by 15 percent (for 2008) of the dependant's income over $5,811.

TO MAKE A LONG STORY SHORT:

- You're entitled to a disability tax credit where you have a severe and prolonged disability that markedly restricts a basic activity of daily living.

- The tax collector has not been generous in allowing these credits.

- Consider filing a Notice of Objection or appealing to the Tax Court of Canada if you disagree with the tax collector's disallowance of your claim (see Chapter 1, Tip 7).

Tim's Tip 18: Choose carefully whether to claim disability support costs as a deduction or a credit.

If you're disabled, you may incur certain costs to allow you to attend and properly function at school or work. In the past, costs related to hiring an attendant were deductible against your income by the attendant care deduction, but certain other costs might not have been deductible. Thanks to the 2004 federal budget, the attendant care deduction was replaced, for 2004 and later years, with a new disability supports deduction. The effect of this new deduction is to ensure that no income tax will be payable on income (including government assistance) used to pay for the expenses.

This deduction is broader than the old attendant care deduction and will allow you to deduct not only the cost of attendant care, but other disability supports as well, such as sign-language interpreter fees, real-time captioning services, teletypewriters or similar devices, devices or equipment to assist the blind in operating a computer or reading print, electronic speech synthesizers for mute individuals, notetaking services, voice recognition software, tutoring services, and talking textbooks.

The disability supports deduction will be limited to the lesser of: (1) the cost of the eligible expenses, or (2) 100 percent of earned income (under the old attendant care deduction, the limit was two-thirds of earned income).

But before you claim the deduction, you should weigh another option first. You see, you're entitled to claim those disability support costs as a medical expense credit instead, if you prefer. Recall that we talked about deductions versus credits in Chapter 1, Tip 3. Normally, a deduction will save you at least as much as the credit ever could, and probably more. But in this situation, there's another point to consider: You can claim all the medical expenses on the tax return of either spouse when you claim them as a credit.

You may be better off classifying the disability support costs as a medical expense, particularly when your income is quite low. To figure out which method is better, your best bet is to use a tax software package. QuickTax comes to mind. Other packages like TaxWiz or MyTaxExpress do a fine job as well. Of course, you can always have a tax professional do the calculations for you.

TO MAKE A LONG STORY SHORT:

- You may be entitled to claim disability support costs if you're disabled and incur the costs in order to earn income or attend school.

- Disability support costs can be claimed as a deduction or as a medical credit. You'll have to do a calculation to figure out which is best for you and your family.

Surviving Separation and Divorce

It's a sad fact, but the truth is that a growing number of Canadian marriages end in divorce each year. In fact, in 2000 there were 156,038 marriages in Canada. What about divorces? There were a staggering 70,292 divorces that same year. That's one divorce for every 2.2 marriages. This is not good news for Canadian families. The question is: How does divorce impact the family financially?

Did You Know?

Under Canadian tax law, it's possible for a taxpayer to have more than one spouse! You may even be eligible to claim spousal credits for each of them. I can't recommend marrying more than one person though—this could land you in prison as a violation of other legislation!

Statistics Canada shows that the average income for a two-parent family in Canada in 2006 was $93,500. Lone-parent families fared much worse, with an average income of just $45,800 in 2006. The message is clear: There are no winners financially (other than the lawyers) when a separation or divorce takes place.

Having said all that, I want to talk to those of you who, for one reason or another, are separated or divorced. There will be definite tax advantages to both you and your spouse or ex-spouse if you can agree to structure your affairs so that you're paying the least amount of tax possible.

Tip 19: Count the tax cost when splitting family assets.

I've seen too many situations where two people split up the family assets at the time of separation and fail to take into account the future tax bill owing on the assets. You see, you may think that you're getting your fair share of the assets in the split-up, but if you subsequently owe the tax collector significantly more than your ex-spouse when you dispose of the assets you received, then was it a fair split-up? Not really. Consider the example of Harrison and Wanda.

Harrison and his ex-wife Wanda separated last year. At the time they split up, they owned the following assets:

Residence	$350,000
Harrison's RRSP	100,000
Wanda's RRSP	80,000
Non-registered investments	170,000
Total Assets	$700,000

They agreed that each would receive 50 percent, or $350,000 of the assets. To make things simple, they agreed that Wanda would receive the family residence worth $350,000. Harrison received the non-registered investments (that is, investments held outside their RRSPs) worth $170,000 (with an adjusted cost base of $70,000), plus the RRSPs worth $180,000. While this may seem like a fair split, let's take a look at how much each receives after taxes. If Wanda were to sell the home today, she would receive the $350,000 tax free due to her principal residence exemption. If Harrison were to liquidate his investments today, he would have to pay tax on a $100,000 capital gain on the open investments, resulting in a $23,205 tax bill, and taxes on the RRSPs of $83,520, since he's in the highest tax bracket in Ontario in 2008. Harrison's total tax bill will equal $106,725, and Wanda's will be nil.

The bottom line is that Wanda will keep $350,000 after tax, and Harrison will keep $243,275 ($350,000 less $106,725 in taxes). Was this really a fair distribution of assets? Perhaps not. If the couple understood the tax impact here and still agreed to distribute the assets in this manner, that's their choice. The important point is that they should at least understand the tax liability that they are each inheriting when splitting up the family assets. Most couples will attempt to split the assets in a fair manner after considering the future tax hit on those assets. In any event, it's important to talk to your lawyer about this issue before finalizing any separation agreement.

TO MAKE A LONG STORY SHORT:

• When dividing up the family assets be sure to count the future tax cost owing on those assets.

• Most couples will attempt to split the assets in a fair manner, looking at the after-tax value of each asset.

• Be sure to discuss this issue with your lawyer before finalizing any separation agreement.

Tim's Tip 20: **Claim the eligible dependant tax credit, if applicable.**

If you're separated or divorced (those who are single and widowed can also claim this credit) and you're supporting another family member living with you, then you may be entitled to the eligible dependant (formerly the equivalent-to-married) tax credit. How much tax can you expect to save? Up to $1,440 federally plus an additional amount from your province (the provincial average is about $718).

Specifically, you'll be entitled to claim this credit if you are supporting a person related to you who is living in your residence and who is under 18. You can ignore the age-18 requirement if the dependent person is your parent or grandparent or suffers from a physical or mental infirmity.

As a general rule, joint custody will mean that one spouse can claim this credit. However, a technical interpretation dated January 7, 2002 (document 2001-0101105), supports the notion that where there is joint custody over more than one child, it is possible that each spouse may be able to claim a full eligible dependant credit on the basis that the children would be wholly dependent on both parents at different times throughout the year. The separation agreement will have to be structured so that one parent can claim the credit for one child while the other can claim it for a second child. This may require one spouse supporting just one of the children in the agreement. If you don't structure your separation agreement correctly, you may be stuck with just one spouse being entitled to the credit. Speak to a tax pro for more information.

TO MAKE A LONG STORY SHORT:

- Claim the eligible dependant (formerly the equivalent-to-married) credit if you are separated, divorced, or otherwise single, and you support a relative who lives with you.

- The credit could save you over $2,000 in tax.

- Joint custody will generally allow one caregiver to claim the credit, but it may be possible to structure your separation agreement so that both parents can claim a full credit when joint custody over more than one child exists.

Tim's Tip 21: **Avoid a tax hit when splitting retirement plan assets.**

I know that things can get ugly when it comes time to divvy up the assets upon separation or divorce. For a lot of people, much of their net worth is tied up in their RRSP or RRIF. The good news is that the tax collector won't add insult to injury by forcing tax to be paid on RRSP or RRIF assets if they're transferred from one spouse's RRSP or RRIF to the other spouse's plan. As long as the payment is made in accordance with a written separation agreement, or a decree, court order, or judgment, then a tax-free transfer can take place without a problem. I should also mention that transferring assets from a Registered Pension Plan (RPP) to an RRSP or another RPP can also be done on a tax-free basis in the event of a marriage breakdown.

> **Caution!**
>
> Upon a marriage breakdown, make sure that any transfers made from one spouse's RRSP, RRIF, or RPP to the other spouse's plan are made directly from one plan to the next to avoid tax on the transfer. That is, the plan assets should never actually pass through the hands (or the bank account) of either spouse; otherwise, the tax collector will take a share of those assets as though they were taxable withdrawals from the plan.

All of this invites the question: Who is going to pay the tax when the withdrawals are made from the RRSPs later? It's quite simple: The annuitant spouse will. If, for example, you transfer some of your RRSP assets to your spouse's plan upon a marriage breakdown, your spouse will be taxed on the withdrawals from his or her plan, and you'll continue to pay tax on any withdrawals made from your own plan. Make sense?

You'll also be glad to know that the rules that would normally apply to discourage withdrawals from a spousal RRSP (see Chapter 6, Tip 79) won't apply here.

TO MAKE A LONG STORY SHORT:

- When dividing up the assets after separation or divorce, avoid taxes on the transfer by splitting RRSP or RRIF assets in accordance with a written separation agreement or a decree, court order, or judgment.

Tim's Tip 22: Maximize Child Tax Benefits by applying for one-income status.

If you happen to have kids under the age of 18, you may be entitled to collect Canada Child Tax Benefits from the tax collector. Now these benefits won't make you rich, but they're better than a kick in the pants. Your benefits are based on the combined income of you and your spouse.

Currently, the benefits are $1,307 annually for each child, plus an additional $91 for the third and subsequent children. Once your family income reaches $37,885, these benefits start to be phased out.

There could be more in store for you. If your income is low, you may be entitled to a *National Child Benefit Supplement* of $2,025 for the first child, $1,792 for the second child, and $1,704 for the third and additional kids. This benefit is phased out beginning at $21,287 of income.

Since your benefits are based on the combined incomes of you and your spouse, the benefits will be clawed back quite quickly for many Canadians. However, when your marriage breaks down, the parent with whom the kids will be living is able to make a special election—within 11 months following the month of marriage break-down—to base the benefits on the income of that spouse only. That is, the estranged spouse's income will be ignored in the benefit calculation. Making this election could put hundreds of extra dollars in the pocket of the spouse making the election.

TO MAKE A LONG STORY SHORT:

- Canada Child Tax Benefits are based on the combined incomes of both spouses and, as a result, often quickly disappear.

- Make an election within 11 months of marriage breakdown to have the benefits based on one income only. This may increase the benefits significantly.

Tim's Tip 23: **Consider splitting real estate when dividing up assets.**

I've already talked about the benefits of the principal residence exemption (see Tip 14). That's the exemption that allows you to sell your home at a profit without paying any tax on the gain. The problem, of course, is that each family unit is entitled to just one exemption. This is a problem, particularly where the family owns more than one property—perhaps a cottage or other vacation property in addition to the family home. Oddly enough, separation or divorce provides an opportunity to multiply the exemption. You see, once you're separated or divorced, you are considered to be your own "family," and you'll be entitled to your own principal residence exemption.

So, where two properties are owned, it makes a whole lot of sense from a tax point of view to give each spouse one property when splitting the spoils. That way, both properties can eventually be sold with any gains sheltered from tax.

TO MAKE A LONG STORY SHORT:

- Each family unit is entitled to just one principal residence exemption, but each separated or divorced person is entitled to his or her own exemption.

- Where the family owns more than one property at the time of a separation or divorce, it makes sense from a tax point of view to give each spouse one property, to multiply the number of exemptions that can be claimed.

Tim's Tip 24: **Deduct legal costs incurred to collect support payments.**

If you're like most, you probably enjoy paying legal fees about as much as getting a root canal. And the tax collector doesn't make things any easier because legal fees are not often deductible unless you're running a business. There are certain situations, however, when legal fees can be claimed, and collecting or establishing a right to support payments may be two of those situations.

CRA's policy on legal costs was relaxed in 2003, thanks to the court decision in *Gallien v. The Queen* (2001). Today you can deduct legal costs incurred for the purpose of:

- establishing a right to spousal or child support under the *Divorce Act*, or under the applicable provincial legislation in a separation agreement;
- enforcing a pre-existing right to interim or permanent spousal or child support;
- obtaining an increase in spousal or child support or to make child support non-taxable under the Federal Child Support Guidelines; or
- defending against the reduction of spousal or child support.

There are four key situations where legal costs are simply not deductible. These are when legal costs are incurred (1) in connection with the receipt of a lump-sum payment that cannot be identified as support payments that were in arrears (although typically that lump-sum payment will not be taxable), (2) by the payer in negotiating or contesting the payment of support, (3) by the payer for the purpose of terminating or reducing the amount of support payments, and (4) to obtain custody or visitation rights to children. Check out CRA's Interpretation Bulletin IT-99R5 for more.

TO MAKE A LONG STORY SHORT:

- Legal fees are not often deductible, but may be deducted when incurred to enforce or establish your right to receive spousal or child support payments.

Tim's Tip 25: **Consider preserving pre–May 1997 support agreements.**

Here's a situation where you're going to have to work closely with your spouse or ex-spouse to beat the tax collector. I know it might be a tall order when the tension between the two of you might be thick enough to cut with a knife, but do yourselves a favour and work together on this. Let me explain.

The Way It Was

Key changes introduced in the 1996 federal budget changed the way child support payments are taxed. It used to be that the payer was able to claim a deduction for the payments made and the recipient spouse was taxed on those payments. While the arrangement may have been frowned upon by many who received the child support (because they were taxed on the payments), it had the advantage of reducing the amount of money ending up in the tax collector's coffers. Here's why: The payer spouse usually has a higher marginal tax rate than the recipient. So the deduction that was claimed usually saved the payer more in tax than it cost the recipient spouse.

Henry and Rosette are separated. Henry earns $70,000 annually and his marginal tax rate is 42 percent, while Rosette earns about $35,000 and has a marginal tax rate of 35 percent. Last year, Henry paid Rosette $10,000 in child support. He claimed a deduction, which saved him $4,200 in taxes ($10,000 × 42 percent). Rosette, on the other hand, reported the $10,000 as income and paid $3,500 in taxes. Combined, Henry and Rosette beat the tax collector by $700 ($4,200 less $3,500). Since the tax savings were in Henry's hands, he agreed to spend the $700 savings directly on his child.

The Way It Is

For child support agreements entered into after April 30, 1997, the payer is not allowed to deduct the payments made. On the flip side, the recipient is no longer required to report the payments as income. If you had an agreement in place before May 1997 that either provided for the deductibility and taxability of payments made, or was simply an agreement entered into prior to the federal budget of March 6, 1996, then your agreement escapes the rules that exclude the payments from being deducted by the payor and taxed to the recipient. If, however, you varied the amounts in the agreement after April 30, 1997, then the new rules will apply. Follow me?

Who really wins under the new rules? The tax collector. If we go back to Henry and Rosette's story, the $700 savings enjoyed on a combined basis is gone under the new rules. Consider keeping pre–May 1997 agreements intact to avoid a windfall to the tax collector. The higher-income parent should consider spending the tax savings on the children to convince the lower-income parent to keep the pre–May 1997 agreement in place.

TO MAKE A LONG STORY SHORT:

- Our tax law says that child support agreements made or varied after April 30, 1997, provide for payments that are non-deductible to the payor and non-taxable to the recipient. The tax collector comes out ahead under these rules.

- Consider keeping pre-May 1997 agreements intact to avoid the tax collector's win here.

Getting into the Game

It's time to turn to the Tax Planning Tip Sheet at the front of the book and review the strategies introduced in Chapter 2. Ask yourself, "Can this tip apply to me?" Each *Yes* or *Not Sure* could lead to big tax savings for you and your family.

SIGNING WITH THE TEAM: STRATEGIES FOR EMPLOYEES

I'm not sure, but I think my pay deductions finally caught up with my salary.

3

If you happen to be one of the millions of employees in Canada today, then you know that the Canada Revenue Agency (CRA) is not exactly bending over backward to provide you with tax relief. Sure, I'll be talking to you about the specific deductions that you're entitled to, but here's a tip for those of you who are employees: While it's important to claim all the deductions possible, you need to focus your energy on other tax planning opportunities. Why? Simply put, the deductions available to employees are very limited, except in special situations. You're going to do yourself a favour by reading this chapter and working with your employer to minimize your tax bill.

Optimizing Employment Benefits

Tim's Tip 26: **Take non-taxable benefits as part of your compensation, with smart strategies from A to Z.**

You know, I'd have to give most employers a 4 out of 10 on the creativity scale when it comes to compensating employees in Canada. I mean, most employees simply receive a flat salary or hourly wage for the work they perform, with no thought given to the tax bill that the employee is going to face. If employers and employees would give just a little more thought to the manner in which compensation is paid, the results could be very tax efficient. I'm talking about non-taxable benefits.

A llison works for a software company, Software Inc. She has one child, age *seven, and the childcare costs that enable her to work can be very high— about $6,000 annually after factoring in the tax savings from her childcare deductions. How much additional salary does Allison have to earn just to pay for these childcare costs? Since her marginal tax rate is 46 percent, the answer is $11,111. That is, an additional $11,111 in salary would leave Allison with just $6,000 after taxes—just enough to pay for the child care. Last year, Software Inc. decided to open a daycare facility right in the building for the benefit of employees. Allison no longer has to pay for daycare services. This benefit to Allison is worth the equivalent of $11,111 in additional salary! The best part, of course, is that Allison is not taxed on the value of the daycare provided to her. This is a non-taxable benefit.*

The best part about non-taxable benefits is that they never show up on your personal tax return as income. Now, here's my question: Can you list all the non-taxable benefits you're currently receiving? If the list isn't long, consider negotiating with your employer the next time you take on a new job or are due for a salary review. The following A-to-Z list of non-taxable benefits will help you get started. It's divided into four categories: home benefits, family benefits, individual benefits, and workplace benefits. You'll find more information on many of these in the CRA's Interpretation Bulletin IT-470R.

Home Benefits

a. Home Loan

If you receive a loan by virtue of your employment to buy or refinance a home, you won't face a taxable benefit as long as you pay interest equal to the prescribed rate charged by the CRA. And that prescribed rate which is in effect when the loan is set up is locked in for five years. The rate is re-set on the fifth anniversary of the loan at the prescribed rate in effect at that time. See Tip 28 for more on this benefit.

b. Relocation costs

If your employer requires you to relocate and reimburses you for costs associated with making the move, this reimbursement is not taxable in your hands. An allowance is different, in that you're not required to provide any receipts to your employer—and a non-accountable allowance of $650 or less is not taxable provided you've certified in writing to your employer that you used the allowance to cover moving costs.

A non-accountable allowance over $650 is taxable (although you may be able to deduct your actual moving costs in this case).

> Since 1998, any interest subsidies that your employer provides upon your relocation will now be taxable. I'm talking about situations where you relocate for work and take on a larger mortgage or higher mortgage rate as a result. Any help from your employer will now give rise to a taxable benefit, where it would not have in the past! Sorry for the news.
>
> **Caution!**

c. Loss-on-home reimbursement

A woman I know found a new job last year that required her to move from Toronto to Vancouver. She had paid $350,000 for her home in Toronto, and she sold the place for just $335,000 when she made the move. Her new employer picked up the tab for the $15,000 loss she incurred on the sale. The best part is this: She wasn't taxed on this loss reimbursement.

Provided your employer requires you to relocate and doesn't reimburse you for more than $15,000 of losses, you won't face a taxable benefit. Thanks to the 1998 federal budget, you'll face a taxable benefit equal to one-half of any loss reimbursement over $15,000 for relocations after September 30, 1998. Reimbursements for relocations made before this date were tax free as long as they were paid before the year 2001.

d. Fair market value guarantee

Suppose for a minute that an employer asks you to relocate, and you're forced to sell your home fairly quickly for a lower price than you might otherwise receive if you weren't in such a hurry. Well, there's good news for you. Your employer can actually guarantee that you'll receive fair market value for your home—to a maximum of $15,000—and you won't be taxed on this benefit. For example, if it can be established that the true fair market value of your home is $375,000, and you're forced to sell quickly for $360,000, your employer can pay the $15,000 difference to you—tax free. Not a bad deal. If your employer pays you more than $15,000 for a relocation after September 30, 1998, you'll be taxed on one-half of the excess as a result of the 1998 federal budget. For relocations before that date, the payment was tax free as long as you received it before the year 2001.

e. Employer home-purchase

I've seen a number of situations where an employer will buy a home from an employee to enable the employee to relocate to a new workplace. Typically, the company will then turn around and sell the home on the open market. This allows an employee to move right away, rather than wait for the right offer on the home. In this case, the benefit to the employee will be tax free as long as the price paid to the employee does not exceed the fair market value of the home.

f. Remote location benefits

Do you work in a remote location? A remote location is called a *prescribed area*, and it includes many places far south of the Arctic Circle. There's no need to move to Nunavut to receive these tax-free benefits! If you happen to work in a prescribed area, you may be eligible for tax-free benefits in the form of board and lodging, rent-free or low-rent housing, travel benefits, and allowances for a child's education—all paid for by your employer. Generally, it will have been necessary for you to reside in this pre-scribed area for at least six months.

g. Assets of personal value

Let's suppose for a minute that you've found a computer or a desk that you would really like to have. And what if your employer were to buy the asset for use in the busi-ness and let you make use of the asset for work? This would be a definite benefit to you, but it would be a non-taxable benefit. Here's the best part: After two or three years, you could simply buy the asset from your employer for its fair market value at that time. Chances are pretty good that the asset will have depreciated in value enough to make the purchase very affordable. By the way, your employer doesn't need to buy the asset to make this idea work. Leasing the asset and allowing you to buy it at the end of the lease term can work just as well.

> **Action Step**
>
> Looking for a non-taxable benefit? Consider buying from your employer the vehicle that your employer has been providing for use in the business. You'll manage to save a bundle by buying the vehicle used. Your employer may be willing to offer this opportunity if it's time to upgrade the vehicles anyway. And by the way, making this kind of purchase may minimize the tax cost of the dreaded standby charge that applies when an employer's vehicle is made available to you (see Tip 31).

Family Benefits

h. Personal counselling

This is one of the lesser-known benefits that could really lend you a hand—not only financially, but mentally or physically as well. If your employer pays for counselling related to the mental or physical health of you or someone related to you, the benefit is non-taxable. This might include counselling related to stress management or an addiction, for example. Financial counselling related to your re-employment or retirement is also non-taxable, so if you're due for a severance or retirement package, be sure to negotiate a number of counselling sessions with a tax professional or financial advisor.

i. Daycare services

If your employer provides in-house daycare services, this benefit will be tax-free. You should note that this is different from your employer paying for daycare provided by a third party. Third-party daycare paid for by your employer is a taxable benefit to you, although I should mention that, in this case, you may still be entitled to claim a deduction for those childcare expenses included in your income as a taxable benefit. The deduction is claimed under the regular rules for childcare expenses, described in Chapter 2, Tip 16.

j. Transportation passes

If you're an employee of a bus or railway company, you'll be able to accept transportation passes from your employer—tax-free. Things work a bit differently if you're an employee of an airline. In this case, your passes will be tax-free as long as you're not travelling on a space-confirmed basis, and provided you pay at least 50 percent of the economy fare for the flight you're on. There's good news if you're a retired employee of any transportation company at all: You won't be taxed on any passes that you receive.

k. Group plan premiums

Most employees these days are members of a group plan for sickness, disability, or accident insurance. You'll be glad to know that the premiums paid by your employer to this type of plan are tax-free benefits to you. You'll want to make sure, however, that any premiums paid on a disability insurance plan are paid by you and not your employer. You see, if your employer pays any part of these premiums, any benefits that you receive under the policy will be taxable payments to you. Not so if *you* pay the premiums. Check out your plan at work to ensure that your disability payments would be tax-free if you had to collect.

l. Private health services plans

A private health services plan (PHSP) is a plan set up to cover certain costs not covered by public health insurance. I'm referring to costs like prescription drugs, hospital charges, and dental fees. Any contributions to a PHSP will be a non-taxable benefit to you. By the way, the government changed the rules in 1998 to allow self-employed proprietors to deduct PHSP premiums from business income.

m. Disability top-ups

A number of Canadians ran into some difficulty a few years ago when the life insurance company that held their disability policy could no longer make good on disability payments. Where your employer tops up disability payments made to you so that you receive all the benefits you were expecting under your disability policy, those payments will not be taxable to you. This applies to all payments made after August 10, 1994.

n. Death benefits

Next time you're talking to your employer about non-taxable benefits, ask that a death benefit be paid to your heirs if you happen to die while in the employ of the company. You see, a benefit of up to $10,000 can be paid to your heirs tax-free once you're gone. It's not going to make your family rich, but hey, it's going to cover the cost of your funeral! How's that for practical?

Individual Benefits

o. Commissions on sales

Picture this. You're an insurance agent or broker and you purchase a life insurance policy for yourself. The commissions owing on the sale are paid to you, just as though you had sold the policy to a third party. Are you taxed on the commissions you receive? No! In fact, any commissions on merchandise that you acquire for your own personal use will not be taxable. Evidently, commissions on sales of investment products to yourself are *not* tax-free. This hardly seems fair in light of CRA's position on life insurance sales.

p. Discounts on merchandise

If your employer sells, say, soap or toothpaste, and you're able to buy those items at a discount, the benefit is not taxable to you. But this benefit doesn't apply to personal hygiene products alone. Any discounts offered by any employer to its employees will generally be a non-taxable benefit. The only catch is that these discounts must be generally available to all employees.

q. Membership fees

Perhaps you like to play golf, squash, or tennis—or just hang out at the social club? Membership fees paid by your employer for social or recreational clubs will generally be a non-taxable benefit so long as the membership is principally for your employer's advantage, rather than your own. Generally, your employer will not be able to deduct these fees for tax purposes. But that may not be a concern—particularly if your employer is a non-profit organization where tax deductions are not important.

r. Gifts and awards

You're entitled to receive certain non-cash gifts from your employer. CRA's policy was relaxed in 2001 when it announced that employers can now give up to two non-cash gifts to each employee on a tax-free basis provided the aggregate cost of those gifts does not exceed $500 (including GST, HST, and PST). In addition, employers can give up to two non-cash awards to an employee each year, tax free, provided the aggregate cost of the awards does not exceed $500 (including GST, HST, and PST). By the way, some gifts, like air miles, are considered akin to cash and will be taxable.

s. Education costs

Revenue Canada's policy on education benefits changed in 1998. It's now clear that there are three types of education costs: two are tax-free but the third is taxable. (1) First there's *specific employment-related training*, which involves education directly related to the skills you use at work. It's tax-free. (2) Then there's *general employment-related training*, which does not relate directly to your required work skills but may be generally relevant, and could include courses such as stress management or employment equity training. It's also tax-free. (3) Finally, there's *personal interest training* in areas that have nothing to do with your work, like ballroom dancing or furniture recovering (unless you dance or upholster furniture for a living, of course). This benefit is taxable.

t. Vacation property use

How would you like a few days away at the company condominium in California? If you're required to spend a few days at the firm's property, in Canada or abroad, the benefit will not be taxable to you to the extent that the trip is business-related. Be sure to keep an itinerary of scheduled meetings and events as evidence to the tax collector that business activities actually took place.

u. Out-of-town trips

Next time your employer sends you on a business trip, why not extend the trip and turn it into a personal vacation too? Once I was forced to spend a week in Whistler, BC, learning about advanced tax issues. I thoroughly enjoyed extending that trip by another week just to relax. You see, turning a business trip into a personal vacation will mean that costs paid by your employer will be tax-free benefits to the extent that the trip is business-related. This can really cut the cost of any vacation!

v. Host or hostess trip

I was asked to speak at a conference of financial advisors in Halifax. On that trip, a woman who worked for a financial planning firm was asked to come along to act as a hostess. The majority of her time was spent helping to organize events and generally keeping the event running smoothly. But she told me that she did have some time to relax and take in the scenery. While she was still able to enjoy her time there, the trip was a tax-free benefit to her because her hostess duties took up a substantial part of each day. If you happen to take a similar trip, you'll enjoy non-taxable benefits as well.

Workplace Benefits

w. Meal subsidies

Before you get too excited, I'm not talking here about your employer picking up the weekly grocery tab. But where your employer provides subsidized meals—most commonly at a workplace cafeteria—the benefit will be tax-free, provided you're still required to pay a reasonable charge.

x. Recreational and fitness facilities

More and more employers are recognizing the importance of having healthy employees. As a result, it's more common than ever for employers to provide in-house fitness and recreational facilities. I know of some corporations that go so far as to reward employees financially for maintaining a certain level of fitness. If your employer provides these facilities, the benefit is non-taxable.

y. Special clothing and uniforms

Some employers are keen on presenting a certain image or look and, as a result, will provide uniforms or special clothing to their employees. If you're in this boat, you'll be glad to know that the clothing is a non-taxable benefit to you. I met a guy once who really enjoyed wearing his employer-provided pants and jacket out on the town. Let's just say that this guy enjoyed an extra benefit—non-taxable, of course.

z. Transportation to work

How would you like it if your boss insisted on sending a stretch limo to pick you up each morning? The truth is, where your employer provides you with transportation to or from work for security or other reasons, the value of that transportation is a non-taxable benefit. This is not the same, however, as your employer giving you an allowance or reimbursement for transportation that you provide yourself: You could be taxed on that type of benefit. (See Tip 32 for more.)

TO MAKE A LONG STORY SHORT:

- Most Canadian employers lack creativity when structuring employment compensation.

- Receiving a non-taxable benefit is the same as receiving salary or wages that will never show up on your tax return.

- Next time you change employers or renegotiate your salary or wages, ask for non-taxable benefits to form part of your compensation package.

Tim's Tip 27: Calculate whether a taxable benefit works to your advantage.

There's no question that most benefits your employer provides to you will be taxable as regular income. Want some examples? If your employer pays the premiums on a life insurance policy for you, provides you with a company car, allows you to keep the frequent-flier air miles earned on business trips, or provides you with many other benefits—you can expect the value of the benefits to show up on your T4 slip at tax time.

Is this a bad thing? Not necessarily. Where the benefit that your employer provides is acquired by your employer for less than you'd have to pay yourself, you'll come out ahead. Further, you'd have to pay your out-of-pocket cost sooner if you were to pay for the item yourself. Consider Floyd's story.

*F*loyd wanted very much to have a new computer system for home. He *priced out the new system at $5,000. Floyd's employer agreed to pay $5,000 this year for the system on his behalf. His employer has two options: (1) pay the computer supplier the $5,000 for the system, or (2) pay Floyd the $5,000 so that he can pay for the system himself. In the first case, a $5,000 taxable benefit is added to Floyd's T4 slip, and this will cost him $2,500 in tax at a marginal tax rate of 50 percent. This $2,500 tax bill will not be owing until April 30 next year when he files his tax return for this year. In the second case, Floyd's employer will pay him the $5,000 directly, and $2,500 in taxes deducted at-source will be withheld immediately. Floyd will have to come up with another $2,500 to bring his available cash to $5,000 in order to buy the computer system. In both cases, the out-of-pocket cost to Floyd is $2,500. The difference is in the timing of that outlay. In the first case, the $2,500 is paid as additional taxes when Floyd files his tax return next April. In the second case, Floyd pays the $2,500 to the computer store today in order to buy the computer. Better to pay that $2,500 next year than this year.*

If you're going to be taxed on a benefit received from your employer, exactly how much will be added to your income? Simple. You'll be taxed on your employer's cost of the benefit. In Floyd's example, the computer system cost his employer $5,000, so Floyd's taxable benefit is $5,000. The good news is that your employer may be able to negotiate lower prices on certain things because of your employer's size and number of employees. If this is the case, the amount of your taxable benefit may be reduced—and your true cost will shrink even further.

TO MAKE A LONG STORY SHORT:

- A taxable benefit will still leave you better off than if you had purchased the item yourself since your out-of-pocket cost will be delayed until you file your tax return for the year you received the benefit.

- In addition, your employer may be able to buy the item at a lower cost than you can on your own. This will reduce your taxable benefit and your true cost will shrink further.

- The value of the benefit added to your income is simply your employer's cost of the item.

Tim's Tip 28: **Negotiate a loan from your employer instead of from a bank.**

Next time you're thinking of borrowing money from the bank for any reason, why not consider approaching your employer for a loan instead? Loans from your employer should be viewed by you—and your employer—as a perk that forms just another part of any creative and tax-efficient compensation package!

Interest Savings

You see, you could save interest costs if the loan is made at a lower interest rate than you'd pay to the bank. You may have to include a taxable interest benefit in your income, but you're still bound to enjoy savings. How much will your taxable benefit be? Simple. It's calculated as CRA's (or Revenue Quebec's) prescribed interest rate minus the actual rate of interest you pay. By the way, if you're paying interest to your employer, you've got to make those payments during the year or within 30 days following the end of the year (January 30).

John wanted to buy a new car. He figured it would help him in his work since he is always driving clients here and there. He needed to borrow $10,000 to make the purchase. John approached his employer, who agreed to lend him the $10,000 at an interest rate of 3 percent, although CRA's prescribed rate throughout the year was 8 percent. What is John's taxable benefit? It amounts to $500, which is simply 5 percent (8 percent minus 3 percent) of $10,000. This taxable interest benefit will appear on John's T4 slip. John's true cost of borrowing is just $550 ($250 in tax on the benefit plus $300 in interest paid to his employer). If John had borrowed from the bank at, say, 8 percent, he would have paid $800 in interest. John saved $250 ($800 minus $550), or 2.5 percent, just by borrowing from his employer.

It's worth mentioning that you won't face any taxable benefit at all if the rate of interest charged by your employer is equal to or greater than commercial rates available from your local bank or other financial institution. This is true even if these commercial rates are lower than CRA's prescribed rate.

Home Loans

If your employer lends you money to buy or refinance a home, some special rules apply. And these rules will work to your advantage. In this case, the prescribed rate used to calculate your taxable interest benefit will be either the rate in effect at the start of the loan or the current prescribed rate, whichever is less. The loan is deemed to be a new loan every five years. As a result, the prescribed rate in effect at that time will be the maximum rate for the next five years.

There's more good news if the purpose of your loan was to buy a home because of a job relocation (rather than to refinance your existing home). In this case, the tax collector will allow you to claim a deduction for the taxable interest benefit on the first $25,000 of the loan. This interest deduction is available only for the first five years of the loan and, to qualify, your relocation must have moved you at least 40 kilometres closer to your new workplace.

Investment or Automobile Loans

There may be other situations where you'll be entitled to claim a deduction for all or part of the taxable interest benefit. In a nutshell, if you'd be entitled to an interest deduction had you borrowed from the bank instead, you'll also be entitled to a deduction for the interest paid to your employer. And by the way, even where you haven't paid your employer any interest, the amount of the resulting taxable interest benefit is considered by the tax collector to be interest paid by you, and may entitle you to a deduction. So if you borrow from your employer to invest, to buy a car for use in your work, or for some other purpose that normally provides you with the ability to deduct interest, you'll reduce your taxable interest benefit.

TO MAKE A LONG STORY SHORT:

- Borrowing from your employer rather than from a financial institution will normally save you interest costs.

- While you will normally have a taxable interest benefit to include in your income, there may be special relief from this taxable benefit if you are borrowing to buy or refinance a home, or for a purpose that would normally entitle you to deduct interest.

Tim's Tip 29: **Opt for stock options or similar tax-efficient compensation.**

One of the more creative methods to compensate employees is the good ol' stock option plan. Not sure how this works? Let me explain. A stock option plan will entitle you to buy shares of the company that employs you—or shares of a related company. This purchase will take place at a predetermined price— called the *exercise price*. Normally, you'll exercise your right to buy the shares only when the fair market value of those shares is higher than your exercise price. After all, why would you want to buy company shares for $10 if the shares are only worth $8? If the shares are ripe for the picking because the market value is higher than your exercise price, then your stock options are said to be *in the money*.

If you're going to borrow for both deductible and non-deductible purposes, and your employer isn't willing to lend you money for everything, borrow the non-deductible funds from your employer and the deductible from your bank. Here's why: Your true interest cost when borrowing from your employer is likely to be less than the bank's interest, so borrow the funds from your employer that will otherwise cost you the most— the non-deductible funds. Since borrowing from your bank is going to cost you more interest, you might as well get all the breaks you can through deductions.

If you exercise your stock options for, say, $20,000 while the fair market value of those shares is $30,000, then you've received a benefit from your employment. In fact, you'll face tax on that $10,000 benefit. But here's where stock options can be very attractive. Provided certain conditions are met, you'll be able to claim an offsetting deduction equal to 50 percent of the stock option benefit you've reported as income. Further, the benefit may not be taxable until the year that you actually sell the stocks acquired under the option, thanks to the 2000 federal budget (more on this in a minute). In my example, you'd include $10,000 on your tax return as income from employment in the year the option is taxed, but you may be entitled to an offsetting deduction of $5,000. This can make a stock option very tax-efficient.

What conditions have to be met to entitle you to the 50-percent deduction? There are three:

(a) you must deal with the company at arm's length (basically, you and your family members must not control the corporation);

(b) the shares must be common shares, not preferred shares;

(c) the stock options cannot be in the money on the day the option is granted.

That is, the fair market value of the shares on the date the options are granted must be no greater than your exercise price. Otherwise, you could exercise your stock options right away and sell your shares that same day for a profit. This is no different than receiving cash, so the tax collector won't allow the 50-percent deduction.

*C*ary's employer, Option Corp., set up a stock option plan for its employees. Cary was granted stock options in 2008 at a time when Option Corp. shares were selling for $10 on the stock market. Cary was granted options to purchase 1,000 shares of Option Corp. at a price of $10 per share—his exercise price. In the year 2009, shares of Option Corp. were trading on the stock market for $15, so Cary decided to exercise all his options. Cary paid $10,000 for his Option Corp. shares ($10 × 1,000 shares), but they were worth $15,000 on the date he exercised them ($15 × 1,000 shares). Cary will have to report the $5,000 difference as employment income. In fact, this amount will appear on a T4 slip for him. The good news? Since the conditions for the 50-percent deduction were met, Cary will also be entitled to claim a deduction of $2,500 (50 percent of $5,000) on line 249 of his tax return.

Things are a bit different if your employer is a Canadian-controlled private corporation (CCPC) and you buy your shares at arm's length from the company. It has been the case for quite a while that you will not have to report your taxable stock option benefit in this situation until the year you actually dispose of your shares. What's more, you'll be entitled to the 50-percent deduction I've been talking about, even if you haven't met conditions (b) and (c) noted above, as long as you hold the shares for two years before selling them.

Deferral Rules for Options

The Department of Finance had been under pressure over the last few years to help Canadian corporations—particularly high-tech businesses—attract and retain top-notch, talented workers and make our tax treatment of employee stock options more competitive with conditions in the United States. The outcome? The 2000 federal budget proposed to allow employees to defer the taxable benefit from exercising employee stock options for publicly listed shares until the disposition of the shares, subject to an annual $100,000 limit, which I'll talk more about in a minute.

Employees who sell their shares will be eligible to claim the 50-percent stock option deduction in the year the benefit is included in income. The rules also apply to employee options to acquire units of a mutual fund trust. By the way, employee stock options granted by CCPCs are not affected by the proposed measure (we've been able to defer the taxable benefit on these types of options until the year of sale for some time now).

Who is eligible for this deferral? If you're an employee who, at the time the option was granted, dealt with your employer (or any related company) at arm's length and was not a specified shareholder (generally, one who owns 10 percent or more of the company's shares), then you may be eligible.

What options are eligible? An eligible option is one under which the shares to be acquired are ordinary common shares; the shares are of a class of shares traded on a prescribed Canadian or foreign stock exchange, and the total of all amounts payable to acquire the shares, including the exercise price and any amount payable to acquire the options, is not less than the fair market value of the shares at the time the option is granted. Follow me? You should be aware that the rules apply to eligible options exercised after February 27, 2000, regardless of when the option was granted or became vested (first became exercisable).

Now, back to the $100,000 limit. You'll be limited to exercising $100,000 worth of options *per year of vesting* to enjoy the deferral. If you exercise more than this amount, the taxable benefit arising on the excess options will be taxed in the year you exercise the options (not the year you sell the shares). The $100,000 limit applies to the value of the stock options in the year that they vest (the year that you first have the right to exercise the options under the option agreement), and not the year you exercise the options. The value of a stock option here is simply the fair market value of the underlying share at the time the option was granted, and the $100,000 limit applies across all stock option plans of the employer corporation and related corporations.

Finally, the taxable benefit will be deferred until the time you dispose of the shares acquired under the option or, if earlier, the time you die or become a non-resident of Canada for tax purposes.

What are the reporting requirements? If you exercise stock options that qualify for the deferral, be sure to:

- Notify your employer in writing of the amount of the stock option benefit you want to defer. The deadline for options exercised in 2008 is January 15, 2009. Your stock option benefit could be subject to payroll withholdings unless you submit your notification immediately after exercising your options (some provinces may still levy payroll withholding taxes).
- Designate the options that will provide the greatest tax deferral.
- Consider whether it's beneficial to sell some of your shares within 30 days after exercising your options. (This would allow you to designate those option shares as the specific shares being sold rather than having to blend the cost of these shares with other shares you might already own in the same company. Doing so could reduce your taxable capital gain on the sale.)
- File Form T1212, Statement of Deferred Stock Option Benefits, with your tax return.

Will this deferral really help you? While it may seem like a windfall that the tax collector is willing to defer the taxation of your stock option benefits, you're not likely to take advantage of this provision if you're handling your stock options properly. You see, in most cases you shouldn't exercise your stock options unless you're planning to sell the shares right away. What's the benefit of exercising your stock options if you're going to hold the shares for any length of time beyond that exercise date? "Tim, my shares could go up in value if I hold them; isn't that a

good enough reason?" you might ask. My response is this: You can simply hold
the options for that same length of time. Your options will go up in value just as the
stocks would have. You don't need to hold the shares themselves to benefit from
the stock price increasing. In fact, it's preferable simply to hold the options rather
than the stock in most cases for two reasons:

- if you hold the shares and they drop in value after
  exercising your options, you won't be able to apply
  the capital loss against the taxable employment benefit you faced (or will face) on the stock options; and
- there's ugly paperwork and accounting to look after if
  you're going to hold your shares after exercising the
  options and you want to defer the tax under the
  deferral rules (see the filing requirements above).

There may be one situation where you may exercise
your options and hold the shares beyond that date:
when your options would otherwise expire (for
example, after a certain length of time or when you
leave the company) but you like the future prospects of
the company. In this case, the new rules permitting a
deferral of tax could come in handy.

> When you acquire shares
> under a stock option plan,
> there's always the risk that
> you could acquire too much
> stock in one company—your
> employer. Make sure that your
> overall investment portfolio
> remains properly diversified.
> This may mean selling some
> of those option shares from
> time to time and reinvesting
> in other securities. Speak to
> your financial advisor about
> proper diversification.

Caution!

Are Stock Options Always a Good Idea?

Do stock options always make sense? Well, not always. You want to be confident of
two things. First, you should feel confident that the shares in the company are going
to increase in value over time. Only then will you be *in the money*. Second, you
want to be confident that you'll be able to sell the shares later. Think back to Cary's
example. Cary's purchase may look good on paper, but he won't actually realize a
profit unless he sells those shares for a higher value than what he paid. You've got
to be able to sell those shares. This can be a problem with private company shares
in particular. Before exercising stock options in a private company, you'd better
have a way out—in other words, someone to sell the shares to.

Phantom Stock Plans and Stock Appreciation Rights

A phantom stock plan works much like a stock option plan, except that you don't actually acquire shares. Rather, your employer will simply pay, in cash, the difference between your exercise price and the fair market value of the company's shares on the date you exercise your phantom stock options. With a phantom plan, you don't have to worry about raising the money to buy the shares and, best of all, you don't have to worry about how you're going to sell the shares later. The drawback? You're not entitled to the 50-percent deduction against your taxable benefit and you won't be able to defer tax on the benefit.

A stock appreciation right (SAR) is a combination of a phantom plan and a stock option plan. When it comes time to exercise your SARs, you'll have two choices: Buy shares in your employer, or take cash as you would under a phantom plan. Talk about flexibility! The best part of a SAR is this: So long as the employee has the right to choose between shares and cash, and this decision isn't influenced by the employer, then the employee will still be entitled to claim the 50-percent deduction against the taxable benefit reported as income (assuming the usual conditions are met), and to defer the taxable benefit until the year the shares are sold (where you take shares rather than cash). In my mind, this makes SARs a better choice than straight stock options or phantom plans.

TO MAKE A LONG STORY SHORT:

- Stock option plans can be a very tax-efficient source of compensation, since the plan may entitle you to a 50-percent deduction to offset the taxable benefits and the taxable benefit may be deferred until you sell your shares.

- These plans are best when you're confident that your employer's shares will increase in value and you'll be able to sell the shares down the road.

- Phantom plans and stock appreciation rights (SARs) are hybrids of a stock option plan, except that they don't require you to buy shares. SARs are especially attractive, since they still offer the potential for the 50-percent deduction and the tax deferral.

Claiming Employment Deductions

The fact is, employees are provided with very little in the way of deductions. Unless something is specifically allowed as a deduction, then don't count on claiming it. Nevertheless, you certainly don't want to pass up the opportunity to claim what you are entitled to.

Tim's Tip 30: **Claim all the employment deductions you're entitled to.**

Let's take a look at the things our tax law will specifically allow employees to deduct.

a. Commissioned employee expenses

If you're an employee selling a product or service and you're compensated partially or fully by commissions, you may be able to claim expenses against that commission income. Your employment contract must require you to pay your own expenses, and you must ordinarily be required to carry on your employment duties away from your employer's workplace. The types of expenses you can deduct are as varied as those available to a self-employed person (see Chapter 4), with some exceptions. Most notably, you can only claim expenses up to the limit of your commission income. That is, you can't create a loss with your expenses.

b. Travel expenses

You can count on deducting any travel costs related to your employment if you were required to pay these costs and did not receive a reimbursement or tax-free allowance to cover those costs. I'm talking about costs such as taxis, trains, planes, buses, parking, or hotels. If you work for a transportation company (as a bus or truck driver or as a flight attendant, for example) and you incur costs for meals and lodging, you can deduct those costs if you weren't reimbursed. Just 50 percent of your meals will be deductible in this case.

c. Automobile expenses

If your employer required you to use your own vehicle in your employment and you did not receive a reimbursement or tax-free allowance to cover your automobile costs, you'll be entitled to claim a deduction for a portion of all your car costs. I'll talk more about this in Tips 31 and 32.

> **Action Step**
>
> Many of the employment deductions I refer to are available only if your employer requires you to pay for certain costs. To ensure that you're entitled to claim the costs, your best bet is to put in writing the requirement that you pay for these things. This is done most easily before you start working for an employer.

d. Aircraft expenses

If you provided your own aircraft for use in your employer's business, and you did not receive a reimbursement or tax-free allowance to cover your costs of flying the aircraft, you'll be able to claim a deduction for a portion of those costs. Your deductible portion is based on the percentage of flying hours that were spent on business in the year.

e. Cost of supplies

Did you incur any costs for supplies consumed directly in your employment activities? If so, you may be able to deduct these costs at tax time. Your employer will have to verify (on Form T2200) that you were required to pay these costs yourself and that you did not receive a reimbursement or tax-free allowance to cover them. By the way, supplies can include cellular phone air time and long distance calls, but won't include connection or monthly service charges, or Internet service fees.

f. Assistant's salary

If your employer required you to pay for an assistant, you'll be entitled to deduct the cost of hiring that person. This includes the wages or salary paid plus your share of any Canada Pension Plan and Employment Insurance premiums paid.

g. Home office expenses

In certain situations, you'll be entitled to claim costs for an office in your home. Before you deduct anything, you've got to meet some tests. First, your employer must require you to have an office in your home. Second, your home must either be your principal place of employment (meaning half your work or more is performed there), or it must be used on a regular and continual basis to meet people as part of your work. Employees will generally be restricted to claiming a portion of any rent, utilities, repairs, maintenance, and supplies associated with the office space. Commissioned employees can add a portion of property taxes and home insurance to the list of eligible expenses (note that mortgage interest and property taxes are excluded here). The deductible portion depends on the percentage of your home used as your office. I'll deal with home offices for the self-employed in Chapter 4.

h. Office rent

If your employer required you to pay your own office rent, you'll be able to deduct the cost of that rent. Sorry, this does not include rent for space in your own residence. See my previous point on home office expenses for more information on using your home as your workplace.

i. Disability support costs

When you have a severe and prolonged impairment and you need to hire an attendant or otherwise incur costs in order to perform your duties of employment, you can claim a deduction for these disability support costs, up to a maximum of 100 percent of your earned income. See Tip 18 for more details.

j. Union and professional dues

You can deduct union or professional dues if you had to pay those dues to maintain your membership in a union or to maintain your professional status in an organization recognized by statute. Sorry to disappoint you, but you can't claim a deduction for dues to a voluntary organization: Only the self-employed can write off those costs.

Did You Know?

A 1998 court decision in the case of *Alan Wayne Scott v. The Queen* established that couriers who perform their work by bicycle or on foot can deduct the cost of additional food and water consumed to provide energy for the job. In the case, the taxpayer travelled 150 kilometres per day and carried a backpack weighing 10 to 20 kilograms or more (about 20 to 50 pounds). He consumed $11 extra in food and beverages each day, which was considered by the court as "fuel" necessary to do his job.

Did You Know?

Here's another possible employment deduction for you: If you happen to need an assistant in your work, consider hiring your lower-income spouse. Even if your employer is not willing to pick up the tab, you can hire your spouse yourself. You'll be entitled to a deduction against your employment income, and your lower-income spouse will pay the tax instead. This will reduce your overall family tax bill. To make this work, you'll need to have your employment contract worded so that you're required to provide your own assistant.

k. Musician's instruments

If you are employed as a musician and are required to provide your own instruments, you'll be able to claim a deduction for the cost of any rental, maintenance, or insurance on the instruments. In addition, if you own the instruments, you'll be entitled to claim capital cost allowance (CCA) (depreciation) on your instruments. Keep in mind that your total deductions cannot exceed your employment income as a musician.

l. Artist's expenses

If you earn employment income from artistic activities, then you'll be entitled to claim a deduction for virtually any unreimbursed costs incurred to earn that employment income. Your total deduction is limited to 20 percent of your income from artistic employment activities, or $1,000, whichever is less. Oh, yeah. I should mention that this $1,000 limit is reduced by any interest or capital cost allowance claimed for work-related use of your automobile or by any claim for musician's instruments.

m. Legal fees

If you had to pay a lawyer to collect or establish a right to salary, wages, retiring allowances, severance payments, private pension plan benefits, or spousal or child support payments, then those fees will normally be deductible. The general rule is this: If you pay legal fees to recover income that will be taxable to you, you'll very likely be entitled to a deduction for those costs. You'll also be entitled to claim a deduction for legal fees paid to file a Notice of Objection or Appeal against the tax collector. See Tip 7 (page 12).

n. Clergy deduction

Are you a member of the clergy? If so, you may be entitled to a deduction with respect to your residence. Now, the government changed the rules in 2001, but proper planning can result in continued tax savings for virtually all clergy.

The rules work this way: Where you're a member of the clergy and you provide your own residence (whether you rent or own), your clergy residence deduction will be limited for 2001 and subsequent years to the least of the following two amounts: (a) one-third of your total remuneration from the office or employment or $10,000, whichever is greater, and (b) the fair rental value of the residence (reduced by other amounts deducted in connection with that residence). In addition, you're now required to file a prescribed form with your income tax return that will have to be signed by your employer to verify that you meet the status and function requirements of a clergy member.

Where your employer provides you with a residence, you can deduct all amounts that were included in your income with respect to that accommodation, including utilities. In any event, whether you provide your own residence or it's provided for you, the deduction you claim cannot exceed your income from that employment in the year.

If you're a member of the clergy, speak to your employer about these rules, and visit the Department of Finance's Web site at **www.fin.gc.ca** for a copy of the December 21, 2000, news release that contains the details, or call the Public Affairs and Operations Division of the Department of Finance at (613) 996-8080. Also, visit my Web site at **www.timcestnick.com**, where you'll find a handy calculator in the Tax Tools area to assist with your clergy residence deduction.

Last Thoughts

When claiming certain employment expenses, you must file Form T777 (Statement of Employment Expenses). In addition, your employer will have to sign Form T2200 (Declaration of Conditions of Employment), although you don't need to file Form T2200 with your tax return; keep it on file in case the tax collector wants to see it. Ask your employer for a signed T2200 each January, and if you leave an employer during the year, get a signed T2200 before you go.

I should also mention that, when you make a claim for employment expenses and your employer happens to be registered for GST purposes, you'll generally be able to claim a GST rebate for the GST paid on the expenses you're deducting. To claim this rebate, you'll have to file Form GST370. The GST rebate is taxable in the calendar year in which it's received.

Finally, always be sure to keep the receipts that support any expenses you claim, if the receipts are not filed with your tax return. The tax collector may ask to see them later.

TO MAKE A LONG STORY SHORT:

- Employees aren't given a lot of breaks in the form of deductions.

- Claim all the deductions you're entitled to, and make sure you obtain a signed Form T2200 where necessary and file Form T777 with your tax return.

- Remember to claim a GST rebate where possible, using Form GST370.

- Always keep your receipts on file in case the tax collector wants to see them.

Driving Automobiles on the Job

I was sitting in a restaurant in Red Deer, Alberta, not long ago, and I couldn't help but overhear a rancher bragging to the owner of a small farm from Lloydminster, Saskatchewan. "I can get in my car at six in the morning," he said, "drive for six hours, spend an hour eating lunch, drive for another six hours, and I still wouldn't have reached the end of my property." "Yeah," the farmer said, nodding sympathetically. "I had a car like that once."

Now there's a man using his car—regardless of its condition—for his work. Do you use your car in your employment? Now, I'm not talking about driving from home to work and back again. I'm talking about using your car for other employment activities on a regular basis. Perhaps you're one of the few who has been provided with a car by your employer. What a perk that is! Or is it? Let's talk about automobiles and employment.

Tim's Tip 31: Say "thanks, but no thanks" when offered a company car.

There's a definite misconception that an employer-provided vehicle is a sign that you've "made it." You've arrived. You're loved so much by the company that they insist on showering you with benefits, not the least of which is a luxurious company car.

Yeah, right.

In many cases, it's going to hurt you to have a company car at your disposal. Why? Because the tax collector may require you to pay tax on two separate benefits. The first is called a *standby charge*, and the second is an *operating cost benefit*.

Standby Charge

There's nothing uglier than a standby charge in my estimation. Here's how the rule works: A taxable benefit called a standby charge will be added to your income and reported on your T4 slip just for having a company car at your disposal. The government figures that there's got to be some personal benefit to you, so you ought to be taxed somehow. The standby charge is calculated as 2 percent of the original cost of the car (or two-thirds of the lease payments, if the car is leased) for each month that the car is available to you. That works out to be 24 percent of the original cost of the car each year! You'll be able to reduce this taxable standby charge only if two conditions are met. First, your business use must account for 50 percent or more of the total kilometres driven; and second, your personal use of the car must be less than 1,667 km per month in the year. Don't bother counting those trips straight from home to the office and back again as business kilometres— they won't generally qualify.

By the way, to add insult to injury, the tax collector will also add 5 percent GST to your taxable benefit (13 percent HST in Nova Scotia, New Brunswick, and Newfoundland). In Quebec, the additional tax amounts to 5 percent GST plus 7.5 percent QST.

Operating Cost Benefit

If your employer pays for any operating costs on the car (insurance, gas, repairs, etc.), then you'll face an operating cost benefit. For 2008, the calculation is 24 cents

Caution!

If your employer provides you with a company car, your taxable benefit from the standby charge every year could be high enough that, after just four years, you will have effectively paid tax on the original purchase price of the car! How's that for a tax hit? Reduce the tax hit by keeping your personal use to under 20,000 kilometres each year and to less than 50 percent of total time the car is available for use. If you can't manage this, then consider giving up the company car!

per kilometre for each kilometre of personal use (21 cents per kilometre for automobile salespeople). If you reimburse your employer for all operating costs within 45 days after the end of the year (that is, by February 14 each year for the previous year's operating costs), then you'll avoid this operating cost benefit altogether.

There's another acceptable way to calculate your operating cost benefit where your business use of the car is greater than 50 percent. To take advantage of this second method, you've got to inform your employer in writing before December 31 that you'd rather use the alternative method of calculating the operating cost benefit. This method allows you to simply take 50 percent of your standby charge as your operating cost benefit. Which method is best for you? In a nutshell, you'll prefer this second method if the cost of the car is fairly low and your personal kilometres are close to 50 percent of the total kilometres driven. But remember: Not more than 50 percent is allowed here.

Know Your Options

Should you always say "no thanks" to a company car? Generally, I discourage employees from taking a company car. Here's why: The standby charge you're going to face is always based on the original cost of the car, even as the car depreciates in value over time. This is a bad deal if there ever was one. In most cases, it'll be better for you to provide your own car, and then take an allowance or reimbursement from your employer to cover the costs of using your car for work. I'll talk more about this in a minute.

If you're going to accept a company car, here are three things to keep in mind:

! Consider buying the car from your employer after two or three years to avoid a consistently high standby charge on a vehicle that has depreciated in value.

! Avoid company cars that cost over $30,000. You see, this will lead to a double-tax problem. Your standby charge will be based on the full cost of the car, but your employer will only be entitled to depreciate $30,000 (plus GST and PST) of that car in 2008. The excess over $30,000 is effectively taxed twice.

! Minimize the amount of time the car is available to you for personal use. If, for example, you park the car at your employer's place of business at the end of the workday, you could argue that the car is not available to you for personal use that day. You should be aware, however, that the tax collector will generally take the view that the car is still available to you unless your employer requires you to park it at the office in the evenings or while you're on vacation. At any rate, if the car is only available to you 345 days each year, rather than 365, you'll effectively face a standby charge for just 11 months instead of 12 months because of the way the calculation is done.

TO MAKE A LONG STORY SHORT:

- You may face two different taxable benefits if your company provides you with a car: a standby charge and an operating cost benefit.

- In most cases, you'll be better off providing your own car to avoid these taxable benefits and then taking an allowance or reimbursement from your employer for use of your car at work.

Tim's Tip 32: Claim automobile expenses that exceed your allowance or reimbursements.

So, you're convinced that providing your own car for use at work is better than using a company car. Great. Now, how is this use of your car going to save you tax? The rules can be kind of tricky, but I'll walk you through them.

Reimbursements and Allowances

First, you need to understand the difference between a reimbursement and an allowance. A *reimbursement* is never taxable. If, for example, you incurred certain car expenses on the job and you submitted actual receipts to your employer for reimbursement, you would not be required to include that reimbursement in your income.

An *allowance* is different. It's a payment from your employer for which you are not required to provide actual receipts. That is, you're not required to account for the payments received. Is an allowance taxable to you? It all depends. Let me explain.

An allowance paid to you for using your own car for work will be non-taxable if it is considered *reasonable*. The allowance will generally be considered reasonable if it's based on actual kilometres driven for work (CRA considers a reasonable allowance for 2008 to be $0.52 per kilometre for the first 5,000 kilometres, and $0.46 for each additional kilometre; the rates are 4 cents higher in the Yukon, Northwest Territories, and Nunavut; these amounts are what your employer is permitted to deduct). That means you'll need to keep a daily driver's log showing how many kilometres you've driven and the purpose of the trip. If you meet this test, then the allowance is tax-free. If the allowance is not based on distance driven, then it is not considered to be reasonable, and it must be included in your income. In fact, this type of allowance is supposed to be reported by your employer on your T4 slip each year.

Claim Those Deductions

When do you suppose you're entitled to claim a deduction for automobile expenses? Well, you can forget about a deduction if you were fully reimbursed for your expenses, or if you received a reasonable allowance and you accepted that allowance as tax-free compensation.

WHEN CAN YOU DEDUCT AUTOMOBILE EXPENSES?

	If you received a reimbursement	If you received an allowance
Amount received is reasonable	Reimbursements are always tax-free. You cannot claim a deduction for automobile expenses that have been fully reimbursed.	Allowances are considered reasonable if they are based on kilometres driven. In this case, the allowance is tax-free and you cannot claim a deduction for automobile expenses.
Amount received is not reasonable	If you were not fully reimbursed for your automobile costs, and no allowance was received, you may deduct the costs incurred over and above your reimbursements.	Allowances are not reasonable when they ignore kilometres driven, or when the employee otherwise considers the allowance not reasonable. In this case, the allowance is taxable and you can claim a deduction for actual expenses.

You're entitled to a deduction if you received an allowance that's not reasonable—in other words, an allowance that is not based on distance driven and that is treated as taxable income. In this case, your deductible expenses help to offset the income.

But what if you received an allowance that is based on distance driven, and therefore would normally be considered reasonable, except that you feel the allowance is not reasonable at all because your actual business-related automobile expenses are greater than the allowance? In this case, you have the option of including that "unreasonable" allowance in your income and claiming a deduction for your actual automobile expenses.

Here's the general rule: If your allowance based on distance driven is less than your actual car expenses, then consider the allowance to be unreasonable, include it in your income, and claim a deduction for those actual car expenses. Likewise, if you have not been fully reimbursed for your actual car expenses, claim a deduction.

What to Claim—and How

You're entitled to claim a portion of all your operating costs. These include gas, oil, repairs, insurance, licence fees, cleaning, and auto club fees—to name a few. In addition, you can claim depreciation—called capital cost allowance (CCA)—on the cost of your car if you purchased it. Keep in mind, however, that the maximum cost you can depreciate is $30,000 (plus GST and PST) for 2008. If your car costs more than this, you won't be entitled to any tax relief for the excess.

Interest costs on a loan to buy your car are also deductible. But there are limits here. For 2008, the maximum that can be deducted is $300 per month for loans on vehicles acquired after 2003.

Finally, if you lease your car rather than own it, you'll be entitled to claim a deduction for a portion of your lease costs. The maximum deduction in 2008 is $800 (plus GST and PST) for each month you leased the car.

To determine the portion of your automobile expenses that you can deduct, add up the kilometres driven for work in the year, divide that by the total kilometres driven in the year, and multiply by 100. The result is the percentage of the expenses you can deduct.

As I mentioned at the end of Tip 30, you'll need to file Form T777 with your tax return, and your employer will have to sign Form T2200 to verify that you were required to use your automobile for work. I also talked about the GST rebate that you may be entitled to claim using Form GST370.

Action Step

Be sure to maximize the employment use of your car to maximize your deduction. This can be done by visiting clients and suppliers or making other business stops on the way to or from work. This will turn non-business kilometres into business kilometres. Also, consider using one car only for work to simplify your record keeping.

TO MAKE A LONG STORY SHORT:

- A reimbursement and an allowance are different things. A reimbursement requires that receipts be provided to your employer, while an allowance does not.

- Reimbursements and reasonable allowances based on kilometres driven are not taxable. Unreasonable allowances are taxable.

- Claim a deduction for automobile expenses if you have not been reimbursed or if your actual expenses are greater than an unreasonable allowance received.

Deferring Compensation

You'll recall from Tip 4 that pushing your tax bill to a future year almost always makes sense. But given today's tax law, it's not so easy to take a portion of your employment income and arrange to pay tax on it a year or two down the road. You see, the *Income Tax Act* has rules to govern these salary deferral arrangements. For example, if you earn $75,000 in 2008 but agree with your employer that you'll take $50,000 in 2008 and $25,000 in 2009, you're going to face tax in 2008 on the full $75,000. Sorry about that. But don't fret. There are some ways you can escape the salary deferral rules. Wherever it's possible and practical, be sure to defer your income to a future year by taking advantage of these ideas. This is especially important, because of the general decline in tax rates from year to year that we've been experiencing.

Tim's Tip 33: Defer tax with a Registered Pension Plan (RPP), RRSP, or Deferred Profit Sharing Plan (DPSP).

Registered Pension Plan (RPP)

A Registered Pension Plan (RPP) at work operates much like your RRSP. Putting money into an RPP, however, will limit your ability to use an RRSP. The government imposes this limitation through something called your *pension adjustment*. You see, the tax collector doesn't want you to have an unfair advantage over those who save through an RRSP alone for retirement. An RPP allows you to defer tax on your employment income by providing a tax deduction for the money you contribute to the plan. You'll face tax when funds are paid to you out of the pension plan, but this won't likely be for a number of years.

I'll make this one comment: I'm not a big fan of company pension plans in many situations. The reason? If you don't plan on staying with the same employer for the better part of your working career, you may actually lose a portion of your retirement savings every time you move from one employer to the next. Since the average Canadian is likely to change jobs a number of times in a lifetime, a lot of people could be short-changed in saving for retirement. I prefer an RRSP alone (since it's portable) in many—but not all—situations. You may want to talk this issue over with a tax professional or a financial advisor.

Registered Retirement Savings Plan (RRSP)

I suppose that Registered Retirement Savings Plans (RRSPs) are one of the more familiar tax-deferral vehicles available today. I won't go into much detail on these now because I've devoted Chapter 6 to retirement savings. Suffice it to say that your RRSP may be the most effective method to push the tax on your employment income to a future year. It's no secret how this works. If you earned $40,000 and had accumulated RRSP contribution room of $10,000, you could contribute the full $10,000 to your RRSP and deduct that amount from your income for the year. In effect, you'd pay tax on only $30,000 of your employment income. And the $10,000 would grow tax-deferred in your RRSP. In fact, you won't pay tax on those funds until you make withdrawals later in life. Can't get a better or more direct deferral than that.

Deferred Profit Sharing Plan (DPSP)

With a Deferred Profit Sharing Plan (DPSP), your employer may contribute up to 18 percent of your income or $10,500 (for 2008), whichever is less. Sorry, but a DPSP is not an option for shareholders or their families who own more than 10 percent of any class of shares of the employer. You can't make contributions to a DPSP—only your employer can. As a result, you're not entitled to a deduction for

DPSP contributions. These contributions are based on your employer's profitability, and so there may not be any contributions in years where the company loses money.

How are these contributions taxed? The funds will grow inside the DPSP tax-deferred, and you'll pay tax on the amounts paid out of the DPSP to you. With most DPSPs, taxable payments can be made to you over a maximum 10-year period, which, by the way, is going to result in a longer deferral of tax than simply paying the funds out in one lump sum. You might even consider rolling some of the payments out of your DPSP into your RRSP, RPP, or a term annuity (with a guarantee period not exceeding 15 years)—just to defer tax even longer. Money contributed to a DPSP will reduce the amount that you can contribute to your RRSP in a manner similar to RPPs. By the way, some of the proceeds out of your DPSP may be tax-free if they represent your pre-1991 contributions made at a time when employees were allowed to contribute to DPSPs.

TO MAKE A LONG STORY SHORT:

- A Registered Pension Plan (RPP) can provide a deferral of tax on your employment income, although in many cases I prefer an RRSP to an RPP when given a choice.

- An RRSP is the most common tax-deferral vehicle in Canada and, like an RPP, provides a direct deferral of tax on employment income.

- A DPSP is a plan to which only your employer can contribute.

- Contributions to RPPs and DPSPs will reduce the amount you can contribute to your RRSP.

Tim's Tip 34: Push the tax on your bonuses to a future year.

If you're entitled to a bonus for work performed in a given year, you'll be able to defer receipt of that bonus for up to three years, and you won't face tax on the bonus until you actually receive it. How much tax will this save? That depends on the rate of return you can generate on the money you would otherwise use to pay the tax, and your marginal tax rate down the road. If you expect to have a lower marginal tax rate in the near future, deferring your bonus can make sense. Consider Eileen's case.

E *ileen earned a $10,000 bonus from her employer in 2008 and would be due to face a tax bill of $4,600 on that bonus, at her marginal tax rate of 46 percent, if she were to receive the bonus in 2008. Eileen expects to have a lower marginal tax rate in the near future since she'll be retiring in 2011. So, she arranged with her employer to defer receipt of her bonus until December 31, 2011 (three years after earning the bonus). The result? She's going to face tax at her expected marginal tax rate of 35 percent, for a tax bill of $3,500, three years from now when she receives the bonus.*

Is there a downside to this idea? Sure. If you're hurting for cash, you may not want to wait for three years to receive your bonus. And your employer won't be able to deduct the bonus until the year it's paid. In addition, if you're concerned about the financial stability of your employer, you may want to take the cash sooner rather than later.

Another good option is this: If you're due to receive a bonus for 2008, ask for payment in January 2009 and contribute that money to your RRSP right away if you have the contribution room. This way, you won't have to wait long to receive the payment from your employer, which gets the money working for you sooner. In addition, you won't face tax on the bonus until 2009 when you receive it, but you'll receive a tax deduction in 2008 for the amount of the bonus thanks to the RRSP contribution. A good deal all around.

TO MAKE A LONG STORY SHORT:

- You're entitled to defer a bonus for up to three years. You won't face tax until the year the bonus is paid.

- Deferring the bonus can make sense when your marginal tax rate is expected to be lower in the future, or where you're only deferring the bonus until early in the new year and you contribute that amount to your RRSP.

Tim's Tip 35: **Consider a leave of absence or sabbatical plan to defer tax.**

Who says you have to be a teacher or professor to take advantage of a leave of absence or sabbatical plan? With the help of your employer, you can set up a similar plan. It works this way: You can set aside up to one-third of your salary each year for up to six years. You won't have to pay tax on the portion of your income set aside. Your leave of absence or sabbatical must begin no later than six years after the deferral begins, and must be at least six months long (three months if you are taking the leave to attend an educational institution full-time). For the plan to qualify, you'll have to return to your workplace for at least as long as your leave, and you'll have to pay tax on the deferred income no later than the seventh year whether you take the leave or sabbatical or not.

> **Caution!**
>
> For a deferred-salary leave or sabbatical plan to be accepted by CRA, you must make sure that your employer documents the plan in writing, and that the main purpose of the plan is to fund a leave of absence and not, for example, to provide retirement benefits. If the tax collector looks at the plan as some kind of attempt to defer tax without really funding a leave of absence, you'll face tax on the full amounts as if they were regular salary.

TO MAKE A LONG STORY SHORT:

- A leave of absence or sabbatical plan will allow you to defer tax on up to one-third of your income for a full six years.

- Certain other conditions must be met for the plan to qualify, and you'll pay tax on the deferred income no later than six years after the deferral begins, whether or not you actually take the leave or sabbatical.

Calling It Quits

There's going to come a day when you won't be working for your employer anymore. Perhaps this is by your own choice—you've put in your dues, and it's time to start a new chapter in life. Maybe it's by your employer's choice—the company might be downsizing, right-sizing, or whatever you want to call it. In any event, you'll do yourself a real favour by working with your employer to make your departure a tax-efficient one.

Tim's Tip 36: Roll as much as possible of your retiring allowance into your RRSP or RPP.

I met a gentleman about two years ago. After we talked over his financial affairs, it became evident that he had been given a bum steer. You see, the gentleman had one thing on his mind: paying down his mortgage with his retiring allowance. When he retired from his last job, a "counsellor" in his former workplace somehow forgot to inform this man that he was able to roll a good portion of his retiring allowance into his RRSP or RPP. It seems that this "counsellor" liked the idea of paying down the mortgage as well. As a result, this man took his $60,000 retiring allowance, handed $27,600 to the tax collector, and used the remaining $32,400 to pay down his mortgage.

Boy, this type of misguided advice makes me steam. Remember this: There is no better option for your retiring allowance than to roll it into your RRSP where you'll defer tax until you make withdrawals. Yes, this is your best option in virtually every case, even if you have a mortgage outstanding. If you don't make this rollover, you're going to face tax, all at once, on any retiring allowances you receive. The gentleman in my story could have made regular withdrawals from his RRSP to meet his mortgage payments, and the mortgage still would have been paid off by the time he was 63 years of age. In the meantime, he would have avoided that immediate $27,600 tax hit, and those assets would have grown tax-deferred in his RRSP.

Action Step

When you receive a retiring allowance, it's not critical that the allowance be transferred directly to your RRSP when it's paid out. But be sure to contribute those funds to your RRSP within 60 days following the end of the year that you received the payment—that is, by March 31, 2009, for retiring allowances received in 2008, or March 1, 2010, for allowances received in 2009. See Tip 75 for more.

How much of your retiring allowance can you roll to your RRSP? The answer is $2,000 per year or part year of pre-1996 service. In addition, you'll be able to roll $1,500 for each year or part year of service prior to 1989 in which you had no vested interest in any employer's contributions into an RPP or DPSP.

TO MAKE A LONG STORY SHORT:

• Your best option when receiving a retiring allowance from your employer is to roll as much of it as possible into your RRSP or RPP to defer tax as long as possible.

• This rollover must be made within 60 days following the year you receive the payment.

Getting into the Game

Whether you're leaving an old job, starting a new one, or heading into this year's performance review, make sure you know all the ways you can maximize your after-tax employment income. Turn now to the Tax Planning Tip Sheet at the front of this book and review the strategies introduced in Chapter 3. Ask yourself, "Can this tip apply to me?" With a little planning, each *Yes* or *Not Sure* might mean more dollars in your pocket.

BECOMING A FREE AGENT: STRATEGIES FOR SELF-EMPLOYMENT

> *"To be successful:*
> *Rise early, work late,*
> *and strike oil."*
>
> *~ J. Paul Getty*

4

I can still remember those long hot summers when I was a kid—you know, after school finished at the end of June each year. In those days, two months of carefree living seemed like an eternity. I laugh now. Two months these days feel more like two weeks!

When it got too hot to play outside, my friends and I would retreat to the rec room. And if it was up to me, we'd pull out a game like Monopoly—something with lots of strategy, luck, and money. From the time I was young, I guess I was destined to be an entrepreneur. It's in my blood.

Now, I'm not going to suggest that if you happen to love Monopoly (even the long version) you're destined to be self-employed. But I will say this: If you have the inclination to run your own business—either full-time or part-time—you will significantly increase your tax planning opportunities. Make no mistake: Self-employment is one of the last great tax shelters.

And, like owning all the yellow, green, and blue properties in Monopoly, winning the tax game through self-employment can leave you feeling on top of the world.

Jumping on the Bandwagon

No doubt about it, a growing number of Canadians are turning to self-employment for their livelihood. Some out of necessity, but many simply because they recognize the benefits—tax and otherwise. In some cases, taxpayers are jumping on the self-employment bandwagon by renegotiating their work arrangements with their employers. This can be an effective strategy *if* you do it properly.

Tim's Tip 37: Structure your work so that you're self-employed, not an employee.

From a tax point of view, it can make a lot of sense to do your work on a contract basis as a self-employed worker, rather than as an employee. You may want to approach your current employer with the idea of resigning and being hired back on this basis. But you'll have to dot your I's and cross your T's here. Just because you call yourself self-employed doesn't mean the tax collector will agree with you. You see, the Canada Revenue Agency (CRA) is more concerned about the true substance of your business relationships than whether you call yourself self-employed. Consider Anwar's story.

Anwar worked as a software programmer for Acme Software Inc. for seven years. In order to provide Anwar with more tax breaks, and to save the company certain costs, his employer agreed last year that Anwar would resign and the company would hire him back on a contract basis. Anwar still performs most of the work at Acme's offices, and he's still enrolled in Acme's benefits plan. Last year, Anwar claimed a number of expenses against his self-employment income from Acme that he wouldn't have been able to claim as an employee. CRA took a close look at his relationship with Acme and decided that he's really still an employee of the company. The tax collector has disallowed Anwar's deductions, and reassessed Acme for its share of the CPP and EI premiums that should have been paid. Sadly, the tax collector is likely right in this case.

A recent court decision, *The Royal Winnipeg Ballet (RWB) v. MNR (2006)*, summarizes nicely the criteria that the CRA will examine to determine whether you're truly self-employed, or just an employee. In the end, the RWB won its case against the CRA, who wanted to call the dancers employees of RWB. There are two broad factors that CRA will consider:

Action Step

Make sure that you sign a written contract with any organization that you work for as a self-employed individual. The contract should clearly spell out the nature, extent, and duration of your services. It should also clearly detail the intention of the parties to create a self-employment arrangement. Set up the contract so that you consider the two key factors: control and economic.

Control Factors

If you're truly self-employed, you'll exercise control over certain aspects of the services you provide. Most commonly you'll control when, where, and how you do your work. The ability to take on work from other sources is also an element of control. Now, the RWB case shed some light on the *control* issue. The dancers could not control when and where they worked because they had to rehearse and perform at pre-scheduled times and locations. But, the judge recognized that, while the degree of control exercised by the RWB over the work of the dancers was extensive, it was no more than was needed to stage a series of ballets over a well-planned season of performances. That is, there had to be *some* control over the dancers to properly stage a ballet. So, the dancers passed the control test and were considered self-employed.

Economic Factors

The courts and CRA will look at certain economic factors as well, to determine whether you're self-employed, or an employee. Specifically, the following is typically considered:

- **Ownership of tools.** Do you provide your own tools, or does the company for whom you're providing services supply the tools you need (whatever those "tools" may be)? If you're self-employed, you'll generally provide your own tools.
- **Degree of financial risks.** Have you assumed any financial risks in your activities, or is there very little financial risk to you? For example, have you made investments of capital in your business? And do you hire your own staff to work for you? Self-employed people generally assume financial risks.
- **Opportunity for profit.** Do you have an opportunity for profit, or is your profit potential limited by the company you're providing services to? Self-employed people tend to have more control over potential profits.
- **Intention of the parties.** This is an important factor. Was the intention of the parties made clear in an agreement? If the intention of both you and the company is that you should be considered self-employed, this should be documented properly. In the end, the RWB ballet won its case because both the RWB and the dancers intended to create a self-employment situation. It was the key deciding factor at the Federal Court of Appeal.

TO MAKE A LONG STORY SHORT:

- Arrange your work relationships so that you're considered self-employed rather than an employee.

- You'll need to consider control and economic factors to convince the tax collector that you're truly self-employed and not simply an employee in disguise.

Choosing Your Business Structure

An important question that you'll face when entering the world of self-employment is this: What business structure are you going to choose?

Tim's Tip 38: Understand the three most common business structures.

There are three common business structures available to you: a proprietorship, partnership, or corporation. Let's take a closer look at them.

Proprietorship

A proprietorship is you, in business for yourself. A proprietor may have employees but owns the business alone. Last week I passed some kids at the side of the road selling lemonade, and since I'm always interested in supporting entrepreneurial efforts, I stopped for a drink. Although the kids seemed a little confused when I explained that they were operating a proprietorship, they'll appreciate the education later in life, I'm sure.

The real benefits of a proprietorship are these: There is little or no cost involved to set up your business as a proprietorship; it's as easy as hanging up a shingle or putting up a sign, and there is little government regulation. The only requirement you might have is to register the business name with the provincial government (for example, "John's Heating and Cooling"). And even this requirement can be waived if you simply operate the business under your own name (for example, "John's" or "John Doe's").

Of course, there can be some drawbacks to a proprietorship, too. First, you'll face unlimited liability for the debts and obligations of the business—effectively, you and the business are one and the same. Second, it may be more difficult as a proprietor

> **Caution!**
> Operating as a proprietorship could leave you vulnerable to creditors and lawsuits if your business involves significant financial or other risks to you or other people, including your employees. Protect yourself with business insurance, and consider operating through a corporation to limit your liability.

to raise financing if you need capital to start or expand the business. Third, there's less flexibility when it's time to plan for the succession of your business. Finally, there's the question of image. Is there a risk that others will view your business as a small, unsophisticated operation? Maybe. But in most cases, the fact that you're a proprietorship will have no effect on whether someone retains your services or buys your products.

If you're a proprietor, the profits of your business are yours personally. You must report all the income and expenses of your business on your personal tax return each year (Form T2124 for business activities or T2032 for professional activities). You don't pay yourself a salary; instead, you simply take cash out of the business for personal use. This is called a *draw*. Of course, if you draw too much, the business may not have enough cash to operate. If you incur losses as a proprietor, those losses are also reported on your tax return, and can be applied against your other sources of income (see Tip 47 for more).

Partnership

A partnership works much like a proprietorship, except that there is more than one business owner. A partnership is really just a group of proprietors joining forces to carry on business together with the idea of generating profits. The benefits to a partnership are these: you're able to share the risks of being in business; you may have greater access to capital; and you can pool your skills.

The truth is, a partnership can also bring new challenges. Think of these as drawbacks if you want. First, you and your partners may not always agree on how the business should be run, and resolving these differences can be tough at times. Second, getting rid of a partner who isn't working out is not exactly an enjoyable task. And finally, a partner is generally liable jointly for the debts and obligations of the partnership (although limited liability partnerships are possible and are often set up by professional accounting and law firms).

If you're a partner, you'll be required to pay tax on your share of the partnership's profits. In fact, as with a proprietor, partners are required to report their profits or losses on their personal tax returns. The partnership itself is required to file a partnership information return annually with CRA.

If you're going to enter into a partnership, even with family members, be sure to visit a lawyer to write up a partnership agreement. This is critical. The agreement should cover issues such as these: how and when the profits of the partnership will be allocated to each partner; how to handle disputes; what to do when a partner dies or leaves the partnership; and whether insurance will be purchased on the lives of each partner.

Corporation

A corporation is a separate legal entity. In fact, a corporation is considered to be a separate *person* for tax purposes. And, just like you, a corporation has to file its own tax returns and financial statements with the tax collector. You can usually tell which businesses are set up as corporations because you'll see the terms *Inc.*, *Incorporated*, *Corp.*, *Corporation*, *Co.*, *Company*, *Ltd.*, or *Limited* after the name of the business.

There are two key benefits to a corporation, and one of these is tax-related. First, a corporation generally offers limited liability protection to its shareholders (the owners). That is, the debts and obligations of the corporation do not become obligations of the shareholders. I should mention that, in some circumstances, a director of a corporation may be liable for certain obligations of the company.

The other benefit is a *tax deferral*. You see, most small Canadian corporations are entitled to an attractive rate of tax on the first $400,000 of *active business income* in 2008. That rate is generally about 18 percent, although this varies slightly by province. Passive income—generally from investments—in that same corporation will face tax at about 50 percent. Quite a difference! It's the low rate of tax on active business income that provides the opportunity to defer tax. Notice that I didn't call this a permanent tax reduction. This is a tax deferral that lets you push taxes to a future year. And this is great tax planning (see Chapter 1, Tip 4). Consider Astrid's case.

*A*strid's corporation expects to generate $170,000 in income this year. Astrid's going to pay herself $120,000 in salary, which keeps her income below the highest marginal tax bracket. If she were to receive much more salary, each additional dollar would face tax at about 46 percent in her hands (see page 288 for actual rates). The remaining $50,000 will be left in her corporation, *where it will be taxed at just 18 percent. Her tax deferral in this case is about 28 percent (46 minus 18 percent). Once Astrid pays the remaining $50,000 out of the company, she'll face tax personally and the tax deferral will be over. But until that point, she saves herself tax dollars.*

There are two drawbacks to a corporation. The first is the cost of setting it up and maintaining it. For the set-up, you're looking at paying between $1,000 and $2,000. Although you can do this yourself, I recommend that you use a lawyer to do the incorporation. There's also the cost of paying an accountant to prepare your corporate financial statements and tax returns each year—a job that must be left to a professional where corporations are involved. Accounting fees can vary widely, depending on the nature of your business and the accuracy of your records.

The second drawback is *trapped losses*. You see, if your business loses money from its operations, it will have *non-capital losses*. These losses can be carried back three years or forward twenty to offset taxable income in those years. If losses are incurred by your corporation in its first few years, they will be trapped in the corporation and will be available to offset income earned by the corporation in the following twenty years. Beyond twenty years, the losses expire. This is not nearly as good as if you had incurred those losses personally as a proprietor or partner. As a proprietor or partner, the losses could be applied to offset your other personal income, and could even be carried back three years to recover taxes you may have paid personally in those prior years.

TO MAKE A LONG STORY SHORT:

- There are three common business structures. A proprietorship is the simplest and least expensive to establish, but offers the least protection from creditors and fewer tax planning opportunities.

- A partnership is slightly more complex. It's much like a group of proprietors working together and sharing the profits and losses.

- A corporation is the most complex. It requires fees to set up and maintain but can provide limited liability and greater tax planning flexibility.

Tim's Tip 39: Consider incorporation once your business has grown, but not before.

I know, I know. You're looking forward to the day when you can incorporate your business and move to a whole new level of sophistication. Besides, it sounds great to be called a founding shareholder of a corporation. Well, hold your horses for a minute.

Remember what I said earlier about the benefits of a corporation? The two key benefits are these: (1) limited liability for shareholders, and (2) opportunities for tax deferral. There's a good chance that you may not even benefit in these ways if you incorporate too soon. Think about it. Will you benefit significantly from the limited liability offered by a corporation? It depends on the industry and the nature of your business. If, for example, you're in the desktop publishing business, your potential liability is likely much lower than if you're in the construction industry. But as your business grows in size, your need for protection from liability will also grow.

What about the tax-deferral issue? If you're not going to leave any of your business earnings in the company, then you won't benefit from the tax deferral I've been talking about. Refer back to Astrid's story in Tip 38. If she had paid the full $170,000 of corporate earnings to herself rather than leaving $50,000 in the company, she would have lost the benefit of the tax deferral. In many situations, it's not until the business has grown in profitability that the owner is in a position to leave some of the earnings in the corporation and really benefit from a tax deferral.

And remember, as I discussed earlier, setting up a corporation from the start of your business could leave losses trapped inside the corporation that could have been used to recover taxes paid personally in previous years.

The general rule, then, is that you should wait until the business has grown in size and profitability before

Action Step

If you're operating as a proprietorship or partnership and decide to incorporate your business, visit a tax pro to arrange for your business assets to be transferred to the new company on a tax-free basis. This is normally done under Section 85 of the *Income Tax Act*. In exchange for transferring those assets to the company, you'll receive payment and/or shares from the company.

you incorporate. As with all tax planning, your circumstances will be different from other people's, and seeking the advice of a tax pro who is familiar with your situation will help you to make the best decision regarding your business structure.

TO MAKE A LONG STORY SHORT:

- The key benefits to setting up your business as a corporation are *limited liability* and the opportunity for *tax deferral* on corporate earnings.

- Normally, you'll experience these benefits most once the business has grown in size and profitability, and so it's often preferable to wait until that time to incorporate.

- Setting up a corporation too soon could result in *trapped losses* in the corporation.

Tim's Tip 40: Choose the right year-end for your business.

Brace yourself, we're now dealing with a very complex area of tax law—choosing a year-end for your proprietorship or partnership. Before 1995, it was fairly easy to pick a year-end for your business. It used to be that you could effectively defer tax for a full year by choosing a non-calendar year-end. Not so anymore. While you'll generally be able to choose any year-end you want for your business, all proprietorships and partnerships are now required to report income on a calendar-year basis. As a result, if you choose a non-calendar year-end, you'll have to adjust your business income each year to reflect a December 31 year-end. Follow me?

In many cases, since you must report your income as though you have a calendar year-end anyway, it may not be worth the hassle to choose a non-calendar year-end. It'll only mean extra work in preparing your tax returns. There may, however, be an opportunity for you to defer tax. Here's the general rule: If your business is growing and you expect your business income to continue increasing for a number of years, then choosing a non-calendar year-end will provide a tax deferral.

If you own a corporation and are trying to determine the best year-end for your company, consider a year-end that falls in the last half of the calendar year. The reason is that you'll be able to claim a deduction for compensation (perhaps a bonus) to yourself at the company's year-end (say, August 31), but defer payment of that amount for up to 179 days (179 days after August 31 is February 26 of the following calendar year). So, the corporation will get the tax deduction at its year-end, but the bonus will not be taxable to you until the following calendar year. This is a nice tax deferral.

Let's briefly look at how the calculation works. Suppose your proprietorship has an October 31 year-end. On your personal tax return for 2008, you'll have to report your income for the 12 months ended October 31, 2008. But you'll have to convert this to a December 31 year-end. This means you'll have to calculate your income from the business for November and December 2008 as well—called the *stub period*—and add this to your October 31 income. When you do this, you will now be reporting income for a 14-month period (the 12 months ended October 31, 2008, plus income for the 2-month stub period). It hardly seems fair that you should report 14 months of income on your tax return each year. Don't panic. You can now deduct from that 14-month income the stub-period income added in the prior year. This brings your income back to a 12-month figure. Make sense?

By the way, the stub-period income that you add each year is not your actual income for those months. It's based on a formula. In my example, we need to add two months' worth of income, so we'd simply take $\frac{2}{12}$ of the October 31 fiscal year income and call this our stub-period income.

If your business is losing money, either because it's new or because it's simply on the decline, you'll be better off with a December 31 year-end. You're able to change to a December 31 year-end at any time, but once you've made this decision, you can't go back to a non-calendar year-end. As you can see, the rules are confusing, and I've only touched the surface here. Be sure to visit a tax pro before making a decision about which year-end is best for you.

TO MAKE A LONG STORY SHORT:

- It can be a difficult decision to choose between a non-calendar and a calendar year-end.

- Generally, if your business income is expected to rise consistently over the next few years, a non-calendar year-end will offer tax-deferral opportunities.

- Be sure to visit a tax pro before making a final decision on a year-end.

Claiming Business Deductions

Why in the world is self-employment such a great tax shelter anyway? Deductions! In fact, our tax law will allow you to claim a deduction for virtually any costs, so long as the costs were incurred for the purpose of producing income from the business, and provided the expenses are reasonable. Let's take a look at the most common expenses you'll be able to claim.

Tim's Tip 41: Maximize your deductions for home office expenses.

There's no getting around it—you've got to pay for a place to live, so why not make a portion of the costs tax deductible? There's nothing like self-employment to make this a reality. However, there are some rules to be aware of. You'll be entitled to claim a deduction for home office expenses where you meet one of two criteria: (1) your home is your principal place of business or (2) you use a specific area in your home exclusively

Did You Know?

As an aside, you might be interested in knowing that in a recent court decision, *Thomas Vanka v. The Queen* (2001), the taxpayer, who was a doctor, was considered to have met the criteria for home office deductions because he met patients regularly from home—but he met them principally by phone. This won't necessarily mean you can do the same, since the facts of your situation may be different, but you should be aware that it may be possible to deduct home office costs as Dr. Vanka did if your facts are substantially the same.

Caution!

I generally tell folks not to claim capital cost allowance (CCA) on the portion of a home used for business. If you do claim CCA, the tax collector will consider that portion of your home to be a business asset. This will jeopardize your ability to claim the principal residence exemption on that portion of your home—which could leave you open to capital gains tax if you sell your home later at a profit.

for earning income from your business and you meet clients there on a regular and ongoing basis.

Once you've met the criteria, there are a number of expenses to consider deducting. The key here is not to forget deductions that you might otherwise overlook. Here's a list to try on for size:

- rent
- mortgage interest
- property taxes
- utilities (heat, hydro, water)
- home insurance
- repairs and maintenance
- landscaping
- snow plowing
- capital cost allowance (but this is not advisable)
- telephone (100-percent deductible if it's a separate business line)

There are a couple of things to note here. You won't be able to deduct the full cost of these expenses I've listed. Rather, you'll be able to deduct the business portion only. If, for example, your office in the house is 200 square feet in size and your home is 2,000 square feet in total, then 10 percent of these costs would generally be deductible. By the way, residents of Quebec will find their deductible home office expenses reduced by 50 percent thanks to changes in Quebec's 1996 budget. Be sure to maximize your deductible expenses by maximizing the business percentage of your home. You can do this by including a portion of your hallway and washrooms as business space if they are used in the business, or by excluding certain non-usable space (an unfinished basement, for example) from the calculation of your total square footage of the home.

Telephone expenses are fully deductible if you have a separate business line, and even where you don't have a separate line, a portion of your personal line (based on time usage) will be deductible. Any additional home costs that were incurred solely because you are running your business from home—additional insurance, for example—are fully deductible.

TO MAKE A LONG STORY SHORT:

- Claim a portion of all eligible home costs when your home is your principal place of business or is used to meet clients on a regular and ongoing basis.

- Maximize the business use of your home by choosing carefully the areas to include in the calculation.

Tim's Tip 42: Maximize deductions related to business use of your automobile.

If you're self-employed, you'll be entitled to a deduction for using your car in the business. The rules work basically the same for employees and the self-employed, so I'll refer you to Tip 32 in Chapter 3, where I talk about deducting automobile costs. Keep in mind that you can deduct a portion of a vehicle's costs based on the percentage of your driving that was business-related.

To satisfy the tax collector, you'll need to keep a log book for each trip, and you'd be wise to maximize your business usage. This can be done, for example, by making stops for business on the way home from work or on the way to work. And don't forget about the wide range of expenses to deduct, including auto club costs, car washes, licence fees, and the more obvious: gas, oil, repairs, insurance, loan interest, lease costs, and capital cost allowance.

A little boy once asked his mother: "Mom, what happens to a car when it's too old to run anymore?"

"Someone sells it to your father," the mother replied.

Folks, if this sounds familiar, take this once piece of advice: Use that old jalopy in your business instead of your newer car! Since repair costs may be high, you'll save more tax by making those repairs deductible.

TO MAKE A LONG STORY SHORT:

- Maximize business use of your car by stopping for business reasons on the way home from work, or on the way to work, and keep a log book of distances driven for business during the year.

- Use your jalopy with the most costly expenses for business purposes.

- Refer to Tip 32 in Chapter 3, where I talk about automobiles at greater length.

Tim's Tip 43: Categorize your meals and entertainment expenses to maximize tax savings.

Did You Know?

If you're a golfer, you'll be glad to know that CRA changed its opinion about meals purchased at a golf course a few years back. You see, the tax collector used to enforce the policy that those meals were not deductible, forcing many to finish a round of golf and then head elsewhere to eat. Talk about crazy. The policy has now changed. Food purchased at a golf course is now deductible, subject to the usual 50-percent limitation.

Leave it to CRA to come up with a way to make any simple subject complex! The rules around meals and entertainment are a perfect example. Generally, 50 percent of any meals and entertainment costs will be deductible if the costs were incurred to earn income from your business.

There are some situations, however, where those costs are 100-percent deductible. In fact, there are six common situations: (1) when the meal or entertainment has been provided to all your employees (a Christmas party, for example, to a maximum of three such occasions each year); (2) when the meal or entertainment costs were incurred by an employee of yours who had to travel out of your metropolitan area to do work and who will be including the allowance or reimbursement in his or her income (in this case, the employee is subject to the 50-percent limitation); (3) when the meal costs were built into the price of a rail, airplane, or bus ticket; (4) when the cost of the meal or entertainment is billed to a client and separately disclosed on your invoice to the client (in this case, your client is subject to the 50-percent restriction); (5) when the cost is incurred as part of a fund-raising event for a registered charity; and (6) when your primary business is the provision of food, beverages, or entertainment.

Given that some meals and entertainment costs are 50-percent deductible and others are fully deductible, you'd be wise to keep track of the categories separately. If you don't, the tax collector could restrict all meals and entertainment to 50-percent deductibility.

TO MAKE A LONG STORY SHORT:

- Meals and entertainment costs are generally 50-percent deductible when they are incurred to earn business income.

- In some situations, these costs are fully deductible.

- Keep track of the categories separately to ensure maximum deductibility.

Tim's Tip 44: **Maximize your eligibility to claim capital cost allowance.**

You've seen the term capital cost allowance (CCA) now and again as you've browsed the pages of this book. CCA is simply our tax law's term for *depreciation*. And CCA is one of the more attractive tax deductions for any self-employed taxpayer. Here's why: There are a number of things that you have probably purchased that will now become tax deductible in the form of CCA because you're running a business.

Want some common examples? Take your home computer. If that computer is now used in the business, even part-time, then it becomes an asset that you can depreciate through the CCA system. Your printer, software, desk, bookcase, fax machine, car, boat, trailer, and tools are all good examples of depreciable assets—provided they are used in the business.

Did You Know?

CRA calculates its prescribed interest rate each quarter by determining the average rate on 90-day treasury bills sold during the first month of the preceding quarter. This figure is then rounded up to the nearest percentage point. The rate charged on overdue taxes is four percentage points above this figure, while interest paid on refunds and over-payments is just two percentage points above this figure. (The rates differ in Quebec.)

There are different *classes* of assets for CCA purposes, and each asset used in your business will fall into one class or another. Each class has an opening balance at the start of every business fiscal year, and that balance can be depreciated at the specified rate for that class. For example, your computer hardware is a Class 10 asset in which the undepreciated capital cost (UCC) can be deducted each year at the rate of 55 percent (45 percent prior to the 2007 federal budget).

In the year you acquire an asset, you're generally entitled to just 50 percent of the CCA you'd otherwise claim. This is called the *half-year rule* because you're only entitled to CCA for half of that first year.

Here are some pointers for dealing with CCA. First, if you're going to acquire new assets, consider buying them before the fiscal year is over and make sure those assets are available for use by the end of the fiscal year. This will provide a CCA claim sooner than if you waited until the start of the next fiscal year. Second, delay the sale of an asset until early in the next fiscal year to permit a CCA claim this year. Third, recognize that CCA is not a mandatory deduction. If you don't want to claim it in a given year, you don't have to. This does not mean you give up that deduction forever. It simply means you're pushing it to a future year. This can make sense, for example, when your business is not yet profitable and you don't need the CCA deduction to bring your taxable income to nil. If you want more information on claiming CCA, CRA's *Business and Professional Income Tax Guide* can help. So can the Interpretation Bulletins available on CRA's Web site at **www.cra.gc.ca**. Use the site's search function to find the term "capital cost allowance."

TO MAKE A LONG STORY SHORT:

- It's possible to claim CCA on assets that you might already own and are now using in the business.

- Maximize your CCA claim by buying new assets before the end of the fiscal year or by selling old assets after the current fiscal year.

- Your CCA claim is not mandatory each year, and it may make sense to postpone the deduction in certain situations.

Tim's Tip 45: Pay salaries to family members for a number of tax benefits.

There's no situation quite like self-employment to allow for effective income splitting between family members. I talked about this strategy briefly in Chapter 2, Tip 10*w*. The idea is this: Your business will be entitled to claim a deduction for any salaries or wages paid to family members, provided the compensation is reasonable for the services provided.

T *ai runs his own carpet cleaning business. Last summer, he hired his daughter, Kim, to work in the office booking appointments and doing various other tasks. Tai paid Kim $8,000 for her work last year. Kim used the money to help pay for her college education, but she paid absolutely no tax on the $8,000 since it was her only source of income and it's below her basic personal credit of $9,600 (for 2008). If the $8,000 had not been paid to Kim, it would have been taxed in Tai's hands as business income, and would have cost Tai $3,680 in taxes at his marginal tax rate of 46 percent ($8,000 × 46 percent). These taxes were saved by splitting income through the payment of a salary. In addition, the $8,000 is earned income to Kim, which provides her with Registered Retirement Savings Plan (RRSP) contribution room. A great deal all around.*

Did you catch the benefits of paying a salary to family members? First, if the salary is paid to a family member who will face no tax, or less tax than the business would have attracted, there are permanent tax savings. Second, the salary provides RRSP contribution room to the family member on the receiving end. Third, the money stays in the family, as opposed to being paid to an unrelated third party. You'll also notice that this strategy works very well when a child needs money for school. Think about it. Tai was able to support his daughter's education in a manner that was tax-deductible to his business and tax-free to Kim. All that's required is that the salary or wages be reasonable for the services provided.

TO MAKE A LONG STORY SHORT:

- Paying salaries or wages to family members with a lower marginal tax rate can result in permanent tax savings and a perfect splitting of income.

- The compensation will provide RRSP contribution room to your family member but must be reasonable for the services provided.

- This strategy offers a great way to cover education costs for children in school.

Tim's Tip 46: Recognize the special tax treatment for certain expenses.

I'd like to talk briefly about a variety of different expenses that have special tax treatment. This list isn't exhaustive, but it covers the key expenses. In most of these cases, the tax collector has simply restricted the amount that can be deducted, similar to the meals and entertainment expenses we looked at in Tip 43. Here we go.

a. Personal or living expenses

You won't generally be able to deduct any costs that are considered personal in nature, such as food or clothing.

b. Prepaid expenses

Sorry, but you can't deduct costs that you've paid for unless the services have already been provided to you. You can deduct them later though, after you receive the services.

c. Personal services business expenses

If you operate your business through a corporation and the tax collector considers you to be really an employee of another employer (that is, simply an "incorporated employee") then you're operating a *personal services business*. You'll be restricted to deducting only salary, wages, benefits, and allowances paid to yourself, plus a few other expenses that would have been deductible personally if you had been working as an employee.

d. Recreational facilities and club dues

Sad to say, but a business is not entitled to deduct costs for using or maintaining a recreational facility (for example, golf fees) or club dues when the main purpose of the club is to provide dining, recreational, or sporting facilities.

e. Private health services plan

Since 1998, self-employed folks have been able to deduct premiums paid for health coverage under a supplementary health plan. To be deductible, your coverage can't exceed the coverage of your non-related employees. If you don't have non-related employees or where they represent fewer than half of all employees in your business, you'll be restricted to deducting premiums of $1,500 for each of yourself, your spouse and children 18 or over in the year, and $750 for each of your minor children.

f. Automobile allowances

If you pay kilometre-based allowances to your employees, including yourself, your business in 2008 is restricted to deducting 52 cents on the first 5,000 kilometres driven by each employee, and 46 cents on the excess. These limits are higher in the Yukon, Northwest Territories, and Nunavut (56 cents on the first 5,000 kilometres and 50 cents thereafter).

g. Conventions

The tax collector will allow you to deduct the costs of attending just two conventions each year that are related to your business. There are some further restrictions if the convention is held on a cruise ship, or in certain other situations.

h. Advertising in certain media

You'll generally have a problem deducting your newspaper, periodical, and broad-cast advertising costs when you're aiming at a Canadian market but advertise through foreign media.

i. Life insurance premiums

If a life insurance policy on your life is paid for by your business, the premiums are not generally deductible. There's an exception when the policy is required as collateral on a loan for the business.

If you're not sure about the deductibility of certain business expenses, speak to a tax pro.

TO MAKE A LONG STORY SHORT:

- Some specific expenses are given special tax treatment. You should be aware of the key ones.

- In most cases, the tax rules restrict the deductibility of these expenses.

Tim's Tip 47: **Deal properly with losses from your business.**

Action Step

If your business has incurred non-capital losses that will expire in the near future, make sure you visit a tax pro to help you plan to use up these losses. There are several strategies for using losses. These include: delaying discretionary deductions like capital cost allowance (CCA); selling assets at a profit and then buying them back; transferring income-generating assets to the business; and other ideas.

It's pretty common in the first few years of business for your expenses to exceed your income from the business. The result? Losses. We call these *non-capital losses*. As long as you're not incorporated (refer to Tip 38), non-capital losses can be applied to reduce any other source of income you might have reported on your personal tax return for the year. This is going to save you tax dollars.

Applying Non-Capital Losses

Your non-capital losses have to be used to offset other income in the year they are incurred, if possible. If you don't have other income, the losses can be carried back to offset taxable income in any of the three previous years, or carried forward for up to twenty years (it used to be ten years) to offset taxable income in the future. If your losses aren't used up by the end of the twentieth year, they expire.

Choosing which years to apply your losses against can be something of an art. Consider this example:

Kevin reported income of $30,000 in 2006 and $60,000 in 2007. In 2008, he reported non-capital losses of $100,000 after starting up a courier service in the year. Kevin has a few options for using his losses. He can carry back $30,000 of the loss to 2006 and $60,000 to 2007 to recover all the taxes he paid in those years, leaving $10,000 in losses to be carried forward for up to twenty years. The problem with this idea, however, is that Kevin doesn't need to carry back losses of $30,000 and $60,000 to 2006 and 2007 respectively in order to wipe out his tax liability for those years. The reason? He's entitled to a basic personal credit for those years, which effectively shelters approximately the first $9,600 of income in those years.

The moral of the story is simple: Your goal is to apply the losses against dollars that will provide the most tax savings. It never makes sense to bring taxable income for a year below the taxable threshold dictated by your basic personal credit (which is $9,600 in 2008). This would be a waste of losses since your tax bill is nil below this threshold.

Similarly, it can be a bright move to bring taxable income down to the first tax bracket of $37,885 in 2008, but not below, if you expect to earn income well in excess of this amount in the next couple of years. In Kevin's example above, he may want to apply his losses to 2007 only, but not to 2006. If he applies the losses to 2006, he'll bring his taxable income in that year below $30,000, which will save him tax at a rate of about 26 cents for each dollar of loss claimed. If he avoids applying the losses to 2006 and carries forward the unused losses, he might be able to apply them against income in excess of $37,885 in future years, which will save him tax at about 35 cents on the dollar. That is, he'll get more bang for his losses if he expects to earn well over $37,885 of taxable income in the next few years and saves some of his losses for those years.

Reasonable Expectation of Profit

In the past, the CRA often denied losses when business owners had claimed losses for several years in a row. The argument was always that there was no "reasonable expectation of profit" (REOP). Two court decisions handed down by the Supreme Court of Canada (SCC) on May 23, 2002, provided relief to business owners in this situation.

In the cases *Brian J. Stewart v. The Queen* and *The Queen v. Jack Walls et al.*, a principle was established: When an activity lacks any personal element to it, then it should be considered a commercial activity and a source of income (whether or not losses have been incurred). The SCC established that there is no opportunity to apply the reasonable expectation of profit test where there is no personal element to the activity being carried on by the taxpayer.

As it turns out, our Department of Finance didn't appreciate the *Stewart* and *Walls* decisions, and proposed changes to our tax law were introduced on October 31, 2003 (which still have not been enacted). Those changes will require a business owner to have a reasonable expectation of profit over the period of time he or she carries on the business (called the *profitability time period*). Suppose, for example, that you start Business X in 2008. Suppose that you report losses from Business X in 2008, 2009 and 2010. For each of these years, a test will have to be applied. For 2008, the test is whether it is reasonable *in that same 2008 tax year* to expect that you will realize a cumulative profit from Business X over the entire profitability time period (the period over which you expect to run the business). For 2009, the test is whether it is reasonable *in the 2009 tax year* to expect a cumulative profit, again over the entire profitability time period.

For each successive year, the same test will be applied: Is it reasonable to expect that you will have a cumulative profit over the profitability time period? Assume that in 2008 and 2009 it's determined that, in those years, it was reasonable to expect that you would report a cumulative profit from Business X over the profitability time period. Then, in 2010 it's determined that it is no longer reasonable to expect profits over that period of time. In this case, your losses for 2010 will be denied. The good news is that this determination in 2010 will not impact the losses you claimed in 2008 and 2009—they will still be allowed.

The bottom line? For years after 2004, you're going to have to demonstrate to the tax collector why you have a reasonable expectation of profit over the long run in order to claim a deduction for losses.

TO MAKE A LONG STORY SHORT:

- Non-capital losses from your business can be carried back three years or forward twenty years to offset taxable income in those years.

- Never use losses to reduce your income below the taxable threshold set by your basic personal tax credit, and consider saving the losses if you can use them in the next few years to offset dollars taxed at a higher rate.

- Proposed changes to our tax law introduced on October 31, 2003 will require you to demonstrate that you have a reasonable expectation of profit from your business over the long run, or else your losses could be denied.

Tim's Tip 48: Avoid tax on loans from your company through a strategy involving your spouse and the bank.

I've noticed that duct tape is like "The Force." It has a light side, a dark side, and holds the universe together. What duct tape is to the universe, two recent Supreme Court of Canada decisions are to taxpayers. I'm referring to the decisions in *Mathew* and *Canada Trustco Mortgage Co.,* where the Supreme Court set out the ground rules in the event that the CRA tries to shut down a tax strategy under the general anti-avoidance rule (GAAR) in our tax law (see Tip 9).

Since those decisions, there have been other court decisions on the issue of GAAR, most of which taxpayers have won. Specifically, a recent case, *Overs v. The Queen (2006),* provides a potential planning opportunity for business owners.

You see, subsection 15(2) of our tax law will generally tax a shareholder on any amounts borrowed from his or her corporation (with few exceptions). One way to escape this tax is to repay the loan by the end of the fiscal year following the fiscal year in which you received the loan. The problem? Most shareholders don't have the cash to pay back these typically large loans.

The Strategy

The *Overs* case sheds light on a strategy that worked for Mr. Overs and may work for you, too. In the case, Mr. Overs had borrowed $2.3 million from his corporation, THL, and had to repay the amount, or face tax on it. The plan he implemented had four steps.

First, his wife borrowed $2.3 million from the bank. Second, she purchased from her husband $2.3 million worth of his shares in THL using the borrowed money. Third, Mr. Overs used the $2.3 million to pay back the loan he owed to THL, thereby avoiding the requirement to pay tax on the $2.3 million loan. Finally, Mr. Overs claimed a deduction for the interest costs and other fees paid by his wife on the loan from the bank.

Now for some details. The bank was willing to lend Mrs. Overs the money because THL ended up with the $2.3 million in cash, which it pledged as security for the loan to her. When Mr. Overs sold THL shares to his wife, the sale was considered to have taken place at his adjusted cost base, not fair market value, because transfers between spouse are always treated this way unless you elect otherwise. The result? No tax to pay on the sale.

Finally, Mrs. Overs had paid over $225,000 in interest costs and guarantee fees related to the loan. Yet, Mr. Overs was able to deduct these amounts. Why? Since the sale of his THL shares to his wife did not take place at fair market value, the attribution rules in our tax law (see Tip 10) apply to tax Mr. Overs on any income his wife receives on the shares, but also attributes back to him any losses she may incur, which included the interest and other fees related to the loan.

Not only did Mr. Overs avoid tax on the $2.3 million shareholder loan, but he received a deduction for the costs his wife incurred to get him out of trouble. Not a bad deal.

Mr. Overs won his case in court, and GAAR did not apply to prevent use of this strategy in his case. An upcoming court decision, *Lipson et al v. The Queen*, could, however, call into question this strategy depending on the decision rendered by the Supreme Court of Canada (no verdict at the time of writing). Visit a tax pro for an update and an opinion.

TO MAKE A LONG STORY SHORT:

- Shareholder loans from your company are generally taxable to you, unless they are repaid by the end of the fiscal year following the fiscal year of the loan.

- Many shareholders do not have the cash to repay these loans from their companies.

- A court decision in *Overs v. The Queen (2006)* may provide a strategy to avoid the tax hit on a shareholder loan. Visit a tax pro for an update on the strategy given the *Lipson* court case.

Adding Up the Tax Hits

Don't be fooled into thinking that income taxes are your only tax burden as a business owner. In fact, there are a number of different "taxes" that your business will be subject to, and while I'm not going to talk about these in detail here, it's important that you become aware of what they are.

Tim's Tip 49: Understand the various "taxes" affecting your business.

In case the income tax burden you'll face on your business profits is not enough to faze you, try a few of these other "taxes" on for size. I call these taxes and, in most cases, that's precisely what they are. In other cases, these are more akin to premiums owing. There are four categories worth talking about.

Canada/Quebec Pension Plan and Employment Insurance

I've got good news and bad news for you. The good news is that, as a self-employed individual, you won't be required to pay any Employment Insurance (EI) premiums on your own earnings. This will save you

> In a family-run business, it may be possible to consider certain family members exempt from Employment Insurance (EI) premiums. This will save you the cost of the premiums, but it means that these family members won't be eligible to collect EI down the road if they find themselves unemployed. If you choose this route, make sure that the salary paid to these family members is reasonable, since the tax collector is more likely to examine the salaries of persons who are EI-exempt.
>
> **Caution!**

$1,706 in 2008 when factoring in both the employee ($711) and employer ($995) portions, although you won't be entitled to collect EI if you decide to try. The bad news is that you'll have to make Canada/Quebec Pension Plan (CPP/QPP) contributions on your self-employment earnings, and you'll have to pick up both the employee and employer portions, amounting to a maximum of $4,099 in 2008. And CPP/QPP contributions could get uglier in the future.

Provincial Payroll Taxes

Provincial payroll taxes originated in Manitoba and have spread like wildfire across the country, and now apply in the following places: Manitoba, Newfoundland, Northwest Territories, Nunavut, Ontario, and Quebec. These payroll taxes normally apply to employment income and in some cases extend to self-employment income. There's good news if you live in Ontario. Ontario's Employer Health Tax (EHT) was eliminated for self-employed individuals in 1999. Only Alberta, British Columbia, and Ontario levy health care premiums on individuals (and some employers pay these on behalf of their employees).

Workers' Compensation

Many businesses are required to pay premiums to the Workers' Compensation Board. The amount of the premiums depends on the type of work that is being undertaken. Be sure to look into this when you start your business.

GST and HST

Every consumer knows first-hand about the Goods and Services Tax (GST) or the Harmonized Sales Tax (HST) in Nova Scotia, New Brunswick, and Newfoundland and Labrador. Your business will need to register for the GST/HST if your taxable sales of goods or services exceed $30,000 in a fiscal year. Once your sales reach this level, you'll be required to register for GST/HST within 29 days and start charging the tax on the sales transaction that puts you over the $30,000 threshold. You'll be required to file GST/HST returns, normally on an annual basis, although some businesses will be required to file quarterly or monthly. In any event, you may be required to remit quarterly installments of GST/HST.

There's an option for many small businesses to calculate the GST/HST owing under the "Quick Method" provided total sales (including tax) are under $200,000. The Quick Method allows you simply to calculate the GST/HST owing as a percentage of total sales (including GST/HST) rather than tracking the actual GST collected and paid throughout the year. CRA has a guide on using the Quick Method, which you can obtain online at **www.cra.gc.ca** or by contacting your local Tax Services Office. By the way, certain businesses can't use the Quick Method (accountants, book-keepers, and a number of others are on this list—check it out first).

TO MAKE A LONG STORY SHORT:

- Income taxes are not the only type of tax that your business will have to deal with.

- Take the time to understand your obligations related to CPP, EI, provincial payroll taxes, workers' compensation, and the GST/HST.

Getting into the Game

If self-employment is in your game plan, there's plenty you can do to minimize the taxes you pay. Turn now to the Tax Planning Tip Sheet at the front of the book and review the strategies introduced in Chapter 4. Ask yourself, "Can this tip apply to me?" Every *Yes* or *Not Sure* could add dollars to your bottom line. When you've finished reading this book, take your Tip Sheet to a tax pro for help in setting up your tax-savvy proprietorship, partnership, or corporation.

BULLS, BEARS, AND BASEBALL: STRATEGIES FOR INVESTORS

To become a millionaire:
Start with 10 million,
then invest in a hot tip.

5

All right, I'll be the first to admit it. My life is a little one-tracked. Here's proof: My career is taxation, and my hobby is investing. Being one-tracked makes me good at what I do, but—according to my wife—something far less than exciting at the dinner table. In fact, my wife Carolyn and I were at a friend's place for dinner once when the conversation turned to investment issues. I was in my element. Evidently, everyone else wished they were in bed.

After dinner, Carolyn said to me privately: "Tim, for the first time in my life, I envied my feet—they were asleep. Why can't you take up another hobby, like insect collecting or something?"

"Insect collecting," I replied. "Great idea! I could liquidate some of my South American holdings, and reassess my short position in that small resource play out west to free up some cash. Then I could undertake a fundamental analysis on any insect-related securities that I can locate in the market. Of course, I'd want to check the price–volume histories and look at other technical analyses. Heck, I could even take a long position in some bug-related futures contracts through my broker in Chicago. Carolyn, you're a genius. We could make millions!"

"Help, I married a financial geek!" my wife replied. "Tim, forget what I said about starting a new hobby."

At this point, I want to talk to those of you who, like me, are investors. And this will include just about everyone. In fact, you can consider yourself an investor for our discussion here if you have any money at all invested outside your Registered Retirement Savings Plan (RRSP), Registered Retirement Income Fund (RRIF), or other tax-deferred plan—or if you expect to have these types of investments down the road. These are called *non-registered assets*, also referred to as your *open money*.

Let's look at some strategies that are sure to keep the tax collector away from your open money. It's time for investors to step up to the plate, because these pages contain some guaranteed home runs.

Investing in a Tax-Smart Manner

Tim's Tip 50: Consider the impact that taxes can have on a non-registered portfolio.

If the truth be known, Canadian investors, financial advisors, and money managers have not focused enough on the impact that taxes can have on your accumulation of wealth over the long run. Now, don't blame your financial advisor for

Did You Know?

A survey by Stats Canada in 2001 showed that 70 percent of all investable wealth in Canada today is outside of RRSPs and RRIFs, where taxes can easily impact the growth of those assets. And don't forget, the next decade will see billions of dollars moving from one generation to the next here in Canada. When money changes generations, it generally ends up in non-registered accounts since RRSP and RRIF assets rarely stay in those tax-deferred plans when moving to the hands of children or grandchildren. The bottom line? A focus on *after-tax* investing is critical!

not paying much attention to after-tax investing if in fact your advisor hasn't been concerned about the issue.

You see, there hasn't been much research on the issue of after-tax returns, so most advisors have not been fed the proper information on the subject. As for money managers in Canada today, most grew up in the pension industry where, quite frankly, income taxes don't matter (money in a pension fund isn't subject to taxes annually).

The bottom line? Canadian investors have not been shown that after-tax investing is critical to building wealth. But times are changing. Canadians are starting to recognize the impact taxes can have on a portfolio. I'm here to tell you that focusing on after-tax returns is so important when investing outside an RRSP or RRIF that it could mean the difference between having plenty in retirement, and moving in with the kids or performing on a street corner to make ends meet (and unless you're Wayne Newton, performing on a street corner is not likely to get you far).

There are two things in particular that will determine how much tax you pay annually on your non-registered investments: portfolio make-up and portfolio turnover.

Portfolio Make-Up Matters

When I talk about portfolio make-up, I'm talking about the types of investments you're holding in your portfolio (remember, I'm referring to those investments outside your RRSP or RRIF; there are no taxes annually on income earned inside those registered plans). You see, the types of investments you hold will determine the type of income you earn from your investments, which will affect how much tax you pay each year.

Generally, your investments will fall into three broad categories:

- money market investments
- fixed income investments
- equity investments

Money market investments include cash and near-cash investments such as Guaranteed Investment Certificates (GICs), Canada Savings Bonds, or money market mutual funds. Fixed income investments, as the name suggests, provide a steady stream of income to the investor, and generally include corporate bonds, government bonds, mortgage-backed securities, preferred shares, income trusts, or mutual funds that invest in these and similar types of investments. Equity investments are different in that you're an owner, not a loaner. That is, equity investments provide you with ownership in something, whether it's a business, real estate, natural resources, or something similar. Equity investments include common shares in publicly traded companies, real estate, or mutual funds that invest in these or similar things.

What's the difference between money market, fixed income, and equity investments from a tax point of view? It's a critical question. Money market and fixed income investments will generally provide you with interest income (and perhaps with dividends in the case of preferred shares), with little opportunity to generate capital gains. Equity investments, on the other hand, provide an opportunity for capital gains (or losses!) and perhaps some dividend income in the case of common shares.

Make no mistake, these differences are crucial. You see, interest income is taxed at a much higher rate than dividends from a Canadian company, and capital gains. Flip to page 283 at the back of the book and you'll see the difference in marginal tax rates that apply to these different types of income in each province. If you're in the highest tax bracket, you'll face marginal tax rates on these types of income approximately as follows (these are averages for Canada in 2008):

- Interest income   45.0 percent
- Canadian ineligible dividends   31.3 percent
- Canadian eligible dividends   25.0 percent
- Capital gains   22.5 percent

The bottom line? Money market and fixed income investments are not generally tax-smart because interest income is downright ugly from a tax perspective. Equities, on the other hand, make more sense from a tax perspective since capital gains are taxed at much lower rates. In fact, only half of any capital gains you realize will have to be included in your income.

Want proof that portfolio make-up can make a difference in your wealth accumulation? Check out Joel's numbers.

*J*oel has $100,000 to invest for a 20-year period. He can earn a 10-percent rate of return annually over that time. Joel's marginal tax rate is 45 percent. He plans to liquidate the portfolio at the end of 20 years. How much will he have at that time after all taxes have been paid? It depends on the type of income he'll be earning—that is, on the make-up of his portfolio. If Joel were to invest strictly in interest-bearing vehicles, he'd have $236,597 in his pocket after taxes at the end of 20 years. On the other hand, if Joel were to invest exclusively in equity investments that grow in value but are not taxed until he liquidates his portfolio, he would have $383,724 after taxes at the end of that time. That is, Joel would have a full $147,127, or 62.2 percent, more at the end of 20 years by changing the make-up of his portfolio. His after-tax portfolio will nearly double in this case! The following table says it all.*

PORTFOLIO MAKE-UP MATTERS			
		$100,000 Invested for 20 Years	
Portfolio Make-Up		Balance Before Taxes	Balance After Taxes
Money Market	(100% interest income)	$236,597	$236,597
Balanced	(50% interest, 50% deferred capital gains)	$333,035	$299,207
Equity	(100% deferred capital gains)	$466,096	$383,724

Assumptions: $100,000 invested; 8% pre-tax annual rate of return; portfolio is liquidated after 20 years; marginal tax rate is 45%; capital gains inclusion rate is 50%.

Portfolio Turnover Matters

In addition to portfolio make-up, the turnover of your portfolio is critical as well. Every time you liquidate an investment and then reinvest the money, you've "turned over" that investment. The more selling and buying that goes on in your portfolio, the higher your rate of turnover. The problem with turnover is that each sale is a taxable event when it takes place outside of a registered plan. If taxes are triggered, it leaves you with less money to reinvest. This means that your next investment has to perform better than you might have thought: It has to provide you with the rate of return you're expecting, but must go further, to replace the dollars you paid in taxes from liquidating the previous investment. Sure, taxes may eventually be paid on your gains, but it's better to defer the tax to the future than to prepay tax today—it's a timing issue.

You need to know that turnover can take place at two levels: the investor level, and the money manager level. That is, there are generally two culprits who can be accused of turning over your investments: you, and/or the money manager (typically the mutual fund manager where you're invested in funds). You create turnover every time you choose to sell a security that you hold in your portfolio, whether it's a stock, bond, mutual fund, or some other investment. The money manager creates turnover in the same way by selling securities inside the fund you're holding. In either case, guess who pays the tax on any taxable capital gains realized. You got it: You pay the tax.

Let's look at Don's example. It'll help you to understand the difference that turnover can make over the long run.

> **Caution!**
>
> Dividends from Canadian companies are taxed at much lower rates than interest income. As a result, many investors think that they're investing in a tax-smart manner when they're earning these dividends. This may not be true. You see, if you need a cash flow from your investments, then earning dividends from Canadian companies can be a good idea. But if you have no need for this cash flow, then receiving dividends annually is creating a tax bill that you could be avoiding. You could instead be investing for long-term growth so that you'll defer your tax hit until you sell the investments, and you'll face tax at the lower rates that apply to capital gains. Now that's tax-smart.

*D*on has $100,000 to invest for a 20-year time period. He knows that capital gains will be taxed at lower rates than interest or dividends in his hands, so he's chosen to invest in equity mutual funds to generate those gains. Don's marginal tax rate is 45 percent. If Don earns an 8-percent rate of return annually, how much will he have, after taxes, at the end of 20 years? The answer depends on the level of turnover in his portfolio over that period. If Don chooses funds with a very low rate of turnover (say, zero turnover in this example), he'll have $383,724 in his hands after taxes in 20 years. If Don instead chooses an equity fund with a higher rate of turnover—say 100 percent (meaning that 100 percent of accrued gains are realized each year)—he'd be left with just $333,035 at the end of that same time. Don will be short-changed by a full $50,689 if he chooses a fund with a high rate of turnover in this example. The following table tells the story.

PORTFOLIO TURNOVER MATTERS			
		$100,000 Invested for 20 Years	
Portfolio Turnover		**Balance Before Taxes**	**Balance After Taxes**
0% Turnover	No capital gains are realized annually	$466,096	$383,724
50% Turnover	50% of accrued gains are realized annually	$394,266	$356,965
100% Turnover	100% of accrued gains are realized annually	$333,035	$333,035

Assumptions: $100,000 invested for 20 years; 8% pre-tax annual rate of return; all returns are capital gains; portfolio is liquidated after 20 years; marginal tax rate is 45%; capital gains inclusion rate is 50%.

By the way, you might think that a turnover rate of 100 percent is not realistic for a mutual fund in a given year. Think again. In any given year, there will be many funds with rates of turnover in excess of 100 percent. I've seen funds with turnover rates as high as 800 percent in a year! If you're not sure what the rates of turnover are for the funds you're investing in, call the fund companies you're dealing with and ask.

Tax-Smart Rules

Want to minimize the tax you're paying on your investments outside your RRSP or RRIF? You should. We've seen that taxes *do* matter—a lot! After the discussion we've had here, you'll now understand that there are two rules to start with to minimize taxes annually on your investments:

1. Focus on capital gains when investing outside of your registered plans.
2. Keep portfolio turnover to an absolute minimum.

Let me make a couple of last points. Earning capital gains outside of a registered plan is important for tax efficiency. Today, there are also a number of mutual funds and income trusts that provide distributions as a return of capital (ROC). A ROC is tax free when the distribution is received. The distribution will reduce your adjusted cost base in the specific investment so that, when you eventually sell it, you'll have a larger capital gain or smaller capital loss at that time. A ROC, then, manages to push the tax hit to the year you sell the investment and results in a capital gain at that time. It's a tax deferral. Not too shabby. See Tip 54 for more on income trusts.

Finally, speak to a trusted financial advisor about which specific money managers attempt to keep turnover to a minimum. Focus on these managers when investing outside your RRSP or RRIF.

TO MAKE A LONG STORY SHORT:

- After-tax investing has been ignored for too long by investors, financial advisors, and money managers alike. Today, Canadians are starting to think about *after-tax* returns, because taxes *do* matter.

- Taxes on a portfolio are affected by two things: portfolio make-up and portfolio turnover.

- Minimize taxes by focusing on earning capital gains or returns of capital outside your registered plans and by keeping turnover to a minimum.

Tim's Tip 51: Call your profits *capital gains* and your losses *business losses*.

Sometimes you're going to make money on your investments, and sometimes you're going to lose it. But are you going to call your profits *capital gains* or *business income*? Similarly, are you going to call your losses *capital losses* or *business losses*? This issue can be as clear as mud. No doubt about it, this is one of the very gray areas in our tax law. And it can be tough making key decisions on the gray issues, where it often comes down to toss-ups and testosterone.

Saya loves to invest. In fact, she follows the stock market closely. In an average month, Saya makes about eight trades on her brokerage account. Last year, she generated $35,000 in profits from her investing. But investing is not Saya's primary source of income. She works as a technician in an architect's office, and she earns $45,000 each year as an employee there. Should Saya's profits from investing be considered capital gains or business income? She could argue either way.

Here's the general rule: Where you have the ability to argue either way, call your profits capital gains. Here's why: Just 50 percent of capital gains are taxable in Canada, while business income is fully taxable. Have you incurred losses? You'll be better off calling these business losses than calling them capital losses. After all, capital losses can only be applied against capital gains to reduce tax, while business losses can be applied against any source of income at all.

Keep in mind that, in many cases, it will be clear whether your profits and losses are capital or income in nature. Consider the analogy of the tree and its fruit. If you bought a tree with the intention of growing and selling fruit, then the tree would be a capital asset to you. So, if you were to sell the tree itself at a profit, that profit would normally be considered a capital gain. The profits from selling the fruit would be considered business income. As far as the tax collector is concerned, your primary intention when you bought the asset will normally determine the proper treatment.

Want a more lifelike example? Suppose you bought a condominium for the purpose of renting it out, and someone offered a good price to buy the condo from you.

Because you bought the condo to generate rents (your "fruit" in this case), the condo is a capital asset, and any profit on the sale is likely a capital gain. If, however, you bought the condo largely to sell it at a profit, and not primarily to rent it, then you could argue that the transaction was income in nature. It's what we call an "adventure in the nature of trade." If you lost money flipping the property in this case, it's arguably a business loss.

In any event, it's important to document your reasoning for the position you take when reporting your gains and losses. And be consistent! That is, don't treat your stock profits as capital gains and your losses from similar investments as business losses. The tax collector doesn't really have a sense of humour in this regard.

Here's one last point: Any profits or losses that you generate from short-selling a stock will generally be considered business income or losses. It only makes sense. You see, a short sale doesn't provide the opportunity for any "fruit from the tree" such as interest, dividends, royalties, or rents. No fruit? Then these securities are more akin to an "adventure in the nature of trade" and will be treated as income.

> You can make a special election to treat all your gains and losses from trading Canadian securities as capital gains and losses. Those who are considered *traders* cannot make this election (although a trader is not defined in the *Income Tax Act*). Normally, I don't recommend making this election. The reason? It's irrevocable—you'll be stuck with it for life. Besides, your profits and losses from trading securities will almost always be considered capital gains and losses anyway, so there's often no need to make the election. Why tie your hands when you don't need to?
>
> **Caution!**

TO MAKE A LONG STORY SHORT:

- It may not always be clear whether you should treat your investment profits and losses as capital or income.

- Where possible, you'll want to argue that your profits are capital gains and your losses are business losses.

- Document your reasoning and be consistent from one transaction to the next.

Tim's Tip 52: **Claim a capital gains reserve to spread your tax bill over time.**

Ah, yes, one of the mysteries of the universe—how to avoid tax on capital gains when an asset has appreciated in value. It's not an easy question to answer. I wish more magic were available here. Your best bet in this situation may be to push the expected tax bill as far off into the future as possible. You can do this simply by not selling the asset. But if you're determined to sell, you can at least minimize the tax hit by spreading it out over a maximum five-year period.

You see, the tax collector will allow you to claim what is called a *capital gains reserve*—a deduction—when you have sold something at a profit but have not yet collected the full amount of your proceeds from the sale.

*L*isa decided last year to sell the family cottage. She had bought it for *$75,000 and was offered $175,000 for it—a $100,000 profit she couldn't refuse. She wasn't able to shelter this $100,000 capital gain in any way, so she decided to take payment from the purchaser over a five-year period—$35,000 each year. This way, the capital gain was not taxed all at once last year. Rather, Lisa will pay tax on the gain over the five-year period—she'll report just $20,000 each year. She reported the full $100,000 capital gain last year, but claimed a capital gains reserve for 80 percent (four-fifths) of the gain. The gain will be taken into income slowly over five years.*

You'll have to take any capital gains into income at a rate not less than 20 percent (one-fifth) each year. If you're not keen on the idea of taking payment over five years because you're giving up use of the proceeds today, there's a simple solution: Build an "interest" charge into the selling price so that you're compensated for the time delay in collecting payment. For example, Lisa could have collected, say, $37,500 each year rather than $35,000—for a total selling price of $187,500. The additional $2,500 each year is like interest income, but the good news is that it should be taxed as a capital gain (only one-half of capital gains are taxable) since it's built into the selling price!

TO MAKE A LONG STORY SHORT:

- It's very difficult to avoid paying tax on accrued capital gains on assets you own.

- Your best bet may be to push the tax bill as far into the future as possible.

- A taxable capital gain can be spread out for up to five years by taking payment of the proceeds over an extended period. This is called a capital gains reserve.

Tim's Tip 53: **Consider investing to earn eligible dividends for big tax savings.**

Some big changes were introduced in 2006 that will impact Canadian investors for years to come. By way of background, the federal government had been concerned about the amount of money being invested by Canadians in income trusts. Why? Because income trusts can result in a significant deferral of tax for investors (see Tip 56 for more). To stem the flow of money invested in income trusts, the federal government proposed to equal the playing field between income trusts and publicly traded shares so that investors may be less inclined to invest in income trusts and more inclined to invest in shares.

What did the feds do? They reduced the tax rate on *eligible dividends* from certain Canadian companies. Let's take a look at the new rules.

Lower Tax Rates

Eligible dividends from Canadian companies will be subject to lower tax rates than ineligible dividends. You see, eligible dividends will benefit from a 45 percent gross-up (as opposed to a 25 percent gross-up for ineligible dividends) and a larger dividend tax credit equal to 18.97 percent of the grossed-up dividend (13.33 percent for ineligible dividends). The end result is a lower marginal tax rate on eligible dividends (see the marginal tax rate tables starting on page 288). In fact, it's interesting to note that, at certain income levels, eligible dividends may have a negative marginal tax rate (more about this in a minute).

By comparison, the average marginal tax rate on eligible dividends is 25 percent, while ineligible dividends have an average marginal tax rate of 31.3 percent.

Eligible Dividends

An eligible dividend is generally a dividend paid by a large publicly traded Canadian corporation. Some dividends paid by a Canadian-controlled private corporation (CCPC) may also qualify.

Okay, let's get more specific here. If a corporation is a CCPC or a deposit insurance corporation, it can pay eligible dividends only to the extent of its "general rate income pool" (GRIP)—a balance generally reflecting taxable income that has not benefited from the low small business tax rate or any of certain other special tax rates.

A corporation resident in Canada that is neither a CCPC nor a deposit insurance corporation (a "non-CCPC") can pay eligible dividends in any amount, unless it has a "low rate income pool" (LRIP), in which case it must pay dividends out of this LRIP before it can pay eligible dividends. The LRIP is generally made up of taxable income that benefited from small business tax rates, either in the hands of the dividend-paying non-CCPC itself (at a time when it was a CCPC) or in the hands of a CCPC that paid an ineligible dividend to the non-CCPC. Many non-CCPCs will never have an LRIP, with the result that the company will be able to designate all of its dividends as eligible dividends.

By the way, a given corporation will have, at most, one GRIP or one LRIP at any time, and that one pool is relevant to the dividends it pays on all classes of its shares. This means that, subject to any constraints in the existing law and the need to avoid artificial manipulations of the pools, a corporation can choose which of its shareholders will receive eligible or ineligible dividends.

Did You Know?

For a dividend to be an eligible dividend, the corporation must give you written notice that the dividend is eligible. If you're the recipient, you can rely on that notice, and you don't have to know anything about the tax status of the corporation yourself. A company that reports a dividend as an eligible dividend but shouldn't have (perhaps due to a LRIP) will be subject to penalties.

Strategies to Consider

The low tax rate available on eligible dividends brings to mind some tax strategies to consider. First, if you own a CCPC, you may want to give thought to creating a general rate income pool (GRIP) by foregoing the small business deduction (and thereby foregoing the small business tax rate). This will enable the CCPC to pay eligible dividends (subject to the LRIP limitation). You see, a new election allows a CCPC to do this without also giving up other benefits of CCPC status. This is simply a number-crunching exercise that your accountant can help you with, to determine if the idea is right for you.

Secondly, given the new, lower marginal tax rate on eligible dividends, it would be a mistake for some investors to hold all of their stocks in their registered plans, if those stocks pay eligible dividends. That is, to the extent you want to hold equities in your portfolio, you may be better off holding certain equities outside your RRSP or registered retirement income fund even if you have the contribution room to hold those assets inside the plan.

Consider this: The dividend tax credit has been increased under the new rules so much that the credit, in some cases, will not only offset the tax owing on the dividend received, but will go further and reduce the tax on other income you have as well. For example, a taxpayer in Ontario earning $30,000 annually will pay $4,350 on that income (2008 tax rates). Add $5,000 of eligible dividends to his income, and his total tax bill drops to $4,032. Did you catch that? The marginal tax rate on those dividends is actually a negative number. Now, once your income hits a certain level ($33,700 in Ontario at 2008 tax rates), your eligible dividends will increase your taxes—albeit at a lower rate than other income.

TO MAKE A LONG STORY SHORT:

- Changes introduced in 2006 will provide a lower marginal tax rate on eligible dividends paid, typically, by large publicly traded Canadian corporations.

- Some private corporations may also be entitled to pay eligible dividends to the extent they have a general rate income pool (GRIP).

- It may now make sense for some private company owners to forego the small business tax rate in exchange for the ability to pay eligible dividends, but this is strategy that your accountant should advise on, depending on your circumstances.

- It may also make sense to hold certain stock outside of registered plans to the extent eligible dividends will be paid on those stocks. This may be particularly true where your income is lower and you may have a negative marginal tax rate on eligible dividends.

Tim's Tip 54: Think about reporting your spouse's dividends on your own tax return where possible.

Sure, it may sound crazy, but taking income from the lower-income spouse and adding it to the income of the higher-income spouse could actually save you taxes. You see, if your spouse earns dividends (eligible or ineligible) from a Canadian company, he or she will be entitled to claim a *dividend tax credit*. This is simply a credit that is deducted from the taxes your spouse would otherwise pay. But what if your spouse isn't going to pay any tax because of not having much income? In this case, the dividend tax credit could go to waste.

The good news? Our tax law will allow you to elect to include *all* (it's all or nothing) of your spouse's Canadian dividends on *your* tax return, where you'll be able to claim the dividend tax credit. How can this possibly save you tax? Simple. By removing the dividend income from your spouse's tax return, your spouse's income will be reduced. This will increase the spousal credit you're entitled to claim for having a spouse who is dependent on you. In fact, the tax collector won't allow you to make this election to report your spouse's dividends unless the spousal credit you're entitled to claim is increased as a result of removing the dividends from your spouse's return. Follow me?

In the end, you'll need to calculate your and your spouse's combined tax bills both ways: (1) having your spouse report his or her own dividends, and (2) reporting your spouse's dividends on your tax return instead. This will tell you whether or not you stand to benefit from the transfer. This is where tax software is going to come in handy. It's easy to do these "what if" calculations with software. The other option is to speak to a tax pro or a financial advisor who may be able to do the calculations for you.

TO MAKE A LONG STORY SHORT:

- It may be possible to save tax by reporting Canadian dividends received by your lower-income spouse on your tax return instead.

- This transfer can be made only where doing so will increase the spousal credit that you're able to claim as a result of your spouse being a dependant.

- You'll need to crunch some numbers to see if this transfer will be beneficial for you.

Tip 55: **Use a tax-free savings account for a number of benefits.**

The 2008 federal budget introduced a new type of savings account, called a Tax-Free Savings Account (TFSA) that will allow you to earn income on a tax-free basis inside the account. Want the basics? You won't be entitled to a deduction for money contributed to the TFSA, but all the earnings inside the TFSA will be tax-free, and all withdrawals from the TFSA are also tax-free. TFSAs will be available beginning in 2009.

Any Canadian resident who is age 18 or older will be able to establish a TFSA. You'll be able to open an account at most financial institutions, such as banks, trust companies, credit unions, and just about any other institution that also offers registered retirement savings plans (RRSPs). You'll have to provide the issuer with your social insurance number when you open the account. And you can open more than one TFSA, but your total contributions to TFSAs in a particular year can't be more than your contribution room.

Contribution Limits

You'll be able to contribute an amount up to your contribution limit for the year. That contribution limit—or contribution "room"—is made up of three amounts:

- $5,000 for each year (this $5,000 will be indexed to inflation and rounded to the nearest $500 on a yearly basis), plus
- Any withdrawals made in the previous year (that is, you'll be able to "re-contribute" any amounts you withdraw from the TFSA, on top of new contribution room you accumulate each year), plus

- Any unused contribution room from prior years.

By the way, the Canada Revenue Agency (CRA) will determine the TFSA contribution room (based on information provided by issuers) for each eligible individual who files an annual T1 individual income tax return. Individuals who have not filed returns for prior years (because for example, there was no tax payable) will be able to establish their entitlement to contribution room by filing a return for those years or by other means acceptable to the CRA. I expect that the CRA will provide information on your notice of assessment annually as to the amount of your available TFSA contribution room.

Jacob is 25 years old, is a Canadian resident, and will therefore be given $5,000 of TFSA contribution room in 2009. He contributes $2,000 to a TFSA in 2009, and so $3,000 of contribution room is carried forward and can be contributed in the future. Jacob's contribution room for 2010, then, is $5,000 (for 2010) plus $3,000 of contribution room carried forward from the prior year, for a total of $8,000. If Jacob does not make a contribution to a TFSA in 2010, but decides to withdraw $1,000, his contribution room for 2011 would be $5,000 (for 2011), plus $8,000 (carried forward from 2010), plus the $1,000 withdrawn, for a total of $14,000.

There is no limit on the length of time you can carry forward unused TFSA contribution room. But be sure not to contribute more than your contribution room. If you make an excess contribution, you'll face a tax of one percent per month on any excess amount, and this tax will apply every month that the excess remains in the TFSA.

Withdrawals from a TFSA

There are no restrictions on the amount of withdrawals you can make, nor are there mandatory withdrawals required, as with a registered retirement income fund (RRIF). And withdrawals are not taxable, and so they will not impact income-tested benefits such as Canada Child Tax Benefits, the Working Income Tax Benefit, Old Age Security benefits, the Guaranteed Income Supplement, Employment Insurance Benefits, age credits, or GST tax credits, for example.

Eligible Investments

What type of investments can you hold in a TFSA? The same investments that you can hold in an RRSP, such as mutual funds, publicly traded securities, GICs, bonds, and even certain shares of small business corporations. For a more complete list of eligible investments, see Tip 70.

Borrowing to Invest

Unlike your RRSP, you can use the assets inside the TFSA as security for a loan if you want. The problem, however, is that you won't be able to deduct the interest on the loan where the loan proceeds have been contributed to a TFSA for investment inside the plan. The rationale is that you're not going to pay tax on any earnings inside the TFSA or upon withdrawing those funds later, so the taxman isn't keen on allowing a deduction for the interest in this case.

Attribution Rules

Here's some welcome news. If you provide funds to your spouse or common-law partner to invest in a TFSA, any income earned in your spouse's plan will not be attributed back to you to be taxed in your hands. That is, the TFSA allows you to side-step the attribution rules which I spoke about back in Tip 10.

Death of a Taxpayer

If you own a TFSA, what happens upon your death? Well, the earnings that accrue in the account after the account holder's death will be taxable, while those earnings that accrue before death would remain exempt. The good news, however, is that it's possible to maintain the tax-free status of the earnings if the account holder names his or her spouse or common-law partner as the successor account holder. Alternatively, the assets of the deceased's TFSA could be transferred to the TFSA of the surviving spouse or common-law partner on a tax-deferred basis without any impact on the survivor's existing contribution room.

Becoming Non-Resident

If you get up and leave Canada—that is, become a non-resident for tax purposes—you'll be allowed to maintain your TFSA, and you won't be taxed on any earnings in the account or on withdrawals. But, you won't be allowed to contribute any more to a TFSA, and no contribution room would accrue for any year throughout which you are a non-resident.

Marriage Breakdown

If your marriage breaks down, any amount can be transferred directly from one spouse or common-law partner's TFSA to the other's. The amount of the transfer would not affect either person's contribution room, and there would be no tax to pay on the transfer of assets from one plan to the next.

Losses Inside a TFSA

Just as your investment losses inside an RRSP cannot be claimed, the same is true for losses inside a TFSA. You cannot simply use those losses against income or capital gains realized outside of the TFSA. And inside the TFSA, those losses will not benefit you since the income inside the plan is not taxable anyway.

TFSA Strategies

Okay, so are TFSAs really a good deal? Should every Canadian have a TFSA? To be honest, I am hard pressed to think of any reason why you would not open a TFSA. Sure, the contribution limits are fairly modest, but some tax free compounding inside a TFSA is better than none at all. So, yes, I think that every eligible person should open a TFSA. Now, consider the following strategies to make the most of a TFSA:

1. **Compare TFSAs to RRSPs.** In all likelihood, it will make sense to set aside money in both a TFSA and RRSP. If you do the math, you'll see that both TFSAs and RRSPs work out to be equal in after-tax returns assuming your marginal tax rate remains the same in retirement as it is today (see the table below). And there's the rub. If your marginal tax rate is going to be different in retirement, then one plan may work better than the other. Here are the three scenarios and how they may affect your choice of account to use:
   - If the two rates are identical, as in the table below, the TFSA and the RRSP are equally effective tax-savings alternatives.
   - If the tax rate at the time of withdrawal is lower than at the time of contribution, the RRSP is the better choice.
   - If the tax rate at the time of withdrawal is higher than at the time of contribution, the advantage goes to the TFSA.

- As a practical matter, the low contribution limits on a TFSA likely make it a poor choice for your sole retirement funding vehicle.

NET PROCEEDS FROM SAVING IN A TFSA RELATIVE TO OTHER SAVINGS VEHICLES

	TFSA	RRSP	Unregistered Savings
Pre-tax income	1,000	1,000	1,000
Tax (40% rate)	400	—	400
Net contribution[1]	600	1,000	600
Investment income (20 years at 5.5%)	1,151	1,918	707[2]
Gross proceeds (Net contribution + investment income)	1,751	2,918	1,307
Tax (40% rate)	—	1,167	—
Net proceeds	1,751	1,751	1,307
Net annual after-tax rate of return[3] (%)	5.5	5.5	4.0

1 Forgone consumption (saving) is $600 in all cases. In the RRSP case, the person contributes $1,000 but receives a $400 reduction in tax, thereby sacrificing net consumption of $600.
2 For unregistered saving case, tax rate on investment income is 28%, representing a weighted average tax rate on an investment portfolio comprised of 30% dividends, 30% capital gains and 40% interest.
3 Measured in relation to forgone consumption of $600. Assumes annual nominal pre-tax rate of return is 5.5 invested for 20 years.

2. **Side-step the attribution rules.** It's possible to use a TFSA to avoid the attribution rules in our tax law. You might recall that, if you simply give money to your spouse to invest, any income earned by your spouse will generally be attributed back to you and will be taxed in your hands (refer back to Tip 10). Not so with a TFSA. For example, you could give your spouse $5,000 in 2009 for him to contribute to his TFSA. Any earnings on that $5,000 inside the TFSA will not be subject to the attribution rules. Now, the attribution rules will be avoided as long as those dollars you've given or loaned to your spouse remain in a TFSA. If you remove those dollars from the account, they will then be subject to the attribution rules if those dollars then earn income outside of the TFSA. Over a period of years, you'll be able to accumulate a fair bit in your spouse's TFSA, growing on a tax-free basis. And so, it makes much sense for both you and your spouse or common-law partner to open TFSAs, and if your spouse doesn't have the means to contribute to his or her plan, you should give the money for that purpose if

you can. Your spouse could then withdraw all $10,000 to invest outside the TFSA, and you could give him $15,000 the following year—and so on. The result? An ever-increasing portfolio in your spouse's hands, outside of the TFSA, that will not be subject to the attribution rules. Now, let me say this: I don't expect this opportunity to last forever because it seems to violate the intention of the attribution rules. In fact, this opportunity may be closed down sooner rather than later—so check with a tax professional to determine whether it is still possible to do.

3. **Save for an education.** Saving for a child's education is still best accomplished by using a registered education savings plan (RESP) provided you are receiving Canada Education Savings Grants (CESGs) on contributions to the RESP. But where the maximum in CESGs has been received already, and further RESP contributions won't attract those grants, I believe it can make sense to save inside a TFSA from that point onward since neither the RESP nor the TFSA provides a tax deduction for contributions, but the TFSA does offer tax-free withdrawals, which the RESP does not offer. While CESGs are being paid into the RESP, you'll still be better off with the RESP, but not beyond that point.

4. **Shelter fixed income.** To the extent you are going to hold interest-bearing investments in your portfolio, you should consider holding those assets in a registered plan (RRSP or RRIF), and in a TFSA. This way, the highly taxed interest income won't present a tax burden annually.

5. **Shelter option or shorting strategies.** If you get involved in certain options strategies, or in short-selling, the profits you make, if any, can be taxed as regular income. If this is the case, consider whether to undertake these strategies inside a TFSA. The advantage is that the income will be sheltered from tax. The disadvantage may be that you won't then be able to claim a deduction for any expenses related to earning that income, but I suspect you'll prefer to have the income fully sheltered inside the TFSA if possible.

6. **Shelter foreign dividends.** Foreign dividends are not subject to the dividend gross-up and tax credit system available on Canadian dividends, and so foreign dividends are taxed as regular income. Earning that income inside a TFSA can shelter that income from tax.

7. **Minimize benefit clawbacks.** By holding income-producing securities inside the TFSA rather than in your personal hands, income that may otherwise increase your net income and thereby reduce certain benefits (Old Age Security benefits, for example) may no longer cause a clawback of those benefits.

8. **Shelter private company shares.** It's possible in some cases to hold private company shares inside an RRSP, and likewise inside a TFSA. The rules are complex, but as a general guideline, the annuitant under the plan cannot be a "connected shareholder" immediately after the time the shares are acquired by the plan. A connected shareholder is one who owns 10 percent or more of any class of shares. So, if your ownership is under 10 percent, you should be fine. There's an exception to the "under 10 percent" limit: If you deal with the company at arm's length and the cost of your shares in the company is less than $25,000, you may own more than 10 percent of the shares. But in any event, if you control the company (or you and related persons control the company), you'll be out of luck—the shares won't qualify. The rules have been simplified here, so visit a tax pro for more information and advice on whether certain shares will qualify. Imagine, however, that you're a minority shareholder in a private company and are able to hold those shares in a TFSA; any gains on the shares would be tax-free if the company grows in value. This could be a huge win if the company's growth is significant.

TO MAKE A LONG STORY SHORT:

- The 2008 federal budget introduced a new Tax-Free Savings Account (TFSA) which offers tax-free compounding of investments, and tax free withdrawals at any time. There is no deduction for contributions to a TFSA.

- Every Canadian resident age 18 or older should open a TFSA starting in 2009.

- There are a number of potential benefits and strategies to consider with TFSAs, and these are generally designed to: Split income between spouses, reduce taxable income, and reduce the clawback of income-tested benefits.

Understanding Tax-Smart Strategies

Tim's Tip 56: Understand the advantages and drawbacks of income trusts.

The last few years saw an incredible proliferation of income trusts in Canada. It seems that every investor and his or her brother has been craving investment yield, and in the wake of weak equity markets, income trusts became the investment of choice. Now, income trusts are not exactly new. They appeared first in the 1980s in the form of real estate investment and oil and gas royalty trusts, which are still common today. In fact, the first three editions of this book spoke at length about real estate and royalty trusts.

More recently, businesses of all kinds converted into income trusts in order to attract the capital of investors. This is no longer the case given recent changes to the taxation of income trusts introduced on October 31, 2006. Let's look at how income trusts work, the recent changes, and more.

Income Trusts: How They Work

There are different forms that income trusts can take, but generally they work this way: Investors purchase units of a mutual fund trust—called an *income trust*. That income trust then uses about 25 percent of the funds raised to invest in the shares of an operating company (the underlying business). The other 75 percent of the cash raised by the fund is loaned to the operating company at a high rate of interest.

The key to making these income trusts work is the interest paid by the operating company to the income trust on the loan. You see, that interest expense to the company is designed to virtually eliminate any profits in the operating company. That is, the interest expense is high enough to offset most of the profits of the operating company. Further, some dividends may be paid by the operating company to the income trust on the shares owned by the trust.

The interest income or dividends received by the income trust is then distributed by the trust to investors. The distributions made to the investors of the fund may be classified as interest, dividends, or a return of capital, and will be taxed in the hands of the investor accordingly (more on taxation in a minute).

Income Trusts: Advantages

The most significant benefits of income trusts used to be the tax benefits, but changes announced on October 31, 2006, have reduced those benefits. You see, it used to be that income trusts provided a significant elimination or deferral of tax. How so? Go back to my explanation of the most common income trust structure. A corporation would earn business income, but this income would be fully or largely offset by interest deductions resulting from money borrowed by the corporation from the income trust. The result? Little or no tax to the corporation. Then, the income trust would distribute the income to the end investor and would claim a deduction for the amount distributed. The result? Little or no tax to the trust. Finally, the end investor may pay little or no tax to the extent the income trust units are held in a registered plan, or the distribution is a return of capital. The government decided that the tax benefits were a little too attractive, and made big changes, which I'll talk about in a minute.

Yet, there are still some benefits to income trusts. Consider these:

- A significant deferral or elimination of tax at the operating company level through the use of high-yield debt owing to the mutual fund trust.

- A deferral of tax on the income distributed by the trust to the unitholders of the trust to the extent that the units are held inside registered plans such as RRSPs, RRIFs, and RPPs.

- Where the units are not held in registered plans, a deferral of tax on the income distributed to unitholders of the trust is available to the extent that the distributions are characterized as a return of capital.

Aside from these tax advantages, the income trust structure appears to be a transparent mechanism for monitoring the company's performance (important at a time when confidence in management integrity is at an all-time low). How so? If cash distributions are made, the company has been successful. If cash distributions are not made, the company has not been successful. Financial statements can be restated if management lacked integrity, but this won't impact the cash distributions to investors. Once the cash has been distributed, it can't be taken back.

Income Trusts: Recent Changes

The changes announced on October 31, 2006, will impact Canadian resident trusts and partnerships whose units are listed on a stock exchange or other public market. The trusts and partnerships that will be impacted are those that hold one or more "non-portfolio properties" (basically, property used in carrying on a business in Canada, including Canadian resource properties, timber resource properties, and more). The government has chosen to call these "Specified Investment Flow-Through" (SIFT) entities. Your typical income trust is now known as a SIFT trust. As an aside, the changes will not impact trusts that hold passive real estate investments (your typical real estate investment trust).

The changes will impact these SIFT trusts by not permitting the trusts to deduct certain distributions that would normally be deductible. Basically, any part of a distribution that can be attributed to a business carried on in Canada or to income from (or capital gains on) non-portfolio properties will not be deductible. The bottom line? The income trust will now pay some tax. That tax will be at the same rate that a corporation would face if it had earned the income. This tax should reduce the level of distributions that an income trust can make to an investor, and therefore should have an impact on income trust values.

But the changes will have other tax impacts. You see, any amount that is not deductible to the SIFT trust and that becomes payable by a SIFT trust to you, the investor, will be taxed in your hands as though it is a taxable dividend from a Canadian corporation. The bottom line is that the tax treatment will be no different to you than if you had invested in a corporation instead of an income trust. By the way, this "deemed dividend" will be an eligible dividend available for the reduced tax rate on certain dividends (see Tip 53).

I will also mention that returns of capital have never been deductible to an income trust, and are not taxable to investors. Returns of capital will remain untouched by these changes. This is not to say that the amount of cash paid out as a return of capital will remain the same, but the tax treatment will remain the same.

Income Trusts: Other Considerations

One drawback to income trusts is that they are often sold by advisors as, and misunderstood by investors to be, fixed income investments. Don't ever forget that income trusts can only make distributions if the underlying operating company is profitable. In this sense, these are equity investments, and should be thought of as equities.

Also, keep in mind that there is a difference between a return on investment and a cash yield. The cash yield you receive from an income trust can be quite high, even though the return on investment from the underlying business may be lower. The reason for this is that the income trust may make a return of capital to you as an investor, and that return of capital is included in your cash yield calculation. If you do receive your original capital back, this is not the same as receiving a return on your investment.

Finally, keep in mind that income trusts are designed to pay out virtually all profits of the underlying business. Therefore, there should not theoretically be significant growth in the value of income trust units over time. Any business that fails to retain its profits should have difficulty growing. The bottom line? Be wary of any income trusts that seem to appreciate in value significantly without any justifiable reason.

TO MAKE A LONG STORY SHORT:

- Income trusts have been a popular investment in Canada over the last few years. They are equity investments that have fixed-income qualities and may be appropriate for investors who require income.

- Income trusts can offer investors interest or dividend income, or a tax-efficient return of capital.

- Recent changes to the taxation of income trusts were introduced on October 31, 2006. The changes reduce the tax benefits, but there are still benefits worth considering, not the least of which is the transperancy into whether management is doing a good job.

Tim's Tip 57: **Look at flow-through shares for a tax deduction and diversification.**

My friend Paul has a good sense of humour, and an even better nine iron. On the way home from a round of golf last summer, he kept me in stitches in the car as he relayed one joke after another. I don't know how he remembers them all. At one point he proclaimed, "Tim, I need some gas."

Thinking he was trying to be funny, I responded, "Great, let's stop for some spicy Mexican food."

He looked at me, straight-faced, and said, "No, I'm talking about my investment portfolio. I have absolutely no exposure to hard assets, and I've heard there are some tax breaks available in the resource sector. Is it true?" He was serious.

"Well, yeah, flow-through shares can offer some tax breaks," I said.

I spent the next half-hour explaining to Paul the benefits and risks of flow-through shares. Let me give you the highlights.

Flow-through Share Basics

Flow-through shares can provide attractive investment returns in addition to the direct tax savings that so many Canadians like Paul are looking for. A flow-through share is a creative, but higher-risk, investment issued by Canadian resource companies looking to raise capital for exploration and development. These shares are designed to provide the investor with tax deductions that generally equal the value of the amount invested—or come close to it.

You see, these resource companies are able to renounce certain deductions and flow them through to the individual investor so that the investor can claim the deduction instead. I'm talking primarily about Canadian exploration expenses (CEE), which are 100-percent deductible by the investor, and Canadian development expenses (CDE), which are 30-percent deductible on a declining balance basis. The fact is, a resource company can renounce these expenditures up to one year before incurring the actual costs. That's right, a company issuing flow-through shares in 2008 is able to renounce its eligible expenditures in calendar 2008 without actually incurring those expenses until the year 2009.

Flow-through Tax Facts

As I said, flow-through shares provide a tax deduction to the investor that is typically equal to the amount invested in the shares. The deduction doesn't usually come all in one year, but you can expect about 90 percent of it in the first year, with the balance in the second and perhaps the third year. Under Canadian tax law, the adjusted cost base of your flow-through shares will be reduced by any deductions you're able to claim. This means that any sale of a flow-through share will give rise to a guaranteed taxable capital gain. But don't let this scare you off. In fact, there may be some tax planning opportunities here. If, for example, you have capital losses to use up, investing in flow-through shares that provide a capital gain down the road will guarantee a way to use some or all of those losses.

Take a look at some of these other tax uses for flow-through shares:

- Minimize the tax hit on RRSP and RRIF withdrawals. The tax deductions available from the flow-through shares can offset the taxable income created by the withdrawal.

- Reduce the clawback of Old Age Security (OAS) or other benefits. The deductions from flow-through shares can help to reduce your net income and minimize the clawback of these social benefits.

- Mitigate the tax impact of receiving a bonus. A taxable bonus from your employer can push your tax bill up significantly, and can even push you into a higher marginal tax bracket. The deduction from the flow-through shares can help to reduce this burden.

- Provide additional deductions once RRSPs have been maximized. Where you haven't got additional RRSP contribution room, flow-through shares can provide the same effect.

Changes in 2006 eliminated the capital gain on publicly traded securities that are donated to a registered charity. Flow-through shares present a special opportunity here. Suppose you purchase $10,000 of flow-through shares, receive your tax deductions, then donate those shares to charity for a value of $10,000 (assume the shares don't change in value). The result? You'll save $9,200 in tax ($4,600 from the deductions, plus $4,600 from the donation tax credit, at a 46-percent marginal tax rate), and you'll pay no tax on the capital gain on the shares (which generally have a zero adjusted cost base). The bottom line: Your $10,000 gift to charity could cost you just $800 ($10,000 less your tax savings of $9,200). Now that's *charitable arbitrage*!

- Reduce the tax impact of realized capital gains. Have you sold any of your assets at a profit this year? If so, the tax deduction from flow-through shares can provide some relief from the taxable capital gain.

Risks and Returns

But the question remains: What kind of return can you expect from a flow-through share? The table shows that you can achieve a 22.5-percent after-tax return on your investment if you sell your shares, one year after claiming the full deductions, for the same price you paid. If you sell the shares for a different price, this return will increase or decrease. You might be interested in knowing that flow-through shares also provide some downside protection. You see, even if your shares drop in value by 29 percent, you'll still break even, thanks to the tax savings you enjoy, assuming a marginal tax rate of 45 percent.

RETURN ON A FLOW-THROUGH SHARE	
Purchase price of shares[1]	$ (10,000)
Tax savings from deductions claimed[2]	$ 4,500
Proceeds received on sale of shares[3]	$ 10,000
Tax on capital gain on sale[4]	$ (2,250)
Dollar return on investment	$ 2,250
Percentage return on investment after taxes	22.5%

Notes:
1. Shares are purchased for $10,000.
2. Tax savings equal $10,000 × 45% marginal tax rate.
3. Shares are sold at the same price for which they were purchased.
4. Tax on capital gain: $10,000 × 50% inclusion rate × 45% tax rate.

There's no doubt that these shares are higher-risk investments and will fluctuate in value with changes in resource prices or interest rates. As resource prices fall, so will the value of your flow-through shares. And a rise in interest rates may cause the same effect as interest-bearing investments become more attractive relative to these shares. The bottom line? You wouldn't want to hold more than 5 to 10 percent of your portfolio in flow-throughs. Nevertheless, oil and gas securities can play an important role in a well-diversified portfolio, and flow-through shares offer tax breaks that little else can today. Your best bet may be to take advantage of the diversification and experienced management offered through a limited partnership or mutual fund that invests in flow-through shares.

Speak to a financial advisor to find out more, or to buy flow-through shares.

TO MAKE A LONG STORY SHORT:

- Flow-through shares are shares in resource companies that are undertaking exploration and development. These shares provide a tax deduction that is typically equal to the amount invested.

- Because of the tax deduction, there are many practical uses for flow-through shares in tax planning, including the ability to help charities at a low cost to you.

- These are higher-risk investments that should not form more than 5 to 10 percent of your portfolio.

Tim's Tip 58: Utilize an equity monetization strategy to diversify without triggering tax.

Recently, *The Wall Street Journal* profiled Gillette Co.'s research lab and reported that the company is working on a new deodorant that blocks odour receptors in the noses of people around you. Evidently, you can't stink if no one can smell you. According to lab director Dr. Ahmet Baydar, Gillette carries out its testing using a synthetic version of underarm odour called the "malodor compound," which can leave an entire office reeking for days. "Just three or four molecules is all it takes," Baydar says. Testing also involves placing five judges in a "hot room" to sniff the armpits of test subjects. Armpits are rated on a scale of 1 to 10, with 10 meaning "your head snaps back," according to one employee.

Dealing with body odour can be a real dilemma. But it's nothing technology can't fix. And if you're an investor, certain tax problems can be fixed with technology too. Investment technology, that is. In fact, there's plenty you can accomplish with an equity monetization strategy.

The Strategy

Picture this. You're the proud owner of a stock that has appreciated in value and you've got too much tied up in this one security. That's right, you've got too many eggs in one basket. The problem? If you sell all or a portion of your holdings in the stock in order to diversify, you're going to trigger a tax liability large enough to wipe out the national debt, give or take. Not to worry. An equity monetization strategy can help.

Under this strategy, you can make use of a customized over-the-counter derivative contract—a forward sale contract—that will allow you to: (1) lock in any gains on paper that you have enjoyed, (2) defer tax on a sale of the stock by avoiding an actual disposition, (3) diversify your holdings through use of a loan, (4) create an interest deduction, and (5) avoid any margin calls that might otherwise apply when borrowing.

The forward contract will allow you to lock-in a selling price at a future pre-determined date. Basically, a financial institution (say, a bank) agrees to buy your stock from you at a set price on a future date. Typically, you'll be restricted to publicly traded securities. Once you've locked in a price, the bank will now lend you money based on the price you'll be collecting for your stock when the forward contract matures. Consider Frank's story.

Frank owns 25,000 shares of XYZ company, which trades at $40 today, for a total value of $1 million. His bank is willing to enter a forward contract with Frank that will give him the right to sell his XYZ shares to that bank for $45 per share five years from now. That is, Frank is guaranteed to receive $1.125 million in five years for his XYZ shares.

In Frank's case, the bank has agreed to a cash settlement in five years when the forward contract

Caution!

Beware of mutual funds that make regular distributions of capital gains to you. You can identify these funds since you'll receive a T3 or T5 slip at tax time, reporting those gains. A fund that distributes primarily capital gains is likely invested in equities. While capital gains are a tax-smart type of income, *you* should control the timing of those gains, not the fund manager. You may be better off choosing a fund with a buy-and-hold strategy where there are no or low distributions. You can then choose the timing of your capital gains tax hit by selling the units or shares of the fund at your own pace. Take back control of your annual tax liability!

matures. Suppose that XYZ stock trades at $40 in five years. In that case, the bank will pay Frank $5 per share, since it guaranteed him a price of $45 ($5 profit per share) for the stock, and Frank will keep the stock. If XYZ is trading at $48 in five years, Frank will have to pay the bank $3 per share because he was only guaranteed to receive a profit of $5 per share, and he'll keep his XYZ shares. Any profit over the forward price of $45 belongs to the bank. Finally, if XYZ trades at $45 per share in five years, no cash will change hands, and Frank will keep his stock.

Under the strategy, the bank will lend Frank $1 million. After all, Frank is guaranteed to receive $1.125 million in five years—so the bank, and Frank, know he'll be able to make good on the loan. Yes, the stock and forward contract will be pledged as collateral.

The result? Frank has now eliminated any future risk of price fluctuations on his XYZ stock, has avoided a taxable disposition of the stock, will manage to diversify his portfolio with the newly borrowed $1 million, and can deduct the annual interest on the borrowed money invested. Finally, there's no potential for margin calls here. The drawback? Frank gives up any upside potential on his shares over the price in the forward contract.

To ensure this strategy works from a tax perspective, it's best to have a cash, not a physical, settlement at maturity of the forward contract. Also, negotiate to retain all rights to dividends and votes attached to the shares during the term of the forward contract. Finally, visit a tax pro to discuss the idea in your situation.

TO MAKE A LONG STORY SHORT:

- An equity monetization strategy will allow you to diversify a portfolio on a tax efficient basis when you have too much invested in one security.

- The strategy allows you to: (1) lock in any gains on paper that you have enjoyed, (2) defer tax on a sale of the stock by avoiding an actual disposition, (3) diversify your holdings through use of a loan, (4) create an interest deduction, and (5) avoid any margin calls that might otherwise apply when borrowing.

- Visit a tax pro to talk over this idea before jumping in.

Tim's Tip 59: Consider an investment in a private company in certain situations.

There are two general types of private companies you might consider investing in: (1) a holding company designed primarily to earn investment income, and (2) an active business corporation. Let's take a look at these separately.

Holding Companies

As a general rule, there has been no use setting up a corporation to hold investments over the last few years because there has been no real opportunity to defer tax by earning income in the corporation as there was in the past. While this is still the case generally, there are other things that can be accomplished by investing inside a corporation. It's time to think outside the typical tax box.

There are four potential benefits to setting up an investment holding corporation. They are:

- to minimize clawback of Old Age Security benefits
- to minimize taxes on death
- to minimize probate fees
- to provide a source for earned income

Is this idea for everyone? Absolutely not. But if you have significant open money (investments outside your RRSP or RRIF)—generally $300,000 or more—then the idea could be for you. Consider Ruth.

*R*uth is 67 years young and makes withdrawals from her RRSP every year, but her main source of income is the interest she earns on $500,000 worth of investments. Because of this interest income, she suffers a clawback of her Old Age Security benefits.

Here's what she did: Ruth transferred the $500,000 of investments to a new holding company. This was set up as a loan by Ruth to the company. Now, the interest income earned on the investments is no longer reported by Ruth on her personal tax return—it's taxed in the corporation instead. As a result, her clawback problem is minimized. Next, the company is going to declare—but not pay—a dividend to Ruth each year that is equal to the after-tax earnings of *the company. Since Ruth needs the investment earnings to meet her costs of living, she withdraws the after-tax income earned by the company each year as a tax-free repayment of the loan the company owes her. Alternatively, she could take a director's fee or salary from the corporation each year, which would count as earned income—providing her with RRSP contribution room.*

Upon her death, two things may happen. First, the dividends still owing to her (that were declared but not paid) will be taxed, but may be reported on a separate tax return called a rights or things return—which will save her tax. Finally, Ruth may be able to pass the shares in her private company to her heirs without probate, by way of a separate will, since the family won't require probate on these shares.

Whoa. Did you catch all that? Let's look at the benefits of an investment holding company once again—in slow motion.

First, you may be able to minimize or eliminate a clawback on OAS benefits by removing income from your personal tax return. You see, when you put your assets into the corporation, the company will report the income and pay the tax from that point forward.

Second, you can minimize taxes upon death. By having the company declare but not pay dividends each year equal to the after-tax earnings of the company, you create an asset for yourself—a dividend receivable. Upon your death, this asset can be reported on a separate tax return called a *rights or things* return. This separate return entitles you to the basic personal credit all over again ($9,600 for 2008) and a lower marginal tax rate on the first $37,885 of income.

By the way, if you need cash flow during your lifetime, you can withdraw cash from the company as a repayment of the loan you made when you transferred your investments to the company. Once this loan has been repaid, the company could make good on the dividends it owes to you.

If you're going to set up an investment holding corporation, keep the following in mind:

- you won't be able to transfer your RRSP or RRIF assets to the company;
- the company will pay taxes at about 50 percent on its investment income, so you're not likely to save any income tax on an annual basis, but the other benefits may still make the idea worthwhile;
- there will be costs to set up the corporation and annual accounting fees for filing tax returns and financial statements.

The moral: Don't try this idea at home. Visit a tax pro!

Caution!

Third, probate fees may be minimized. Here's how: Since family members are shareholders and directors of the company, and heirs of any shares, it may be possible to pass these shares to your heirs through a separate and non-probatable will. After all, who in your family will require probate in this case? Probably no one. But these shares must pass to your heirs outside of your original will, which may have to go through probate. Speak to your lawyer about this idea. It's based on an Ontario court decision in *Granovsky v. The Queen* (1998).

Finally, the corporation can be a source of earned income for you. Earned income is most commonly paid in the form of director's fees or salary and will provide you with RRSP contribution room that will benefit you while you're under age 71—and sometimes beyond (see Chapter 6, Tip 74).

Active Businesses

It's time to take a look at the tax benefits of investing in the shares of a small private company that carries on an active business. Sometimes this type of company is referred to as a Canadian-controlled private corporation (CCPC). A CCPC is simply a corporation that is not controlled by a public corporation or by non-residents of Canada, and is not listed on a prescribed Canadian stock exchange or certain foreign stock exchanges. Typically, these are small to medium- sized companies and normally include most Canadian businesses—maybe even the one next door, or your own business. There can be a number of tax benefits to owning shares in this type of company. Read on.

Enhanced Capital Gains Exemption

If you own shares in a small business, and those shares increase in value over time, there's a strong possibility that you'll be able to shelter up to $750,000 (based on 2007 federal budget changes; formerly $500,00) of that increase from tax—through the $750,000

> **Action Step**
>
> If you haven't yet used up your enhanced capital gains exemption, consider making use of it today. A study on business taxation was undertaken on behalf of our government, and a document known as the *Mintz Report* was released in the spring of 1998, recommending that the exemption be eliminated. Don't delay! Visit a tax pro to determine whether it's worth your while and whether you're able to claim the exemption.

enhanced capital gains exemption. To be eligible, your small company shares will have to be *qualified small business corporation* (QSBC) shares. Using the full $750,000 exemption could save you $168,750 in taxes if your marginal tax rate is 45 percent.

What in the world are QSBC shares? In general, these are shares that you (or a related person) must have owned for a two-year period. In addition, the company must be a CCPC. Finally, at the time the shares are sold, the company must be using 90 percent or more of its assets to carry on an active business primarily in Canada, and the same must hold true for 50 percent or more of its assets throughout the two-year period you've owned the stock. Sound complex? The truth is, the definition has been simplified here. Be sure to have a tax pro review the company's financial statements to determine whether it qualifies for the $750,000 exemption.

Capital Gain Rollover

Thanks to the 2000 federal budget, it may be possible to dispose of your shares in your small private company and to defer the tax on any gain by reinvesting the proceeds in the shares of another small business corporation. In this case, your adjusted cost base of the new shares is simply reduced by the gain that you defer so that, eventually, you'll be taxed on that gain. Certain conditions must be met to qualify for this capital gain rollover, including these: you must acquire newly issued common shares from the treasury of the new small business; you must be an individual (not a trust); and only dispositions after February 27, 2000, qualify. There used to be a cap of $2 million (by reference to your adjusted cost base) on the number of shares on which you could defer your gain, but this cap was eliminated in the 2003 federal budget for dispositions after February 18, 2003. To qualify, the new company you're investing in must have a carrying value for its assets of $50 million or less before and after your investment in the company. Other requirements must also be met. Talk to a tax pro for more details if you think you qualify.

Allowable Business Investment Losses

Okay, so you're still not convinced that shares in a small business are worth owning—despite the enhanced capital gains exemption and the capital gain rollover. Too risky, right? But consider this: Your investment in that small business could also offer greater downside protection than other investments if the investment goes sour. Again, the company has to be a CCPC, and 90 percent or more of its assets must be used in an active business that operates primarily in Canada.

If it becomes evident that you'll never recover your investment in the small business, you'll be entitled to claim an *allowable business investment loss* (ABIL). This ABIL equals one-half of the invested money you've lost and can be deducted on your tax return against *any* source of income. Normally, when you lose money on shares you own, you've incurred a capital loss that can only be used to offset capital gains. You should also be aware that, where you've lent money to a small business instead of buying shares, you may still be eligible for ABIL treatment.

TSX Venture Exchange Stocks

If you happen to own stocks that trade on the TSX Venture Exchange, you might be interested in knowing that presently Tier 3 stocks trading on that exchange are not considered to be traded on a "prescribed" stock exchange. The result? Those stocks are currently considered to be private company shares for tax purposes. This means that you may be able to shelter gains on those shares with the enhanced capital gains exemption or consider any losses to be ABILs. The company will have to meet certain tests to qualify as a Small Business Corporation for these tax benefits, but a call to the company to determine whether it meets the test could save you some tax.

Qualified Farm or Fishing Property

I talked about the enhanced capital gains exemption to shelter any gains on qualified small business corporation shares. This exemption is extended to shelter any capital gains on qualified farm or fishing property—which normally includes most family farms, farm quotas, and fishing quotas. There are some conditions that the farm or fishing property must meet to be eligible, so visit a tax pro to determine for sure whether you'll be eligible. By the way, the eligibility of qualified fishing property was new in 2006, and it applies to dispositions of such property after May 1, 2006.

TO MAKE A LONG STORY SHORT:

- A private company that you invest in can take two forms: (1) a holding company, or (2) an active business corporation.

- A holding company may be used to reduce clawbacks of OAS, minimize taxes on death, reduce probate fees, and provide a source for earned income.

- An investment in an active business that is a Canadian-controlled private corporation can offer tax benefits in the form of an enhanced capital gains exemption if the shares increase in value, a capital gain rollover if the shares are sold, and an allowable business investment loss if the investment turns sour.

- Companies trading on the TSX Venture Exchange (Tier 3) may qualify for this capital gains exemption or ABIL treatment.

- Gains on qualified farm or fishing property can also be sheltered using the enhanced capital gains exemption. Qualified fishing property became eligible in 2006 for dispositions after May 1, 2006.

Sheltering Income with Life Insurance

Tim's Tip 60: Consider an exempt life insurance policy for tax-sheltered growth.

There's no doubt about it: Life insurance can be confusing—and sometimes downright intimidating. But don't let this stop you from considering life insurance as an investment tool. Is this for everyone? Nope. But it may be worth discussing the strategy with a trusted financial advisor who can crunch the numbers for your specific situation to see if the idea makes sense.

As an investment tool, an exempt life insurance policy can provide a tax shelter offered by little else. You see, under an exempt policy, a portion of each premium that you pay will cover the cost of your insurance, and the balance will be deposited in a growing pool of investments. The policy is called *exempt* because the investment component of the policy grows exempt from tax. That's right, tax-sheltered growth can be yours—much like what you experience with your RRSP. The best part of this is that, upon your death, the face value of the policy, plus the accumulated investments, are paid out on a tax-free basis to your beneficiaries.

I know what you're probably thinking: "Tim, the problem is that I can't enjoy those investments during my lifetime. I have to die for anyone to benefit here." Not true. You'll be able to access those investments in a number of ways.

For example, you can simply make withdrawals of the accumulated investments during your lifetime, although there could be a tax bill to pay when you do this. Alternatively, you could borrow, using the investments in the policy as collateral. Upon your death, the life insurance proceeds would be used to pay off the debt. This last idea is called *leveraged life insurance*, and I like it in some cases, but the idea does come with some risks. Provided it's set up properly and conservatively, it can make sense for some.

Where will you find an exempt life insurance policy? Most whole life and universal policies are set up to be exempt, but not all policies are created equal. It's important to find out your investment options. Make sure you're able to invest in equities to maximize your investment growth over the long term. Speak to a financial advisor who is licensed to sell life insurance.

TO MAKE A LONG STORY SHORT:

- An exempt life insurance policy will allow the tax-sheltered growth of investments inside the policy.

- The face value of the policy plus the accumulated investments will be paid out tax-free to your beneficiaries upon your death.

- There are ways of accessing the investments in the policy during your lifetime, although there may be tax or interest costs involved in doing this.

Tim's Tip 61: **Learn how to use cascading life insurance to shelter investment growth from tax for years.**

Do yourself a favour. Speak to your insurance broker this week. Insurance brokers always have a good story or two about insurance claims. My broker recently shared with me the true story of Arlene Evans. You see, in December 1990, the Kansas Court of Appeals affirmed Arlene Evans' challenge to Provident Life and Accident Insurance Co.'s determination that her husband had committed suicide. Though he was found in his bathtub, clothed and charred, she said it was an accident, that he was a heavy smoker and had often burned himself. Her strongest argument was that he often struck matches after passing gas, to clear the air, and that the fire that killed him was started this way. Hey, accidents happen.

When you speak to your broker, ask about another insurance story: cascading life insurance. It may not be as interesting as the story about Arlene Evans, but it'll save you more tax.

The Rules

The cascading insurance strategy takes advantage of Subsection 148(8) of our tax law, which will allow you to transfer ownership of a life insurance policy to any of your children, free of tax, where a child of yours is the life that is insured under the policy. (A "child" includes any natural or adopted child, a grandchild, stepchild, or a son- or daughter-in-law.)

On the surface, the idea may seem crazy. I mean, who's going to buy insurance on the life of a child? Glad you asked. Canadians who would like to pass assets to the next generation completely free of tax and probate, and then to subsequent generations in the same manner—hence the cascading effect—should consider the strategy.

> **Action Step**
>
> Cascading life insurance can be a terrific tax shelter strategy, provided you arrange it properly. Make sure that you name a child as the contingent owner on the policy, and another or the same child as the life that is insured. These two details are critical to ensuring a tax-free transfer of the policy at the time of your death under Subsection 148(8) of our tax law. It's also important to ensuring that the policy will transfer for no consideration (that is, free) to your child.

The Strategy

The cascading insurance strategy takes advantage of the fact that it's possible to invest money inside a universal life insurance policy on a tax-sheltered basis (see Tip 60), and that the death benefit, along with the accumulated investments in the policy, are all paid out tax-free to the beneficiaries when the insured dies. The best way to understand cascading life insurance is to walk through an example. Consider Barbara.

Barbara is 70 years of age. She has $200,000 of non-registered money that she doesn't need to meet her costs of living. She wants to minimize her tax hit on the income from this money annually. In addition, she wants to shelter the money from tax and probate fees when she passes it to her daughter Allison, who is aged 35, and ultimately to her grandson Mark, Allison's son, who is a minor. Barbara purchased a universal life insurance policy and put the $200,000 into the policy over a five-year period. She named Allison as the contingent owner. The insurance is placed on Allison's life and Barbara's grandson Mark is the beneficiary. When Barbara dies, Allison will become the owner (since she was named the contingent owner) with the result that Allison will then own the accumulated investments inside the policy. The policy will pass to Allison free of tax and probate fees. What are Allison's options? She could make withdrawals from the accumulating investments in the policy (a taxable event), borrow money using the investments in the policy as collateral (providing her with tax-free cash flow), or she could reserve the whole policy for her son Mark (he'll receive the insurance proceeds free of tax and probate fees upon her death).

A cascading life insurance strategy allows you to accomplish a few things, including: transferring money to the next generation without giving up control during your lifetime; eliminating current taxes in your hands on the money invested in the policy; eliminating probate fees on the assets in the policy; and providing you with access to the funds in the policy if needed. Not a bad deal.

Bulls, Bears, and Baseball: Strategies for Investors

TO MAKE A LONG STORY SHORT:

- The cascading insurance strategy takes advantage of our tax law, which allows you to transfer ownership of a life insurance policy free of tax to any of your children when a child's life is insured under the policy.

- The strategy will allow you to transfer money to the next generation free of tax and probate fees, minimize annual tax on the investments placed inside the policy, and maintain control of and access to the funds in the policy during your lifetime.

- Your insurance broker may have some great stories to tell about insurance claims.

Tim's Tip 62: Establish a back-to-back prescribed annuity for tax-efficient cash flow.

Here's a clever idea for those of you who rely on interest-bearing investments for an income stream. It's called a back-to-back prescribed annuity, and it could really boost your income. Here's the deal: A back-to-back simply involves buying a prescribed annuity plus term-to-100 insurance. The best way to understand this tactic is through a couple of examples. Let's look at Howard's situation, then Lily's.

Howard is 70 years old and has $100,000 invested in GICs paying 5.5 percent interest, which provide him with $5,500 of income annually. Howard's marginal tax rate is 45 percent, since he has other income sources, too. The bottom line is that Howard will pay taxes of $2,475 annually on his GIC income, and will be left with $3,025 each year as disposable income. Howard would like to leave the $100,000 to his children, so he likes the GICs because he can use the interest generated without ever touching the $100,000 capital.

It's true that Howard's investment in GICs will successfully preserve his $100,000 capital, but the interest income is highly taxed, and so he's left with very little (just $3,025) each year. Lily's financial advisor had a better idea. Here's her story.

*L*ily is also 70 years of age and has $100,000 that used to be invested in GICs, providing the same $3,025 after taxes that Howard receives. Lily's advisor had another plan: to use a back-to-back prescribed annuity. Here's what Lily did: She bought a prescribed life annuity with the $100,000 she had sitting in GICs. The annuity will pay her $12,491 a year. Since only a portion of each annuity payment is taxable, the tax on the annuity will be just $2,077 each year. You see, each annuity payment is made up of interest income plus a return of capital, and the capital is returned tax-free. The interest portion attracts some tax—but much less than she was paying with the GICs. After taxes, Lily is left with $10,414 ($12,491 minus $2,077) which is much higher than the $3,025 she received annually with the GICs.

Did You Know?

A "prescribed" annuity is different from other annuities. Normally, payments in the early years of an annuity are mostly taxable interest income, with only a small portion being a tax-free return of capital. Under a prescribed annuity, the taxable interest portion remains constant from one payment to the next. This means that in the early years of a prescribed annuity, you'll actually report less taxable interest than you would have otherwise. What a great tax deferral!

The moral of the story is that a prescribed annuity can provide much more cash than GICs and similar investments, and a smaller tax bill to boot. The drawback? Each time Lily receives an annuity payment, she's getting back some of her original $100,000 capital, so that she won't be able to leave her children the $100,000 that she could have with the GICs. In fact, aside from buying an annuity with a guaranteed payment period, there's no way to leave any of that $100,000 to her kids since the insurance company will keep whatever's left of her capital on her death.

But there is a solution. With the extra cash she's re-ceiving, Lily can buy a term-to-100 life insurance policy that will pay her children $100,000 when she dies. The cost of the policy? About $3,281 each year. So follow the numbers here. Lily takes the $10,414 she has been receiving after taxes, pays her insurance premiums of $3,281, and is still left with $7,133 in her pocket each year. This $7,133 is a full $4,108 more than the $3,025 of after-tax income she used to receive on her GICs.

Now you'll understand why this strategy is called a back-to-back prescribed annuity. The idea involves buying both a life annuity and an insurance policy back-to-back.

There's one more twist on this strategy that you might want to consider. It may be a very good idea to take some of the additional cash generated from the back-to-back annuity and invest in good quality equity mutual funds to protect yourself against inflation and provide an emergency fund. You see, when you buy a life annuity, the interest rate is locked in at the start, and it's a very expensive option to arrange for indexed annuity payments that increase each year with inflation. By investing just a portion of your capital in a back-to-back prescribed annuity (enough to beat the cash flow from the GIC), buying term-to-100 insurance, and investing the rest in equity mutual funds, you will have significantly improved your financial health by reducing taxes, providing a hedge against inflation, and setting aside an emergency fund.

To set this idea in motion, just visit a financial advisor who is licensed to sell life insurance.

TO MAKE A LONG STORY SHORT:

- A back-to-back prescribed annuity involves buying a life annuity to provide increased cash flow and then buying a term-to-100 life insurance policy to replace the capital used to buy the annuity.

- Take this a step further by using some of the additional cash to invest in good quality equity mutual funds as a hedge against inflation and to provide an emergency fund.

Borrowing to Invest: Leveraging

Tim's Tip 63: Consider leverage to accelerate wealth creation and provide tax deductions.

What is this strategy called leveraging? Simply put, it's borrowing money to invest. And make no mistake, leveraging can offer some significant financial benefits. The catch? You've got to do this prudently. If you're not careful to follow the rules of prudent leveraging, you could be in for more harm than good. In this tip I want to look at the rewards, risks, and rules of prudently borrowing money to invest.

The Rewards of Leveraging

There are definite potential rewards to leveraging. Consider these five rewards:

- **Reward 1:** Leveraging is a forced investment plan. The money you borrow is invested up front, and you pay for this investment through required monthly loan payments.
- **Reward 2:** You can build wealth using another's resources. Where you've got cash flow, but little in the way of investments, you can use someone else's resources to jump-start the wealth accumulation process.
- **Reward 3:** Leveraging can boost your effective returns. While leveraging won't improve your *actual* returns, it can increase your *effective* returns (see Jack's story below).
- **Reward 4:** You can reach your financial goals faster. Leveraging gets more money working for you sooner than you might otherwise be able to achieve. The result? You may be able to reach your financial goals sooner.
- **Reward 5:** Leveraging can create a tax deduction for interest costs. Let's not forget about tax deductions. Interest costs are generally deductible for tax purposes when you've invested the borrowed money. I'll talk more about this in Tip 64.

Jack borrowed $50,000 to add to his own $50,000 available to invest, for a total portfolio of $100,000. He earned a 10-percent pre-tax return on the total portfolio last year, or $10,000—all in capital growth. Jack is paying interest of 8 percent on the loan, which cost him $4,000 ($50,000 multiplied by 8 percent) last year. After all taxes and interest have been paid, Jack managed to put $5,500 in his pocket last year. This represents an 11-percent after-tax rate of return for Jack ($5,500 as a percentage of his own $50,000 is 11 percent). That's right, his portfolio grew by 10 percent before tax (which is 7.5 percent

after tax given our assumptions), but Jack's effective rate of return was 11 per-
cent after tax! That is, if Jack had not borrowed any money, his after-tax
return would have been 7.5 percent. His leveraging strategy, however, created
an effective return of 11 percent after tax.

Jack's story is spelled out more clearly in the table below. You'll notice from the table that leveraging can magnify your returns so that your effective return is higher than you could achieve without borrowing money. In Jack's example, a 7.5 percent after-tax return was magnified to 11 percent after taxes.

The Risks of Leveraging

Now, before you hop on the leveraging bandwagon, you need to understand the downside potential too. Check out the table one more time. What would have happened if Jack's portfolio had lost 10 percent of its value last year, rather than gaining 10 percent? Jack's effective loss from a 10-percent decline in value would have been 19 percent! And this calculation assumes that Jack would be able to use the capital loss to offset capital gains on other investments. If he were unable to use the capital losses in this manner, his effective loss would have been 24 percent for the year! Yikes.

As you can see, leveraging is great when your portfolio is growing in value. But when your investments drop in value, the effective loss can sting. In fact, the risks of leveraging include the following:

- **Risk 1:** Your investments could drop in value. We just discussed this one.
- **Risk 2:** Interest rates could rise. As interest rates rise, the break-even rate of return you'll need in order to make leveraging profitable will also rise.
- **Risk 3:** Your cash flow could suffer. Cash flow is critical. If you run short on cash, you may be forced to sell investments at a bad time to meet loan payments.
- **Risk 4:** Margin calls could be made. Depending on the type of loan you assume, you may be required to come up with more cash, or liquidate investments, in the case of a margin call. A margin call can arise if your investments start dropping in value.

EFFECTIVE RETURNS FROM LEVERAGING

		No Leveraging: 10-Percent Gain	Leveraging: 10-Percent Gain	Leveraging: 10-Percent Loss
Personal money	(A)	$ 100,000	$ 50,000	$ 50,000
Borrowed money[1]	(B)		$ 50,000	$ 50,000
Total invested		$100,000	$100,000	$100,000
Return on investment		$ 10,000	$ 10,000	$(10,000)
Less: Interest costs[2]		$ —	$ (4,000)	$ (4,000)
Add: Tax savings from interest deduction[3]		$ —	$ 2,000	$ 2,000
Less: Tax on capital gain[4]		$ (2,500)	$ (2,500)	$ 2,500
After-tax returns ($)	(C)	$ 7,500	$ 5,500	$ (9,500)
Effective after-tax return (%)[5]		7.50%	11.00%	−19.00%

Notes:

1. Assume a 1:1 loan.
2. Assume interest rate on loan of 8%.
3. Assume interest costs are deductible; marginal tax rate is 50%.
   Tax savings from interest deduction = 50% of interest paid.
4. Tax on capital gain = $10,000 × 50% inclusion rate × 50% MTR = $2,500; assume capital losses can be applied against other gains in the year.
5. Effective after-tax returns = After-tax returns (Line C) divided by Personal money (Line A), multiplied by 100.

- **Risk 5:** Tax deductions could be disallowed. A deduction for interest costs is generally available when borrowing to invest—but it's not guaranteed. If interest costs are not deductible, the break-even rate of return in order for leveraging to work will increase. I'll talk more about interest deductibility in Tip 64.
- **Risk 6:** You might just get greedy. Getting greedy could cause you to borrow more than you should. You then run the risk of not being able to meet loan payments if interest rates rise or your cash flow suffers.

- **Risk 7:** You could lose sleep at night. Leveraging could keep you up at night if you're not conservative in how much you borrow.

The Rules of Prudent Leveraging

Don't let the risks I've just mentioned scare you too much. As long as you follow the rules of prudent leveraging, you'll largely be able to manage those risks. Here are the eight rules you should follow:

- **Rule 1:** Understand the risks and rewards of leveraging. I've talked briefly about these risks and rewards above.
- Rule 2: Borrow only a reasonable amount of money. As a general rule, don't borrow more than 30 percent of your net worth.
- **Rule 3:** Make sure you've got sufficient and stable cash flow. Stay conservative. If you can afford loan payments of, say, $300 monthly, then take out a loan that will cost you $100 monthly—about 30 percent of what you can afford. This leaves room for increases to interest rates or other changes in your circumstances. Leveraging is only for those with a stable source of cash flow.
- **Rule 4:** Leverage for the long term only. Over the long term—10 years or more—there is a greater probability that your investments will have increased in value—which is critical when leveraging. Over the short term, your investments could be up or down—who knows?
- **Rule 5:** Make sure you're diversified. It's critical that your portfolio grow in value over time when leveraging. Minimizing volatility is done best by prudent diversification.

> **Action Step**
>
> The concept of leveraging, or borrowing to invest, should be seriously considered if you have sufficient cash flow to easily afford the monthly loan payments and are willing to take the necessary steps to mitigate the risks—including investing for the long term only. Why borrow to invest? The wealthiest people in the world have, at one time or another, borrowed money to create their wealth. If you implement this strategy prudently, you will be able to accelerate your own wealth creation. Remember: There are risks to the strategy, but they can be managed.

- **Rule 6:** Keep your interest costs deductible. Deductible interest costs will reduce your break-even rate of return required to benefit from leveraging.
- **Rule 7:** Choose the most appropriate type of loan. I like loans that have no potential for margin calls (a home equity loan, for example). An interest-only loan requires payments of interest only each month, which will enable you to borrow more money for a given monthly payment. If your cash flow is stable and sufficient, I prefer this type of loan. Granted, a blended payment of principal and interest is more conservative since the loan balance drops over time.
- **Rule 8:** Work with a trusted financial advisor. This is key. You see, a good advisor will ensure that your emotions don't drive bad investment decisions. Leveraging can be an emotional experience if your investments drop in value. Your advisor is there to help you stick to a proper game plan.

TO MAKE A LONG STORY SHORT:

- Leveraging is the idea of borrowing money to invest, and should be done prudently.

- Leveraging can significantly increase your effective rate of return. It can also magnify your losses.

- Be sure to understand the rewards, risks, and rules of prudent leveraging before trying the strategy.

- Find more information on leveraging in the booklet *Don't Just Invest, Upvest*, written by me and published by AIC Limited. Your financial advisor can get you a copy.

Tim's Tip 64: **Deduct as much of your interest cost as possible.**

Generally, the tax collector will allow you a deduction for your interest costs when you've borrowed for business purposes or to make investments. But a deduction is not guaranteed.

The Rules

Our tax law says that you're entitled to claim a deduction for your interest costs if you've used the borrowed money to earn income from a business, or income from property. Income from property includes interest, dividends, rents, and royalties—but not capital gains. This is not to say that you'll have to avoid earning capital gains when investing borrowed money. It simply means that you must have a reasonable expectation of earning interest, dividends, rents, or royalties, perhaps in addition to capital gains.

The Proposed Changes

On October 31, 2003, both the Department of Finance and the CRA made announcements on the issue of interest deductibility. Like most tax professionals, I was quite upset about the proposed changes. You see, these two departments of the federal government released differing views on interest deductibility. Talk about confusing. Let me briefly tell you what each department said:

Canada Revenue Agency: The CRA released Interpretation Bulletin IT-533 on October 31, 2003. That bulletin announced that the CRA will permit full interest deductions provided you have a reasonable expectation of earning *some income* from property. It's not necessary that the income you expect to earn be higher than the interest costs you're paying to the bank on the loan. The test is really a "reasonable expectation of income" test. This position is consistent with the Supreme Court of Canada decision in the case *Ludco Enterprises Inc. v. The Queen* (2001).

Department of Finance: On October 31, 2003, Finance announced proposed changes to our tax law which differ from CRA's assessment policy as outlined in IT-533. Finance announced that, in order to deduct full interest costs, you must have a reasonable expectation of *profit.* What this means is that you must reasonably expect to earn more interest, dividends, rents, or royalties from your investment than the interest you are paying to the bank on the loan, over the time you expect to own the investment (called the "profitability time period").

It's simply not realistic to expect the income from an investment in, say, common shares, to exceed the interest costs on the loan (investors will often invest for capital

Did You Know?

The Supreme Court of Canada in 2001 heard the case of *The Queen v. Singleton*, which confirms your interest deductibility where you've completed a debt swap. A debt swap is a strategy where you liquidate an existing investment, pay off some non-deductible debt (a mortgage, for example) with the proceeds, and then borrow to replace those investments. This strategy allows you to convert non-deductible interest into deductible interest since the newly borrowed money is used for investment. In recent years there was some doubt as to whether or not this strategy would work. On September 28, 2001, the Supreme Court confirmed its validity!

growth, not income). For example, the average dividend yield on common shares is about 2 percent, while a loan at your bank is going to cost you more than 2 percent without a doubt. The difference, then, would not be deductible under Finance's proposals. What an impact this tax policy would have on capital markets in Canada!

In short, our government was saying on October 31, 2003 that "we are going to change the tax law to at least partially deny interest deductions in most situations (Department of Finance announcement), but don't worry, we won't enforce the new tax law (CRA announcement)." Gee, thanks for the certainty.

Now, don't panic. I fully expect that, when the dust settles, investors will be entitled to deduct interest costs when they have a reasonable expectation of earning some interest, dividends, rents, or royalties. The question remains: Will this be the result because the CRA has said it will administer the law this way in IT-533, or because our tax law is worded to allow this treatment? I'll feel much better if our tax law explicitly allows this treatment.

Where are we today with these proposed changes? Although the 2008 budget did not announce any changes to these proposals, the Department of Finance did say in the 2005 budget that they have "sought to respond by developing a more modest legislation initiative that will respond to these concerns while still achieving the Government's objectives." Finance also said that they will release alternative proposals "at an early opportunity." Check with a local tax professional on the status of interest deductibility before jumping into any leveraged investing program.

By the way, the rules around interest deductibility changed significantly in Quebec in 2004. Quebec will only allow an interest deduction to the extent interest, dividends, or taxable capital gains are reported in a year.

Keep It Deductible

Even if it turns out that you can fully deduct your interest costs, you could lose your interest deduction in future years. You see, the tax collector is going to trace your borrowed money to its current use to determine whether the interest remains deductible year after year. Let's say, for argument's sake, that you borrow $100,000 to invest in units of a mutual fund, and your units grow to a total of $150,000. At that time, you sell $50,000 of those units. If your loan remains outstanding after this sale, what portion of your interest will remain deductible? The tax collector will look to where your sale proceeds are today. If you were to reinvest those proceeds of $50,000, you'd be entitled to continue deducting the full amount of the interest on your loan. If, however, you took that $50,000 and used it for personal purposes—to take a vacation, renovate your home, pay down debt, or even pay down interest on your debt—you'd lose the ability to deduct one-third ($50,000 is one-third of $150,000) of your remaining interest costs.

Consider these ideas to keep your interest deductible:

! **Skim the interest, dividends, or other income from property** (but not capital gains) from your leveraged investments before these amounts are reinvested, and spend this income in any way you'd like. This won't jeopardize your interest deduction because you're not dipping into your principal, or invested capital. However, once this income is reinvested in additional units or shares, it forms part of your capital, and you may run into an interest deductibility problem when you make withdrawals later.

! **Pay down your investment loans** with income from your investments, or by using proceeds from the sale of investments in the leveraged investment account. Normally, when you withdraw capital from your leveraged investment account and use the proceeds for any purpose other than investing, you'll lose a portion of your interest deductibility, as I just discussed in the example above. There's an exception, however, if you take capital from the account and use the proceeds to pay down the very same loan used to make that investment. In this case, the CRA has said (in technical interpretation 2001-0081025, dated February 12, 2002) that they will not reduce the percentage of interest costs that remain deductible. Any remaining interest costs on the debt should remain fully deductible. Intuitively this makes some sense, since the investment loan in this case will itself be reduced, thereby reducing the interest that will be deducted by the investor going forward.

Action Step

If you borrowed to make an investment that subsequently turned sour, and then sold this investment at a loss, be sure to continue deducting a portion of your interest costs. You see, Section 20.1 of the *Income Tax Act* says that you'll be able to continue deducting the interest on your *loss portion* of the investment. This applies to dispositions after 1993 (except for sales of real estate or depreciable assets). But the rules are complex enough to leave your head spinning, so visit a tax pro for help.

TO MAKE A LONG STORY SHORT:

- Interest is normally deductible when the borrowed money is used for business or investment purposes.

- Proposed changes to the tax law will require that you have a reasonable expectation of profit in order to deduct full interest costs. These proposed changes may not be enacted as currently written. Check with a tax pro for an update.

- The tax collector will look to your current use of borrowed money to determine whether your interest costs will remain deductible. Keep your borrowed money invested to preserve interest deductions.

Getting into the Game

From mutual funds to flow-through shares, investing properly can make you a clear winner in the tax game. Turn now to the Tax Planning Tip Sheet at the front of the book and review the strategies you've read about in Chapter 5. Ask yourself, "Can this tip apply to me?" When you've finished this book, take your Tip Sheet to a tax professional if you'd like more information on each strategy or help in implementing the ideas.

EARNING THE GOLD GLOVE: STRATEGIES FOR RETIREMENT

*"If you don't know
where you're going,
you might not get there."*
~ *Yogi Berra*

6

In major league baseball, the Gold Glove is a coveted symbol of
achievement. It's awarded to the best fielders in the game—those
who rarely make mistakes when the ball comes their way. To earn it, you've
got to keep your head up and your errors down. Most important, you've got to
know the turf.

You know, retirement planning is a lot like that. If you want to make the most of
your golden years, you've got to be alert, keep your mistakes to a minimum, and

understand the world of retirement planning. It's going to take some perseverance and good coaching. Tell you what: You provide the perseverance and I'll provide the coaching. Sound good? Great.

Understanding RRSP Basics

A Registered Retirement Savings Plan (RRSP) is a plan registered with the Canada Revenue Agency (CRA) that is designed to encourage and help you save for your retirement. While placing some of your retirement savings outside an RRSP can make sense in some situations (which I'll talk about in Tip 66), the general rule is that an RRSP should form an important part of your retirement savings.

Tim's Tip 65: Contribute to an RRSP for tax deferral and tax-free growth.

Your RRSP offers two attractive benefits that can't be ignored: a tax deferral and tax-free growth of your investments.

A Tax Deferral

Your RRSP contributions offer a deferral of tax because you'll be permitted to push a portion of your taxable income to a future year. No kidding. When you contribute to your RRSP within your contribution limit, the amount of that contribution may be deducted on your tax return, reducing your taxable income. You won't face tax on those funds until they're withdrawn from your RRSP—usually in a much later year.

For example, suppose you contribute $5,000 to your RRSP at age 35. So long as this is within your contribution limit, you'll be able to deduct the full amount from your total income. If your marginal tax rate is 45 percent, your tax saving will be $2,250 in the year you make the contribution. Now let's say you leave the $5,000 to grow in your RRSP until you reach age 65 and then withdraw $5,000 from your plan. In that year—a full 30 years later—you'll face a $2,250 tax bill. Here's what you could do now to pay that $2,250 tax bill 30 years down the road: You could take $521 today, invest it for 30 years at an after-tax return of 5 percent annually, and watch it grow to be worth $2,250 in 30 years. You could then pay your tax bill with that money. Because of the tax deferral resulting from your RRSP deduction, your tax bill would really cost just $521 in today's dollars, not $2,250. Effectively, you would have reduced your tax bill by pushing it to a future year. This is the value of tax deferral.

Tax-Free Growth

Your RRSP offers another significant benefit. I'm talking about tax-free growth inside the plan. Unlike many investments held outside your RRSP (your *open money*), the investments inside your RRSP will not be taxed as they grow each year, regardless of how much you earn inside the plan.

Don't underestimate the value of this tax-free growth! Just look at how much more you could have by investing inside your RRSP rather than outside. If you

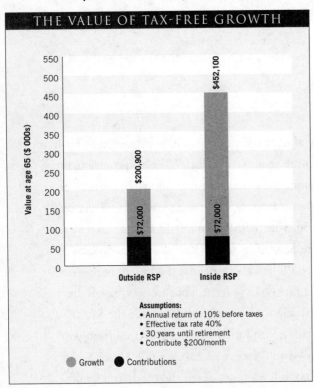

socked away $200 each month for 30 years and enjoyed annual growth on your money of 10 percent, you'd have $200,900 at the end of that period if you invested outside your RRSP, assuming an effective tax rate of 40 percent. But what if you made those same monthly contributions for the same length of time, earned that same 10 percent, but invested *inside* your RRSP? When all is said and done, your investments would be worth a whopping $452,100—more than double what you'd have outside your RRSP.

I should clarify something here. It may be possible to invest outside your RRSP in a manner that is very tax-efficient as well (more tax-efficient than my example above).

For example, investing in certain equity investments can be tax-smart (see Tip 50). In fact, it may be possible to nearly eliminate annual taxable income simply by buying and holding good quality equity investments.

The point is this: Investing outside your RRSP can work in addition to your RRSP when it comes to building a retirement nest egg—but only if it's done in a tax-smart manner. More on this in Tip 66.

Now, back to RRSPs. The earlier in life you start your RRSP contributions, the more you'll benefit from the tax-free growth. For example, suppose that you contributed $3,000 to your RRSP each year for 10 years, starting at age 30, and then left those funds to grow at 10 percent each year until you were 65. How much would you have at age 65? The graph shows a value of $518,030. Not bad on total contributions of just $30,000!

But what if you waited just five short years until age 35 before making any RRSP contributions, and then contributed $3,000 every year until age 65—a total of $90,000 in contributions? At age 65 you'd have just $493,480. That's right, you'd end up with *less* by waiting five years, even though you would have invested more of your money.

The moral of the story is simple: The earlier you start your RRSP savings, the better off you'll be in retirement.

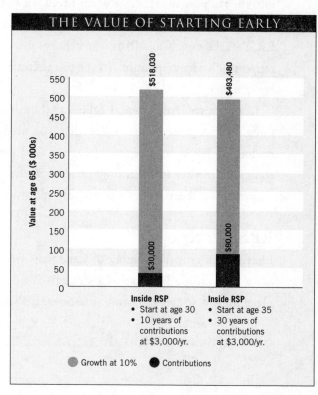

THE VALUE OF STARTING EARLY

Value at age 65 ($ 000s)

$518,030

$493,480

$30,000

$90,000

Inside RSP
• Start at age 30
• 10 years of contributions at $3,000/yr.

Inside RSP
• Start at age 35
• 30 years of contributions at $3,000/yr.

● Growth at 10%   ● Contributions

TO MAKE A LONG STORY SHORT:

- An RRSP offers two significant benefits: a deferral of tax and tax-free growth inside the plan.

- The earlier in life that you start, the greater the benefit to you in retirement.

- Having some retirement savings outside an RRSP can make sense in some situations, but only where it's done in a tax-smart manner. More on this in Tip 66.

Tim's Tip 66: Recognize that it's possible to have too much in your RRSP.

I shared with my wife, Carolyn, last week that, at the pace we're going, we'll end up with far too much in our RRSPs in retirement. I nearly pushed her over the edge into the realm of amazement when I told her this. She wasn't so surprised that we'll have enough in retirement, but shocked that I suggested we'd have *too much* in our RRSPs. Like most Canadians, she believes that an RRSP is the cornerstone of any retirement savings program. To suggest that we'll have too much in an RRSP seems crazy to her.

Don't get me wrong here. I believe that having enough in your RRSP is a good thing. Having more in your RRSP than you need to support yourself comfortably in retirement, however, doesn't make sense. And why not? Simple. Every dollar that comes out of your RRSP is fully taxable. With the capital gains inclusion rate at just 50 percent, you can create a pretty tax-smart portfolio outside your RRSP as well.

RRSP Excess

I have met a growing number of Canadians who have too much inside their RRSPs. Some are taking advantage of a strategy called the "RRSP freeze." I believe there's a place for this strategy in some situations. Let's consider Charlie's example.

Charlie is a gentleman who is 50 and plans to retire at 65, just 15 years from now. He expects to live to about age 90 and wants to plan for an income in retirement until that age—a 25-year retirement period. Charlie wants a retirement income of $50,000 after taxes annually (in today's dollars) beginning at age 65. By the way, that $50,000 annually will equal $77,898 after taxes in the year Charlie reaches age 65, assuming a 3-percent inflation rate. The bottom line is that Charlie will need $2,285,000 in his RRSP at age 65 to provide him with the income he needs in retirement (assuming a 7-percent annual return and 3-percent inflation annually). Here's the issue: Charlie already has $1,200,000 in his RRSP today. Do the math. That $1,200,000 will turn into about $3,300,000 by the time Charlie reaches age 65—even if he doesn't make another RRSP contribution (assuming a 7-percent annual return). Do you follow? Charlie will have about $3.3 million in his RRSP at age 65, but only needs about $2.3 million. He'll have nearly $1 million too much in his RRSP at age 65 even without further contributions.

Action Step

How much is enough in your RRSP? How do you know when you've got too much in your plan? First, you need to determine how much income you'd like each year in retirement, in today's dollars. Next, figure out how much money you need sitting in your RRSP on your retirement date to provide that income. You'll have to make assumptions about your rate of return on investments, inflation, tax rates, and perhaps how long you're going to live. Your best bet may be to visit a trusted financial advisor who can crunch the numbers for you.

The problem with having so much in an RRSP is that every dollar in the plan is fully taxable when withdrawn. Compare this to making withdrawals from an investment account outside of a registered plan where you'll face tax on any capital gains only. And just one-half of capital gains are taxable.

RRSP Freeze

What if there were a way for Charlie to remove some of the excess assets in his RRSP without any negative tax implications? Would it make sense? Arguably, it would—particularly when he could then invest those assets outside of his RRSP in a manner that would result in more in his hands after taxes later. Charlie has done that very thing. Here's how: Charlie borrowed $125,000 at 8-percent interest and invested the money in high quality, conservative equity investments. Charlie makes interest-only payments on the loan, and the $10,000 of interest cost annually is deductible on his tax return. Charlie then withdraws $10,000 from his RRSP annually to pay the interest costs. The interest deduction offsets the taxable RRSP withdrawal so that he is effectively not taxed on the RRSP withdrawal.

What has Charlie really accomplished here? He has managed to convert some of his registered money (in his RRSP) into non-registered money on a tax-free basis. Think about it. The $125,000 that Charlie borrowed is invested and growing. It more than replaces the $10,000 withdrawn from the RRSP each year that was used to pay the interest costs on the loan. In fact, Charlie will end up with more after-tax money in retirement through this strategy for two reasons: (1) By borrowing and investing $125,000, Charlie gets more money working for him sooner (compared to simply leaving the $10,000 annually in the RRSP and not borrowing any money), and (2) the withdrawals from the non-registered investments are taxed at much lower rates since capital gains are just 50-percent taxable, and *only the growth* on the $125,000 is taxed. In Charlie's case, his *after-tax* retirement nest egg (dollars he can actually spend!) will be greater by $98,000 assuming a 7-percent investment return both inside and outside the RRSP over that 15-year period until he reaches age 65, and a marginal tax rate of 46 percent.

Some people refer to this strategy as the *RRSP meltdown*. I prefer to call it an *RRSP freeze*. To melt down an RRSP (that is, to actually reduce the amount of money in the RRSP over time) you've got to borrow a heckuva lot of money (upwards of twice the value of your RRSP may be necessary). An RRSP freeze is easier to accomplish and this is what Charlie did. A freeze simply caps the amount in the RRSP by making withdrawals annually to limit the growth in the plan.

Now, I'd like to make a point to those who live in Quebec. The RRSP freeze strategy only works when you're able to deduct the interest costs on your investment loan so that it offsets the taxable RRSP withdrawal. In 2004, Quebec changed its rules so that the interest deduction will not be available to offset those withdrawals. The bottom line? The RRSP freeze strategy will not work as advertised, in Quebec.

Drawbacks

Okay, there have got to be some drawbacks to the RRSP freeze or meltdown, right? Right. Consider these.

- You've got to have too much in your RRSP already. Not everyone is in that situation. If you can't crunch the numbers to figure this out, visit a financial advisor who can help.

- Borrowing to invest has to make sense for you—but it's not for everyone. This is the most important issue when deciding whether or not to use the strategy. If you're not a good candidate to borrow money, the strategy is not for you (see Tip 63 for the criteria you should meet before borrowing money to invest).

- Your non-registered investments might be subject to tax annually that could reduce your growth outside the RRSP. You can mitigate this problem by keeping portfolio turnover very low (see Tip 50 for more on turnover).

- The capital gains inclusion rate could be increased in the future, making non-registered investments less tax-efficient—although I believe that the likelihood of this is slim unless capital gains tax rates in the U.S. increase. And this is just not likely to happen in the foreseeable future.

- You can't turn around and recontribute the money you've withdrawn from the RRSP; the contribution room is lost forever (this generally won't matter to you if you stand to benefit from the strategy).

- There may be a greater temptation to access the money outside your RRSP before you ought to because it's not as highly taxed as withdrawals from an RRSP. In this way, there may be a psychological advantage to RRSPs. Working with a financial advisor who can gently remind you that you're better off leaving your investments untouched until retirement can be a great solution here.

Since borrowing to invest is such a significant part of the RRSP freeze or meltdown, you should re-read Tip 63 before considering this strategy.

TO MAKE A LONG STORY SHORT:

- It's possible to have too much in an RRSP. You may need to visit a trusted financial advisor to determine whether this is the case for you.

- The RRSP freeze or meltdown involves borrowing money to invest and using the interest deduction to offset taxable RRSP withdrawals. The strategy can provide higher after-tax income in retirement. This strategy will no longer work in Quebec.

- There are some drawbacks to the strategy. Most notably, you've got to borrow money, and if this is not prudent for you, the strategy won't work.

Tim's Tip 67: Open a self-directed RRSP once your plan assets reach $20,000.

RRSPs can come in all shapes and sizes. The easiest way to understand the differences is to picture an RRSP as a "basket." When you buy an investment, you can choose to hold the investment inside an RRSP basket or outside the RRSP in your own hands (called your *open money*). Now, RRSP baskets can differ. Some will allow you to hold just one specific type of investment—like a Canada Savings Bond (CSB) or Guaranteed Investment Certificate (GIC)—while others will allow you to hold many and varied investments.

Here are two examples of single-purpose baskets. If you visit your local bank and buy a GIC in any amount, but buy it as an RRSP investment (that is, inside an RRSP basket), the GIC will come in its own RRSP basket. Don't even think about holding other investments in the basket because you won't be able to. Similarly, if you open an RRSP with your favourite mutual fund company, the RRSP basket you receive will hold any mutual funds you buy from that company, but can't generally hold, say, stocks or other investments at the same time.

That's where a self-directed RRSP comes in. A self-directed RRSP is simply an RRSP basket (or account) that can hold virtually any type of investment that qualifies to be held in an RRSP (see Tip 70 for a list). The annual administration fees on a self-directed RRSP are usually higher than with other plans (over $100 in most cases), and so I don't recommend that you move to a self-directed plan until your RRSP assets reach $20,000. But once you've hit this threshold, a self-directed RRSP makes a lot of sense, for three key reasons.

- *Simplicity*. If you've been living with more than one RRSP account, you'll understand the aggravation of receiving a barrage of paper from each institution each month. It can be confusing trying to track what investments you own and where they are. A self-directed RRSP lets you hold all those investments in one account. You'll get just one monthly statement rather than the pile you've been used to getting. By the way, this will make it much easier for your financial advisor (where you use an advisor) to make sure your total retirement portfolio is properly balanced and diversified.

- *Flexibility*. With a self-directed RRSP, your investment options are wide open and can include any investments that are eligible for RRSPs in general. Don't underestimate the value of this. As you age and your circumstances change, you may want to adjust the overall asset mix in your portfolio, and having all your retirement assets in one place will make this job much easier.

- *Diversification*. In order to maximize your investment returns, it's important to diversify globally. After all, Canada represents under 3 percent of markets worldwide. This means that 97 percent of all investment choices fall outside Canada. Allocating your assets to different regions of the world becomes easier when you have fewer investment accounts to monitor. When your investments are held in multiple accounts, there is more room for duplication of investments without recognizing that one of your accounts may have inappropriate diversification when seen in the context of your investment portfolio as a whole (all of your accounts together). Imagine using just one RRSP account—a self-directed

Action Step

If you were to open a self-directed RRSP of $10,000 and pay an annual fee of $100, the fee would represent 1 percent of your total assets in the plan. That is, your investment returns would be reduced by 1 percent just because of the fee. With $20,000 in the plan, a $100 fee represents just 0.5 percent of the assets—a more tolerable ratio. This is why a self-directed plan makes the most sense once you've reached $20,000 in assets. Of course, if you can find a self-directed plan that doesn't charge a fee, you may be smart to opt for that account right away.

account—rather than many. In this case, it will be easier to ensure that your asset allocation by asset class (equities, fixed income, and cash) and region (North America, Europe, Asia, Latin America) is appropriate.

TO MAKE A LONG STORY SHORT:

- A self-directed RRSP is a "basket" (an account) that can hold a wide variety of investments. It should be considered once RRSP assets reach $20,000.

- The benefits of a self-directed RRSP include simplicity, flexibility, and diversification.

Tim's Tip 68: Pay your RRSP fees from outside your plan up to age 71.

Talk about confusing. I need two hands and a foot to count the number of times the tax collector has changed opinions on how your RRSP and Registered Retirement Income Fund (RRIF) fees will be treated for tax purposes. You may recall that, back in 1996, the rules were changed to disallow any kind of deduction for RRSP or RRIF fees. This rule still holds today. Regardless of whether it's your annual administration fee (typically between $40 and $125), or investment management fees (often a percentage of your assets), the fees are not deductible.

If these fees happen to be paid from inside your RRSP or RRIF (that is, paid using assets inside your plan), these payments *will not* be considered taxable withdrawals by you, which is great news. Likewise, if you pay these fees from outside your plan, the payments *will not* be considered a contribution to the plan. This, too, is great news.

Here's the game plan: Pay these fees from outside your plan up to age 71. This will allow your plan assets to grow untouched, and will result in more assets in your plan at retirement. However, once you've reached age 71, start paying these annual fees from inside your plan. This makes sense because, at age 71, you've got to start making withdrawals on a regular basis, and each fee payment is like a tax-free withdrawal from the plan.

TO MAKE A LONG STORY SHORT:

- Administration and investment management fees for your RRSP or RRIF are not deductible for tax purposes.

- Pay these fees from outside your plan up to age 71 to preserve the growth of your plan assets. From age 71 onward, pay the fees from inside the plan as a way to make tax-free withdrawals from the plan.

Contributing to Your RRSP

Tim's Tip 69: Know your RRSP contribution limit each year, then avoid an accumulation of contribution room.

How much are you entitled to contribute to your RRSP each year? Well, that depends on your earned income in the previous year. You're entitled to contribute up to 18 percent of your earned income from the previous year, to a yearly maximum amount. If, for example, you had $116,667 of earned income in 2008, you'd be entitled to $21,000 ($116,667 multiplied by 18 percent) of RRSP contribution room in 2009. See page 194 for RRSP contribution limits by year.

What is *earned income*? Basically, it includes employment income, rental income (minus losses), self-employment income (minus losses), royalties if you're an author or inventor, and alimony or separation payments received (subtract these payments if you made them). But the following don't qualify: investment income, pension income, RRSP or RRIF income, Old Age Security (OAS) or Canada Pension Plan (CPP) income, retiring allowances or death benefits, scholarships or bursaries, or income from limited partnerships.

The most obvious place to find out how much you're entitled to contribute to an RRSP is your Notice of Assessment—that form you get in the mail each year after filing your tax return. Your assessment will detail the amount of your contribution room and is usually accurate. But if you disagree with yours, don't hesitate to get a tax pro involved to check it, since you don't want to rob yourself of contribution room.

By the way, if you don't make the maximum contribution to your RRSP in a given year, your contribution room will be carried forward for use in any future year. But don't get in the habit of allowing that room to accumulate for too long. After all, if you had trouble making a $5,000 contribution this year, it's going to be that much harder to make an even larger contribution next year! Besides, you could be enjoying a deferral of tax and that tax-free growth I spoke about earlier.

There's an exception to this general rule. Where you already have enough in an RRSP and you've opted for the RRSP freeze strategy I spoke about in Tip 66, then you may be willing to allow your RRSP room to accumulate.

MAXIMUM RRSP CONTRIBUTIONS	
Year	18% of earned income from the prior year, to a maximum of:
2008	$20,000
2009	$21,000
2010	$22,000
2011	Indexed

TO MAKE A LONG STORY SHORT:

- You're entitled to contribute 18 percent of your earned income from the prior year to an RRSP, to a yearly maximum.

- Even though unused contribution room can be carried forward, don't let this happen, since you'll be giving up a valuable tax deferral and tax-free growth of your money.

- The exception to this rule is where you've opted for the RRSP freeze strategy I spoke about in Tip 66.

Tim's Tip 70: **Make a contribution** *in kind* **to your RRSP if you're low on cash.**

Who says that your RRSP contributions have to be in the form of cash? It's just not true. In fact, you'll be able to contribute a whole host of qualifying assets to your RRSP, including:

- cash
- Guaranteed Investment Certificates
- most mutual funds
- government-guaranteed debt obligations
- corporate bonds or other debt obligations
- shares and most other securities listed on a pre-scribed stock exchange (Canadian and foreign)
- shares of certain private corporations
- mortgages secured by real property in Canada
- certain annuities
- certain life insurance policies
- certain rights and warrants
- investment-grade gold and silver bullion coins and bars, and certificates of such investments (after February 22, 2005)
- other less common investments

Make sure that you don't contribute a non-qualifying asset to your RRSP—the effect could be ugly. In fact, you could face tax on some of the earnings inside your RRSP, tax on the value of those non-qualifying assets, or deregistration of your plan. Do you know what deregistration means? It means you could pay tax on the full amount of your RRSP assets in a single year! While this is not likely to happen, it's a possibility.

Caution!

If you're going to contribute *in kind* rather than in cash, there are two tax consequences:

First, you'll be entitled to a deduction just as you would with any RRSP contribution in cash. The value of the contribution simply equals the fair market value of the assets being contributed to your plan.

Second, you'll be deemed to have sold those assets when you contribute them to the plan. So, where those assets have gone up in value, you might face a taxable capital gain. Of course, the RRSP deduction will always offset any taxable gain provided you've got enough contribution room. On the flip side, if the asset you're contributing has gone down in value, the tax collector won't let you claim a capital loss on this transfer to your RRSP. Sorry. In this case, sell your investment at a loss outside your RRSP, then contribute the cash to your plan. This way, you can utilize the loss.

Make sure you've got enough RRSP contribution room available before making any contribution, including one in-kind. By the way, you'll generally have to set up a self-directed RRSP in order to make a contribution in kind.

TO MAKE A LONG STORY SHORT:

- If you haven't got the cash, contribute in kind to your RRSP.

- You'll be deemed to have sold any investment that is contributed in kind, which could mean a taxable capital gain, but you'll also be entitled to a deduction for your contribution in kind, within your contribution limits.

- Set up a self-directed RRSP to make a contribution in kind.

Tim's Tip 71: Consider borrowing to make RRSP contributions if you haven't got the cash.

Truthfully, in most situations you'll be better off borrowing to make your RRSP contribution than not contributing at all or making that contribution two or three years down the road. You won't be entitled to claim a deduction for the interest on your RRSP loan, but don't worry—it still works to your benefit to borrow because that money is working for you by growing tax-free. If you have investments outside your RRSP, you may be better off to contribute those to your RRSP and then borrow to replace the non-registered investments. That way, the interest will be deductible. This is a contribution in-kind, as I discussed in Tip 70.

TO MAKE A LONG STORY SHORT:

- Borrowing to contribute to your RRSP makes sense when your other choices are to make no contribution or to delay the contribution for even two or three years.

- The interest on your RRSP loan will not be deductible.

Tim's Tip 72: **Have your employer contribute directly to your RRSP.**

What if I told you that there's a way to nearly double your ability to contribute to your RRSP? Arranging for your employer to send a portion of your pay directly to your RRSP could accomplish this. These are called *employer-direct contributions*. All that's necessary is enough contribution room and some cooperation from the boss.

Let me buck a trend here. It's been commonly held that you should borrow for your RRSP and pay back that loan over a period of no more than one year. I don't buy this advice. Even a 5- or 10-year loan can leave you better off in the long run when it lets you use up more of your contribution room. Besides, many Canadians have accumulated so much room that it would be impossible to borrow and pay back the loan over one year. The general rule? Keep your loan interest rate 2 percent below your rate of return inside your RRSP, and your loan term 10 years or less.

*R*ob's employer was due to pay him a bonus of $10,000 at the end of last year. If the bonus had been paid directly to Rob, his employer would have been required to deduct withholding tax for remittance to CRA. This would have left Rob with about $5,400, which he planned to contribute to his RRSP. But Rob managed to contribute much more. Rather than taking payment of the $10,000 bonus in his own hands, Rob arranged for his employer to send the amount directly to his RRSP carrier. As a result, his employer was not required to deduct the withholding tax; only Canada Pension Plan (CPP) and

Employment Insurance (EI) contributions were required. Because almost all of the $10,000 was contributed to his RRSP, Rob effectively doubled his RRSP contribution without even borrowing to make it happen!

Maybe your situation is a little different from Rob's. He received a bonus. But if you're not slated to receive a bonus of any kind, the employer-direct idea still works well where your employer deducts a set amount from each pay, or simply sends one or two paycheques each year to your RRSP. I like the idea better than most group RRSPs because it will give you more flexibility.

If you do receive a bonus from your employer, there's one other trick you can play. It worked well for Rob. He arranged for his employer to send his 2008 bonus directly to his RRSP carrier, but also arranged for this to happen in the first 60 days of 2009. The result? Rob gets a deduction on his 2008 tax return for the RRSP contribution, but he won't be taxed on the bonus until 2009, since it wasn't paid out until 2009. In short, he has managed to defer tax on the bonus for a year *and* claim a deduction for the amount of that income a year earlier.

TO MAKE A LONG STORY SHORT:

- Employer-direct RRSP contributions can significantly increase the amount you're able to contribute to your RRSP without borrowing.

- Your employer will simply send a portion of your pay directly to your RRSP carrier and will avoid income tax withholdings (although CPP and EI will still be payable).

Tim's Tip 73: **Avoid over-contributing to your RRSP and invest any excess outside the plan.**

For the most part, you can expect to face some penalties if you contribute too much to your RRSP. In fact, this penalty equals 1 percent of the excess amount per month. You should know, however, that the tax collector will allow you a $2,000 cushion. That is, the first $2,000 of over-contributions to your RRSP will not attract a penalty. You won't be entitled to claim a deduction for this over-contribution, although the money will still grow tax-free while it's in the plan.

Some argue that the over-contribution doesn't make sense because you're going to be taxed on that $2,000 when you eventually withdraw it from your RRSP, without having ever received a deduction when you put it into the plan. In other words, you'll face double tax here. While this is true, this is not the real reason I believe that you should skip the $2,000 over-contribution. You see, if you've got 10 years or more before you start making withdrawals from your RRSP, then the growth on that money inside the plan will outweigh any double-tax problem you might face.

The reason you should skip the $2,000 over-contribution is that you can invest that same $2,000 in a non-registered account and accomplish the following: You'll have no restrictions on the types of investments that you can hold when you invest this money outside an RRSP, and withdrawals from a non-registered account are much more tax-efficient than withdrawals from an RRSP, since only the growth will be taxed, and at capital gains tax rates to boot (just 50 percent of capital gains are taxable).

If you've read previous editions of this book (2000 and prior years), you'll note that this advice is a departure from what I have said in the past. Since the federal mini-budget of October 18, 2000 reduced the tax rate on capital gains, however, I believe that this new advice makes more sense provided that: (1) you already have a non-registered investment account or are committed to building some assets outside your RRSP, and (2) you're going to invest this money outside your RRSP in tax-smart investments (generating capital gains or a return of capital and keeping turnover low—see Tip 50).

TO MAKE A LONG STORY SHORT:

• Excess contributions to an RRSP attract a monthly penalty of 1 percent of the excess amount.

• You're entitled to a $2,000 over-contribution but you should skip the opportunity to make this contribution. Instead, invest that $2,000 in tax-smart investments in a non-registered account.

Tim's Tip 74: Over-contribute to your RRSP just before winding up the plan at age 71, if you have earned income.

While an RRSP is going to help you save for retirement, you won't be able to keep your plan forever. Because of changes introduced in the 2007 federal budget, you're permitted to keep your RRSP around until the end of the year in which you reach age 71. Wouldn't it be nice if you could somehow contribute to an RRSP even beyond age 71? Well, you can. One option is a spousal RRSP, which I'll talk about in Tip 79. Your other option is known as the *senior's over-contribution*.

*P**avel turned 71 in July 2009, and so he's going to have to wind up his RRSP by the end of 2009. But he has earned income for RRSP purposes in 2009 of $122,223. The result? Pavel is entitled to $22,000 (18 percent of $122,223) of RRSP contribution room in the year 2010. The problem, however, is that Pavel won't be able to contribute to an RRSP in the year 2010 since his RRSP must be wound up by the end of 2009. Does he lose the ability to make an RRSP contribution for the year 2010? No!*

Pavel is going to take advantage of his 2010 contribution room by making his 2010 RRSP contribution in December 2009, before he winds up his RRSP forever. Provided that Pavel has already maximized his RRSP contributions for 2009, making an additional contribution of $22,000 in December will result in an over-contribution to his RRSP, and will mean a penalty of $200 for that month. Effective January 1, 2010, Pavel's over-contribution problem disappears, because he's entitled to new contribution room of $22,000 on that date (due *to his 2009 earned income). The over-contribution made in December 2009 will provide Pavel with a $22,000 RRSP deduction in the year 2010, saving him $9,900 in taxes at a marginal tax rate of 45 percent. Even a tax accountant can see that $9,900 in tax savings is greater than a $200 penalty!*

The key here is that you're going to need earned income for RRSP purposes in the year you turn 71 for this to work. With some active tax planning, it may be possible to generate earned income for yourself to allow you to use this tactic. Your tax pro or financial advisor can help.

TO MAKE A LONG STORY SHORT:

- You'll have to wind up your RRSP by December 31 of the year you turn 71.

- You may be able to take advantage of RRSP deductions beyond age 71 through the senior's over-contribution, which involves making one last over-contribution to your RRSP just before winding up the plan at age 71.

- The tax savings from the future RRSP deduction will outweigh any penalties owing from the over-contribution.

Tim's Tip 75: Boost the value of your RRSP with tax-free rollovers.

If the name of the game is saving for retirement, and you're committed to using your RRSP to do this, then you need to be aware of the opportunities to transfer potentially large sums to your RRSP, tax-free. These are called *tax-free rollovers*. I want to tell you about six rollover scenarios.

Transfers from One RRSP to the Next

I have a friend named Pat. He's always been the kind of guy who is never really satisfied with the return on his investments. So, Pat has jumped from one mutual fund RRSP account to the next at least five times in the last six years. Good thing

Action Step

By making large lump-sum transfers to your RRSP, you may significantly boost the level of the assets in your plan. While an RRSP is a great retirement vehicle, large lump-sum transfers may leave you with more in your RRSP than you need to provide a comfortable income in retirement. If this is the case, consider an RRSP freeze or meltdown strategy, which can leave you with more after-tax income in retirement than you would otherwise have. The strategy is not for everyone. See Tip 66 for more.

for Pat that assets can be transferred tax-free between RRSP accounts. I, on the other hand, have changed RRSP accounts only once. I moved from an account at my bank where I held mutual funds to a self-directed RRSP. A self-directed plan let me continue holding those mutual funds I owned, but I'm now able to hold many other kinds of investments as well. I like the flexibility. Whatever your reasons for changing, rest assured that the tax collector doesn't mind a move from one RRSP account to the next. Too bad Martin didn't know that. Here's his story.

Since Martin has not been thrilled with his RRSP's investment performance, he has decided to switch from one RRSP to another with different investment options. Last week, he withdrew the full $30,000 sitting in his original RRSP and then wrote a cheque for $30,000 to his new RRSP carrier. In doing this, Martin made a mistake that cost him nearly $10,000 in tax! You see, Martin only has $10,000 of RRSP contribution room available. Because he made a $30,000 withdrawal, he has to report this amount as income this year. But he's only entitled to contribute $10,000 this year to an RRSP and claim a deduction for it. The remaining $20,000 will be exposed to tax this year. Yikes—bad move by Martin. He could have avoided any tax on the $30,000 by arranging for a direct transfer of his RRSP assets to the new account.

Retiring Allowance Rollovers

It could be that you're entitled to receive a retiring allowance when you leave your current job. A retiring allowance could include any number of payments received by you, or by your loved ones after your death, in recognition of your service. These payments might also include early retirement incentives or even damages received as a result of wrongful dismissal. At any rate, a retiring allowance can be rolled to your RRSP tax-free—up to certain limits.

The maximum that can be rolled into an RRSP tax-free is $2,000 for each year or part-year of pre-1996 service, plus an extra $1,500 for each year before 1989 in which you had no vested interest in any employer's contributions to a Registered Pension Plan (RPP) or Deferred Profit Sharing Plan (DPSP). You'll be glad to know that this rollover does not have to be direct from your employer to your RRSP. That is, you'll be able to take the money into your hands personally and still roll those funds to an RRSP as long as you make that contribution within 60 days after the end of the year in which you received the payment. This rollover is made over and above your available contribution room.

Here's one last point: The 1998 federal budget improved things for those who transfer retiring allowances to RRSPs. This rollover often creates a sizeable RRSP deduction for the individual in the year the rollover is made. This used to create an Alternative Minimum Tax (AMT) problem in some cases. AMT is simply an amount of tax that CRA will require you to pay, as a minimum, if you claim certain large deductions. This is no longer an issue. The feds have said that RRSP deductions will no longer be factored into the calculation of AMT.

RPP Assets to an RRSP

While most Registered Pension Plans (RPPs) discourage or prohibit some transfers from the RPP to an RRSP, there are four situations where this can be done. Keep in mind that transfers from an RPP to an RRSP have to be made directly—you can't take these funds into your own hands first.

- If you leave your job for any reason, you may be entitled to take with you certain funds in the company pension plan that are earmarked for you. The amount you can take is generally called the *commuted value* of your pension. Before you get too excited about walking away with thousands of pension dollars at your disposal, be aware that a portion of the commuted value can generally be transferred to a locked-in RRSP only, while the balance is generally taxable. You won't be able to make any old withdrawal from a locked-in plan. Locked-in RRSPs will restrict your withdrawals in a way that is consistent with the payments you would have received under the terms of your pension plan. The benefit of a locked-in plan is that, unlike your pension plan, you have complete control over your investments and could quite possibly generate a greater return on those assets than your pension plan would have offered you. This could spell greater income in retirement.

- If you die while still a member of your company pension plan, a tax-free transfer can be made to the RRSP or RPP of a surviving spouse.
- If you separate or divorce, and you have a written separation agreement or court order, a lump-sum amount can be transferred from your RPP to the RRSP or RPP of your spouse or ex-spouse.
- If your pension plan has been amended to retroactively reduce or remove the requirement for you to make contributions to your company's registered pension plan, you may be entitled to receive a return of your pre-1991 contributions plus accumulated interest. If you transfer this money directly to your RRSP, the transfer will be tax-free.

Inherited RRSP Assets

Your RRSP could cause you some grief as you try to come up with a way to avoid a tax hit on those assets when you die. In many cases, RRSP assets will be taxed on the deceased's final tax return, and whatever is left will pass to the heirs. There are two ways to transfer RRSP assets from the deceased's plan to another RRSP, RRIF, or annuity to defer tax a little longer. The first is to leave your plan assets to your spouse or common-law partner. The second is to transfer the plan's assets for the benefit of a dependant. Check out Chapter 9, Tip 100, for all the details.

Transfers upon Marriage Breakdown

If you're planning to make an equalization payment to your spouse after separating or divorcing, you can use your RRSP assets to do it. You see, any payments transferred directly from your RRSP to your spouse's RRSP, RRIF, or RPP as a result of a marriage breakdown can be transferred tax-free. Before making a transfer, keep in mind that this rollover must follow a written separation agreement, or a decree, order, or judgment by a competent tribunal. I dealt with tax issues around separation and divorce in Chapter 2.

U.S. IRA to an RRSP

You'd be surprised how often I'm asked whether or not it's possible to transfer assets to an RRSP from a U.S. Individual Retirement Account (IRA), which is effectively the U.S. version of an RRSP. The short answer is yes. Our tax law will allow a tax-free transfer to take place—and so I'm including this item in my list of tax-free rollovers. Here's the problem: You won't be able to avoid the long arm of the IRS on withdrawals from an IRA. You'll face tax at graduated U.S. tax rates, plus you'll face a 10-percent early withdrawal penalty if the withdrawal is made before age 59 and a half. The bottom line? Unless the U.S. tax hit is minimal, I usually advise that an IRA be kept intact, although each case deserves its own look. I'll deal with other U.S. tax issues in Chapter 7.

TO MAKE A LONG STORY SHORT:

- There are a few ways to boost the assets in your RRSP through tax-free transfers of other assets to your plan.

- Most of these transfers will require a direct transfer from the original plan to your RRSP, while retiring allowances can be received directly in your hands and then contributed within certain time limits.

Tim's Tip 76: **Ensure that your child files a tax return to maximize RRSP contribution room.**

Several years ago, when I told my cousin Erik that he should file a tax return, he gave me that I-dunno-what-you're-talking-about-and-sounds-like-a-grown-up-kind-of-thing-to-do sort of look. Erik was 15 years old at the time. But he took my advice, and today he's reaping the benefits. If that special child in your life has earned any income at all, make sure he or she files a tax return. In fact, there's no requirement to file a return in most cases, unless the child's income exceeds the basic personal amount of $9,600 in 2008, or if the child has capital gains to report, in which case CRA expects a return to be filed. But the benefits of filing a tax return when your child has earned income can't be ignored.

*W*hen Erik was 15 years old, he started his own lawncare service. It didn't make him rich, but it gave him some spending money and later helped to pay for his university education. Even though his income each summer was well under $6,000, he filed tax returns anyway. The income he reported qualified as earned income and created RRSP contribution room. By the time Erik finished university, he had $5,000 worth of contribution room. This year, in his first year of full-time work after graduation, Erik is going to make that $5,000 contribution to his RRSP. This is going to save him about $2,000 in tax.

Filing a tax return will benefit your child in two important ways. First, it's going to create valuable RRSP contribution room, which will save your child taxes down the road and provide a good head start in saving for retirement. Second, it will teach your child something about money and taxes if you keep him or her involved in the process.

TO MAKE A LONG STORY SHORT:

- There's no requirement to file a tax return unless income is over $9,600 in 2008 or there are capital gains to report.

- Even if it's not required, helping your child file a tax return can be worthwhile because it will create valuable RRSP contribution room that will save your child tax down the road and provide a good head start in saving for retirement.

Tim's Tip 77: **Claim your RRSP deduction in the right year.**

Patience, my friend, patience. It's so tempting to make a contribution to an RRSP and claim the deduction on your tax return as soon as possible. But this doesn't always make sense. You see, you're not required to claim a deduction for your RRSP contribution in the year you make the contribution. Did you know that? In fact, you're able to claim that deduction in any future year. I'll admit, there are few things harder in life than forgoing a tax deduction when you know you could be claiming it today. The only thing harder is opening a bag of potato chips and eating just one. It takes willpower. Nevertheless, I'm going to suggest that in certain situations it makes a whole lot of sense to exercise some of that willpower and put off your RRSP deduction to a future year.

> **Action Step**
>
> If you're in your early sixties and you're concerned about the clawback of Old Age Security benefits, consider making contributions to your RRSP but saving the deduction for a future year when the clawback might be an issue.

Picture this. You earn $40,000 annually and make a $10,000 contribution to your RRSP in February of 2009. The RRSP rules actually say that you can make your RRSP contribution for a particular year as late as 60 days following the end of that year (your 2008 contribution can be made as late as March 1, 2009). As a result, your $10,000 contribution in early 2009 can entitle you to a deduction in 2008 or any subsequent year.

The question is: When should you deduct that contribution? Simple. You should deduct that contribution against income that is taxed at a high rate. Specifically, I'm talking about dollars of income over and above the lowest federal tax bracket of $37,885. You see, if you earn $40,000 in 2008 and deduct the full $10,000 in the same year, the first $2,115 of that deduction will save you taxes of about $677 (approximately 32 percent of the deduction). The next $7,885 of the deduction will bring your taxable income below $37,885, and will save you taxes of about $1,971 (approximately 25 percent). Your marginal tax rate is lower on dollars of income below $37,885, so you'll save less tax when claiming a deduction against those dollars.

You may want to consider claiming the first $2,115 of the deduction in 2008, and saving the remaining $7,885 of the deduction for 2009 if it means you'll be able to claim that amount against income in excess of $37,885 in 2009.

Similarly, you may be in a situation where you expect to earn more income next year, which could push you into a higher marginal tax bracket (see the tax brackets starting on page 288). In this case, you may be better off delaying your RRSP deduction in order to claim it against income taxed at a higher rate in the following year.

TO MAKE A LONG STORY SHORT:

- Your RRSP contributions will entitle you to a deduction on your tax return, but that deduction may be put off and claimed in any future year.

- Delaying the deduction may make sense when you can claim the deduction in a future year against dollars that will be taxed at a higher rate.

Tim's Tip 78: Contribute to your RRSP instead of paying down your mortgage.

Canadians love real estate. Canadians also love to pay down the mortgage on that real estate as quickly as possible. I can understand why. On a $100,000 mortgage amortized over 25 years with an interest rate of 8 percent, you're on course to pay over $128,000 in interest alone over 25 years. Scary, isn't it? But hold on a minute. When you've got to make a decision between paying down the mortgage or contributing to an RRSP, many Canadians make the wrong move. Your best bet, in almost every case, is to contribute to your RRSP. If you took the time to do the math, you'd agree with me.

Only in very rare circumstances does it actually make sense to pay down the mortgage first. If the following two conditions are *both* met, then by all means pay down the mortgage as your first priority:

- the interest rate on your mortgage is 3 percent higher than the expected rate of return in your RRSP, and
- you're committed to contributing your annual mortgage payments to your RRSP once the mortgage is paid off.

Meeting the first of these conditions is going to be unlikely, so your best option will generally be contributing to your RRSP first. But why not have your cake and eat it too? Here's how: Contribute to your RRSP each year, and use the tax savings to pay down the mortgage.

TO MAKE A LONG STORY SHORT:

- Except in very rare situations, you'll be better off making contributions to your RRSP than paying down the mortgage.

- Get the best of both worlds by contributing to your RRSP and then using the tax savings to pay down the mortgage.

Tim's Tip 79: **Contribute to a spousal RRSP to equalize incomes in retirement.**

Share and share alike. I think that the soul who first spoke these words was actually a Canadian looking to keep a lid on the family tax bill. I'm talking about one very effective strategy: splitting income with your spouse or common-law partner. You see, in an ideal situation, you and your spouse should have equal incomes during retirement (and prior to retirement for that matter). This keeps the total family tax bill at a minimum. The most practical tool for accomplishing this splitting of income is a spousal RRSP. A spousal RRSP is simply one that you will contribute to, but that your spouse will make withdrawals from. You'll get a deduction for making the contribution, but your spouse, being the annuitant, will pay the tax on any withdrawals. How's that for moving income directly from one spouse to the next? Let me share with you a few facts and strategies surrounding spousal RRSPs.

> **Caution!**
>
> Keep in mind that you won't be entitled to additional RRSP contribution room to contribute to a spousal RRSP. That is, the total contributions to your own RRSP and to a spousal RRSP combined must be within your annual contribution limits. If you exceed your limit, you'll generally be able to withdraw the excess tax-free, but you'll face a penalty of 1 percent per month on the excess contribution until you withdraw it.

Avoiding Attribution on Withdrawals

Our tax law has been designed to avoid abuses of spousal RRSPs. To this end, any withdrawals your spouse makes from a spousal RRSP will actually be taxed in your hands to the extent you made contributions to a spousal RRSP in the year of withdrawal or in the previous two years. For example, if your last contribution to a spousal RRSP was $5,000 in 2007, and your spouse withdraws $7,000 from a spousal plan in 2009, the first $5,000 of that withdrawal will be taxed in your hands since that's the amount of the withdrawal that can be attributed to contributions you made in the year of the withdrawal or the previous two years. To avoid this attribution, the withdrawals will have to wait until the third calendar year after you make your last contribution.

Contributing by December 31

You can effectively reduce the waiting period for withdrawals from a spousal RRSP to just two years—and still avoid attribution—by making spousal RRSP contributions by December 31 each year.

*D*ave has been contributing to a spousal RRSP for his wife, Andrea. His last contribution was on December 31, 2006. Dave and Andrea had a child in 2008, and Andrea decided to stay home with the new baby for a couple of years. Since Andrea's income will be quite low during this time, she has decided to withdraw $8,000 from the spousal RRSP in the year 2009. The $8,000 will be taxed in Andrea's hands, not Dave's, since Dave will not have made a contribution to the spousal RRSP in the year of the withdrawal (2009), or in the prior two years (2007 and 2008). The good news is that the funds inside the spousal RRSP were really tied up for just two years plus a day (December 31, 2006, to January 1, 2009). If Dave had made his last contribution to the spousal plan just one day later, in 2007, Andrea would have to wait a whole extra year before she could make withdrawals and avoid attribution of the income back to Dave. As an aside, since Andrea will have no other income in the year 2008, she won't face any tax on the $8,000 withdrawal because this is less than her basic personal credit (which is $9,600 in 2008 and will be even higher starting in 2009).*

Contributing beyond Age 71

A spousal RRSP is a great tool for making contributions to an RRSP even when you pass age 71 and have wound up your own RRSP. You see, as long as your spouse is still 71 or under in the year, you'll be able to make a contribution to a spousal RRSP in the year, regardless of your own age. Of course, you'll need to have RRSP contribution room available before making any contributions.

Other Considerations

You should be aware that, after your death, your executor may be able to make a final contribution to a spousal RRSP on your behalf if you have unused RRSP contribution room available at the time of your death. See Chapter 9, Tip 101, for more. Also, be aware that on October 31, 2006, the government introduced changes that will allow Canadians receiving eligible pension income, which includes certain RRSP withdrawals once you're 65 or older, to split that income with a spouse. This can be a complementary strategy to spousal RRSPs, but doesn't render spousal RRSPs unnecessary. See Tip 10(s) and Tip 86 for more.

TO MAKE A LONG STORY SHORT:

- A spousal RRSP is a plan that you contribute to but your spouse or common-law partner makes withdrawals from.

- You're entitled to a deduction and your spouse will be taxed on any withdrawals, which accomplishes a perfect splitting of income.

- Watch out for attribution rules, which could tax some of the withdrawals in the hands of the contributor.

- A spousal plan can be used to make RRSP contributions beyond age 71, and to reduce taxes upon your death through a contribution by the executor.

Withdrawing from Your RRSP

You've worked hard to put money aside in your RRSP. At some point, those funds are going to be withdrawn from the plan. Most commonly, you'll withdraw them once you've decided to retire and you need a steady income from those investments. But there may be times in life when you decide that you need to make RRSP withdrawals sooner.

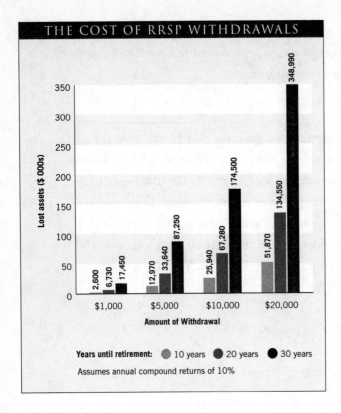

THE COST OF RRSP WITHDRAWALS

Lost assets ($ 000s)

Amount of Withdrawal

Years until retirement: ● 10 years ● 20 years ● 30 years
Assumes annual compound returns of 10%

Before jumping at the chance to pull money out of your RRSP for reasons other than retirement, stop and think twice. You stand to give up plenty of growth in your RRSP by making withdrawals early. Want proof? Consider the cost of RRSP withdrawals shown in the graph. If you make a $5,000 withdrawal from your RRSP and you have 30 years to go before retirement, you'll give up $87,250 in retirement savings because of your withdrawal, assuming a 10-percent return on your money. A $20,000 withdrawal with 20 years to go before retirement will cost you $134,550!

In some cases it may make sense to withdraw money from your RRSP when you're undertaking an RRSP freeze (see Tip 65), but in this case you're building up investments outside of your RRSP, so you're not giving up growth of your assets. Making withdrawals to meet your costs of living or to make a special purchase can often be a bad idea.

If you still plan to make withdrawals from your RRSP, there are some tax-efficient ways to do this. Let's take a look at them.

Tim's Tip 80: Make RRSP withdrawals during periods of no or low income.

There's no doubt that at certain times in your life you might find yourself strapped for cash. During these times, your RRSP can act as a source of income if need be.

It could be that you're unemployed, on disability leave, or on maternity or parental leave. Perhaps you're launching a new business and haven't started generating any income yet. In any event, these times of no or low income may allow you to make very tax-efficient withdrawals from your RRSP.

You see, every Canadian resident is entitled to the basic personal amount that effectively shelters your first $9,600 of income from any tax in 2008. The bottom line is that, if you have no other income, you'll be able to withdraw $9,600 from your RRSP and not pay a cent of tax on that income. Even if your income is over $9,600, you'll still enjoy Canada's lowest marginal tax rate, about 25 percent, on taxable income below $37,885.

> **Caution!**
>
> If you make withdrawals from your RRSP, the tax collector will not give back contribution room for you to make up that withdrawal later. That is, you'll lose that contribution room forever! This has to be considered a cost of making withdrawals over and above the tax you might pay on any withdrawals.

You should realize that you're going to face withholding taxes when you make withdrawals from your RRSP. The federal withholding tax is 10 percent on withdrawals of $5,000 or less, 20 percent on withdrawals of $5,001 to $15,000, and 30 percent on withdrawals over $15,000. The percentage in Quebec is 16 percent on all withdrawals. By the way, the withholding tax rate applies to the *cumulative* withdrawals you've made in the year. So, if you withdraw $5,000 and then another $5,000 later in the year, the second withdrawal will be subject to the 20-percent withholding rate federally. Think of these withholdings as installments on your taxes. In most cases these withholdings won't be enough to satisfy your full tax bill on the RRSP withdrawal, and you'll have to make up the difference when you file your tax return for the year of the withdrawal. In other cases, if your income is low enough, you may get back some of those withholdings as a refund when you file your return.

TO MAKE A LONG STORY SHORT:

- Withdrawing funds from your RRSP can be done tax-efficiently if your income is low, thanks to the basic personal amount of $9,600 for 2008.

- Withdrawals will be subject to withholding taxes, which are simply installments toward your eventual tax bill.

Tim's Tip 81: Consider the impact of using RRSP assets to buy a home.

If you're thinking of buying a home but are not sure where to find a down payment, your RRSP may be one option. In 1992 the Department of Finance introduced the Home Buyer's Plan (HBP), which was designed to help certain Canadians use RRSP money tax-free in order to buy a home.

Is this idea for everyone? Not really. The younger you are, the less sense the HBP makes. You see, if you take money out of your RRSP at a young age, even for a home purchase, you give up more growth inside your RRSP than someone who has, say, just 10 years to go before retirement. As a general rule, if you have 35 years or more to go before it's time to retire, then the HBP quite likely does not make sense on paper. Having said this, I'm not going to spoil the dreams of any young person intent on owning a home. So, do what your heart desires. But learn how the HBP works first!

Making Withdrawals

You'll be entitled to withdraw up to $20,000 from your RRSP tax-free for buying or building a home, as long as you haven't owned a home in the five calendar years leading up to and including the current year (you can use the plan in the current year up to 30 days after you've purchased your home). If you're married, then you and your spouse will each be entitled to a $20,000 withdrawal, provided neither of you has owned a home in the last five calendar years (including this year) and you're buying the new home jointly. Even if your spouse has owned a home in that time, you're entitled to make a withdrawal under the HBP, provided it was not your principal residence while you were married or living as common-law partners (including same sex partners).

It used to be that the tax collector would only let you make withdrawals in a single calendar year under the HBP. This was changed in 1998 and now you can make withdrawals in a year subsequent to your previous withdrawals provided those previous withdrawals are paid back first. Second, if you are disabled or support a disabled person, you may be eligible to make withdrawals under the HBP even if you have owned a home recently.

Once you've made a withdrawal under the HBP, you've got to close the purchase of a home by October 1 of the following year—called the *completion date*. So, if you make a withdrawal in 2009, your purchase will have to close by October 1, 2010. Can't manage to close the deal that quickly? The tax collector may be willing to provide a one-year extension to that October 1 deadline, and in most cases you have the option of putting the funds back into your RRSP by December 31 following the completion date—without a penalty. Keep in mind, too, that the rules require you to occupy your new home as your principal residence within 12 months after buying the place. Make sure you use Form T1036 (available from your RRSP carrier) when making withdrawals; this will allow the RRSP carrier to bypass tax withholdings on your withdrawal under the HBP.

If you were hoping to buy that boat you've been dreaming of, and call it your home under the HBP, you'll find yourself out of luck. The home must be located on solid ground in Canada, but other than this, most homes will qualify, including: detached and semi-detached homes, townhouses, condominiums, mobile homes, apartment units, and even a share in a cooperative housing corporation.

Making Repayments

If you make withdrawals under the HBP, you've got to pay that money back to your RRSP. You won't get a deduction for these repayments. At a minimum, the repayments must be made in equal annual installments over a 15-year period, and your first payment will have to be made in the second calendar year after the year of your withdrawal. If, for example, you withdrew $20,000 on July 31, 2009, you'd have to make your first repayment in the year 2011, and this repayment could be made within the usual RRSP deadlines for that year. That is, you could make your first repayment in the first 60 days of 2012, for the 2011 year. If you happen to miss a repayment, or repay less than you should, the deficient payment is added to your taxable income—just as any RRSP withdrawal would be.

Don't be afraid to speed up your repayments to your RRSP. In fact, the sooner you repay those borrowed funds, the better. If you do accelerate your repayments, this will reduce the amount of each payment for the balance of the 15-year term.

Timing Your RRSP Contributions

When you're getting involved with the HBP, you've got to carefully plan out your RRSP contributions to ensure you'll be entitled to claim a deduction for them. Here's the deal: If you contribute to your RRSP and then withdraw those same funds within 90 days under the HBP, you won't be able to claim a deduction for that contribution. Any money that was already in your RRSP will be considered withdrawn first, before the new contribution is considered withdrawn. The bottom line is this: Always allow your contributions to sit for 91 days or more before withdrawing them under the HBP.

For more information, get a copy of CRA's booklet No. RC4135 on the Home Buyer's Plan (get it online at **www.cra.gc.ca**).

TO MAKE A LONG STORY SHORT:

- Under the Home Buyers' Plan (HBP), you may be eligible to make tax-free withdrawals from your RRSP in order to buy a home.

- The younger you are, the more it will cost you in lost RRSP growth to use the HBP.

- Money borrowed from your RRSP under the HBP must be paid back over 15 years.

- The rules are many and complex, so take the time to learn how the HBP works first.

Tim's Tip 82: Consider the impact of using RRSP money for full-time education for you or your spouse.

When I first read about the Lifelong Learning Plan (LLP) introduced in the 1998 federal budget, it seemed to me like a waste of effort on the part of the Department of Finance. Since that time, however, I've run into a number of Canadians who are taking advantage of this program, which came into effect in 1999. I'm talking about using RRSP assets to finance full-time training or education for you or your spouse or common-law partner. This plan works much like the Home Buyer's Plan I talked about in the last tip, and complements the other education strategies I presented in Chapter 2.

Making Withdrawals

The feds have made it possible for Canadian residents to withdraw money tax-free from RRSPs for full-time training or education. You'll be able to take up to $10,000 each year, over a four-year period, to a maximum of $20,000 in total from your RRSP for education for you or your spouse. You'll be glad to know that "full-time" doesn't have to mean four years of schooling. It can simply mean a three-month enrollment in a qualifying educational program at an eligible institution. If you're disabled, even full-time isn't a requirement—part-time will also make you eligible for the LLP.

Once you've made a withdrawal from your RRSP under this plan, you'll have to enroll in a qualifying program no later than January of the following calendar year. Sorry, but you won't be able to make any education withdrawals from your RRSP for your spouse if you still have a balance outstanding from withdrawals for yourself. However, your spouse can use his or her own plan to make withdrawals.

> **Action Step**
>
> Making a withdrawal from your RRSP for education may be ideal if you're 40-plus and aren't quite sure what to do with the balance of your career, or if you have a real desire to build on your existing skills to increase your marketability. And if you received a retiring allowance from your former employer that was rolled into your RRSP, then any withdrawal you make won't hurt your RRSP as much—after all, you've just added a few thousand to your RRSP because of the retiring allowance.

Dropping Out

If you don't quite make it through your full-time program, you'll generally face tax on the amount of your RRSP withdrawals made under this plan. But don't panic. There are ways to avoid this tax hit. First, if you meet even *one* of three conditions, you'll manage to sidestep the tax collector:

- You withdraw from the educational program more than three months after the year of your RRSP withdrawal.
- Less than 75 percent of your tuition costs are refundable when you withdraw from the educational program.
- You enroll in another qualifying program on a timely basis.

Second, you can bypass the ugly tax hit by repaying the amount withdrawn by December 31 of the year following the year of withdrawal. Send a copy of the RRSP receipt proving repayment, along with a letter explaining why you are cancelling your withdrawals under the LLP, to the Ottawa Tax Centre, Room 362, 875 Heron Road, Ottawa, ON K1A 1A2.

Making Repayments

You'll have to repay your RRSP withdrawals in equal installments over a 10-year period, and you—not your spouse—must be the annuitant of the RRSP. Your first payment back to your RRSP must be made no later than the first 60 days of the sixth year after your first withdrawal. So, if you make a withdrawal in 2009, your first payment will be due in the first 60 days of 2015. You may have to start your repayments sooner if, after your first withdrawal, you fail to qualify for the full-time education credit for three months in two consecutive years. In this case, you'll have to start your payments in the first 60 days of the year following the second of the two consecutive years. Special rules apply in the year of your death or if you give up Canadian residency.

Kind of confusing, isn't it? Not to worry. CRA will send you notices to explain how much you have to repay and when. By the way, if you fail to make the proper repayments in any given year, you'll face tax on the deficient payments.

Timing Your RRSP Contributions

As with the Home Buyer's Plan, if you make a contribution to your RRSP and then withdraw those funds within 90 days under this plan, you won't be entitled to an RRSP deduction for the contributions. For more information, refer back to Tip 81 dealing with the Home Buyer's Plan. Also, get a copy of CRA's booklet No. RC4112 on the Lifelong Learning Plan (you can get it online at **www.cra.gc.ca**).

TO MAKE A LONG STORY SHORT:

- The 1998 federal budget opened the door to making tax-free withdrawals from an RRSP for full-time training or education under the Lifelong Learning Plan.

- You can withdraw up to $10,000 each year, over four years, to a maximum of $20,000 in total withdrawals.

- The plan is similar to the Home Buyer's Plan in many ways, and the rules can be complex. Take the time to understand the impact on your retirement savings before withdrawing RRSP money.

Tim's Tip 83: Take three steps to minimize the tax hit on RRSP withdrawals if you're planning to leave the country.

If you're thinking of leaving Canada, perhaps to live it up down south in your retirement, make sure that you leave your RRSP intact when you go. You see, regardless of where you move, you're likely to be better off in the long run by making RRSP withdrawals after you've given up Canadian residency, and not before.

*M*ark and his wife Karen decided to move to the U.S. at the end of 2008. They liked the thought of spending their retirement in the warmth of Arizona. Before leaving, they visited their tax advisor and took her advice before packing their bags. As a result, Mark and Karen decided to keep their RRSPs intact, so they simply informed the various mutual fund companies and financial institutions holding their investments that they would be non-residents of Canada from 2009 onward. In addition, they sold all the assets inside their RRSPs that had appreciated in value and reinvested those proceeds just before leaving. Finally, they took great pains to make sure that they gave up Canadian residency properly. The result of all this? Mark and Karen will enjoy extremely tax-efficient withdrawals from their RRSPs.

Did you catch the three steps taken by Mark and Karen? Let's look at them again.

Step 1: Leave the RRSP intact.

If you were to collapse your RRSP before leaving Canada, you'd face a significant tax hit because that withdrawal would be fully taxable in the year of your leaving. Mark and Karen avoided this by leaving their RRSPs intact until they had given up Canadian residency. If you wait until you're a resident of the U.S., or another country for that matter, the only tax you'll pay to CRA will be a 25-percent withholding tax on any withdrawals from your RRSP. Further, the 25-percent rate will generally be reduced to just 15 percent on *periodic* withdrawals, as opposed to *lump-sum* withdrawals from your plan—provided Canada has a tax treaty with your new country of residence.

By the way, to ensure that your withdrawals are considered *periodic* and eligible for the 15-percent withholding tax rate, you'll have to convert your RRSP to a RRIF first. This conversion can be done before or after you leave Canada. Once you're making withdrawals from your RRIF, be sure not to withdraw more than twice the minimum amount each year, or 10 percent of the fair market value of the plan assets at the start of the year, whichever is greater. Otherwise the withdrawals will be considered lump sum, and you'll face the higher 25-percent withholding tax rate.

Step 2: Step up the cost amount.

If you've taken up residency in the U.S., any withdrawals from your RRSP will be taxed by the U.S. (in addition to the Canadian withholding tax), but Uncle Sam won't tax the full amount of your withdrawals. Rather, you'll be entitled to withdraw from your plan, tax-free, the cost amount of your RRSP investments as calculated on the day you took up residency in the U.S. So, if you can maximize that cost amount, you'll be entitled to greater tax-free withdrawals in the U.S. Mark and Karen accomplished this by selling and repurchasing their RRSP assets that had appreciated in value—otherwise known as *stepping up* the cost amount of their RRSPs. You see, if you have investments in your RRSP worth $300,000 but you only paid $100,000 for them, your cost amount is $100,000. If you sell those investments and reinvest the proceeds, your new cost amount will be $300,000. This is a step-up in your cost amount. If an investment inside your plan has dropped in value, selling it and reinvesting the proceeds will cause your cost amount to drop—so it doesn't make sense to sell those investments.

Caution!

Some are under the impression that simply moving RRSP assets from one financial institution or advisor to another will result in a step-up of the cost amount of your investments. Sorry, it won't work. While your new RRSP carrier may not have a record of your true original cost amount, you can bet the U.S. tax authorities will take the time to determine this figure if they decide to look into your RRSP withdrawals.

Keep in mind that you won't face a tax bill in Canada on the sale since it all takes place inside your RRSP where gains are sheltered from the Canadian tax collector. The only drawback is that you may face some commissions or charges on the sale of your plan assets, so consider this cost first.

Step 3: Give up residency properly.

Mark and Karen took great pains to make sure they gave up Canadian residency properly. And if you plan on taking up residency outside Canada, you should do the same. If CRA considers you to be a resident of Canada still, even after you've left the country, you'll face tax on your RRSP withdrawals at full Canadian tax rates, not the lower withholding rates.

Although no single factor will determine whether you're truly a non-resident, the tax collector will consider a number of things, and in particular:

- the permanence and purpose of your stay abroad
- your residential ties within Canada (your primary ties include your dwelling place, spouse and dependants, personal property, and social ties)
- your residential ties elsewhere (the courts have said that you must be a resident somewhere, and you can be a resident in more than one country at the same time)
- the regularity and length of your visits to Canada

To avoid an unpleasant tax hit on RRSP withdrawals once you're gone, be sure to follow all three steps outlined here. Why? Because in this game, it's not three strikes and you're out. Strike out on even one of these steps, and you could cost yourself significant tax dollars. Always visit a tax pro when you're thinking of giving up Canadian residency.

TO MAKE A LONG STORY SHORT:

- If you're planning to leave Canada, leave your RRSP intact and make withdrawals once you're gone. The only tax you'll face in Canada will be a maximum withholding tax of 25 percent, which could be reduced to just 15 percent.

- Be sure to follow these three steps to minimize the tax hit on your RRSP if you plan to leave the country: (1) leave your RRSP intact; (2) step up the cost amount of your plan assets; and (3) give up residency properly (visit a tax pro for help).

Benefiting from RRIFs and Annuities

What would a discussion of retirement be without talking about Registered Retirement Income Funds (call 'em *riffs*) and annuities?

Tim's Tip 84: Roll your RRSP into a RRIF or annuity to defer tax well beyond age 71.

I've said it before: There's going to come a day when your RRSP just won't be around anymore. In fact, your RRSP will mature at the end of the year in which you turn 71. By that date, you'll have to wind up your RRSP and do something with the assets inside your plan. You'll have three options at that time:

- make a lump-sum withdrawal from your RRSP
- buy an annuity with the proceeds of your RRSP
- transfer your RRSP assets to a RRIF

You don't have to choose just one of these options. You can actually do all three without a problem. But which option is your best choice?

Make a Lump-Sum Withdrawal

Now here's an option for the high-flying, fast-living senior. If you want to take your life savings, pay tax on the entire proceeds all in one year, then travel around the world for a year or two until your money runs out, you might like this option. But make no mistake, there is absolutely nothing tax-smart about taking a lump-sum withdrawal from your RRSP when you wind up the plan. This option is, in my view, no option at all. Don't even think about it. You see, you can always make withdrawals at a later date from your RRIF if you want more cash—don't make the withdrawal at age 69 when your RRSP matures. Read on for better alternatives.

Buy an Annuity

The name of this game is deferring taxes. A lump-sum withdrawal won't do it, but an annuity can help. When you buy an annuity you are simply entering into a contract where you pay a sum of money to a company (usually a life insurance company) that agrees to pay to you a guaranteed sum of money each month for a period of time—usually your lifetime. Each annuity payment you receive will be fully taxed—but not until you receive the payment. There are two common types of annuities. The first is a *term-certain* annuity that will pay you a sum each month for a fixed period of years. The second is a *life* annuity that will pay you a sum each month for as long as you live. A life annuity can also be set up so that it's a *joint life* annuity that will make monthly payments to you and your spouse as long as one of you is alive. For additional cost, you can also add other features to your annuity, such as indexation to inflation, or a guaranteed term attached to a life annuity.

Annuities may be for you if you have no interest in investing your own money, and all you want is a guaranteed income for life. One of the drawbacks of an annuity is that once you and your spouse are gone, so is the annuity. That is, you shouldn't expect to leave your annuity to the kids, because they generally won't get anything. Another drawback to annuities is that the amount of your payments is determined by interest rates in effect at the time you buy the annuity. If rates are currently low, you might not end up with as high an income in retirement as you could achieve with a RRIF. Finally, if you choose the annuity option, don't wait until December 31 of the year you turn age 71 to make the purchase—after all, you'll be at the whim of current interest rates if you do this.

Roll into a RRIF

A RRIF is a great retirement plan. It works much like your RRSP. In fact, you can hold all the same investments in a RRIF that you can in your RRSP. However, there are two key differences between a RRIF and your RRSP. First, you can't make contributions to a RRIF. Second, you've got to make withdrawals from a RRIF each year. The amount of your withdrawals will depend on your age or the age of your spouse. A RRIF also works like your RRSP in that any assets in your plan will grow tax-free until they're withdrawn. If you want to transfer assets from one RRIF to the next, you'll be able to do this tax-free.

A RRIF is different from an annuity in that you control the investments that are made. If you're not comfortable with this task, the RRIF can still be a real hands-off option if you link up with a trusted financial advisor who can help with the investment decisions. Further, a RRIF can provide for a more flexible income in retirement because you can control the timing and the amount of your withdrawals, although you must make at least the minimum withdrawal each year (see the table on page 294). With an annuity, your annual income is basically fixed from the start. Another advantage of the RRIF is that it doesn't disappear upon your death or the death of your spouse. Your kids will actually receive the balance of your RRIF, albeit after taxes, once you're gone.

The key drawback to the RRIF is that, if you're not careful, you could make big enough withdrawals in the early years of the RRIF to leave you with very little income in your later years. Proper planning should put this concern to rest, however.

In the end, you'll need to decide which of these three options is best for you. I believe that in most cases the RRIF is the way to go, but speak to a trusted financial advisor before making this final decision—you may have to live with your choice for a lifetime.

TO MAKE A LONG STORY SHORT:

- When your RRSP matures in December of the year you turn 71, you've got three choices for those assets: make a lump-sum withdrawal, buy an annuity, or roll the assets over into a RRIF.

- The annuity and RRIF options will allow you to defer tax, while the lump-sum option won't.

- In most cases, the RRIF option will be best, but speak to a trusted financial advisor about what would be best for you before making a decision that you may have to live with for a lifetime.

Tim's Tip 85: Defer tax on your RRIF withdrawals as long as possible.

The longer you defer withdrawals from your RRIF, the longer you'll enjoy a tax deferral. There are two ways to minimize your RRIF withdrawals.

Base Withdrawals on the Younger Spouse

I remember reading one time about a 70-year-old man from Toronto who married a young woman aged 22. Someone had asked him: "Aren't you concerned about marrying a woman so much younger than you?" "Why should I be?" he said. "She's in great health." If I didn't know that they had married for true love, I would suspect that maybe he had some tax planning in mind.

You see, the required minimum withdrawals from your RRIF each year will equal the balance in your RRIF at the start of the year multiplied by a percentage based on your age or the age of your spouse or common-law partner. If your spouse is younger, then the percentage that you've got to withdraw each year will be less if you use your spouse's age in the calculation. And the tax collector will let you use the younger age, provided you establish this when you set up the RRIF.

When Ken set up his RRIF last year at age 71, he decided to base his RRIF withdrawals on the age of his spouse, Leslie, who was just 63 at the time. Ken had $100,000 in his RRIF at the beginning of this year, and because he was 71 at the start of the year, he would have to withdraw 7.38 percent of his RRIF assets ($7,380) from his plan this year if he based those withdrawals on his own age. However, if he based the withdrawals on Leslie's age, he would only have to withdraw $3,700. As the couple gets older, the savings from using Leslie's age will become more pronounced.

See the table on page 294 for minimum annual RRIF withdrawals based on your age or the age of your spouse.

Delay Your First Withdrawal

You'll be glad to know that you don't actually have to make any withdrawals from your RRIF in the year you set up the plan. For example, if you set up your RRIF in January 2009, you won't have to make any withdrawals until the year 2010. And when in the year

Action Step

If you keep your annual RRIF withdrawals to the minimum amount, you'll avoid having taxes withheld by your financial institution. This will give you more money up front to meet your daily living needs. Keep in mind that the withdrawals are still taxable, so the fact that no withholding taxes are paid may mean you'll face a tax bill next April when you file your tax return, and you may be required to make installments to the tax collector quarterly.

2010 do you suppose you'll have to make those withdrawals? Right—not until December 31! By leaving your assets to grow untouched in your RRIF as long as possible, you'll maximize the growth inside your plan and defer tax as well.

TO MAKE A LONG STORY SHORT:

- Defer tax as long as possible by minimizing how much you take out of your RRIF and by delaying those withdrawals until absolutely necessary.

- You can minimize your withdrawals by basing them on the age of the younger spouse, and you can delay your withdrawals until the end of the year following the year you set up the plan.

Tim's Tip 86: Split eligible pension income for tax savings as a family.

You may be aware that, on October 31, 2006, the federal government announced changes which will allow retirees to transfer up to one half of eligible pension income to a spouse or common-law partner, starting in 2007. Bill C-52, introducing the new changes, received Royal Assent on June 22, 2007, which means that the new rules have now become law. Will the new rules save everyone tax? Not necessarily. But where you and your spouse or common-law partner have different marginal tax rates, pension income splitting could save you significant tax dollars. Consider Peter and Diane's example.

Peter has $60,000 of taxable income, $50,000 of which is eligible pension income that he can split with his wife Diane. Diane has $10,000 of investment income of her own. Peter has decided that he'd like to transfer the maximum (50 percent) of his eligible pension income to Diane. As it turns out, this strategy will save the couple $4,250 in taxes in 2008 (using Ontario tax rates).

BEFORE INCOME SPLITING

	Peter	Diane	Total
Pension Income	$ 50,000	$ —	$ 50,000
Other Income	$ 10,000	$ 10,000	$ 20,000
Total Income	$ 60,000	$ 10,000	$ 70,000
Income Taxes Before			
Pension Credits and Age Credits	$ 12,956	$ 60	$ 13,016
Pension Credits	$ 373	$ —	$ 373
Age Credits	$ 151	$ 60	$ 211
Net Tax Owing - Before	**$ 12,432**	**$ –**	**$ 12,432**

AFTER INCOME SPLITING

	Peter	Diane	Total
Pension Income	$ 25,000	$ 25,000	$ 50,000
Other Income	$ 10,000	$ 10,000	$ 20,000
Total Income	$ 35,000	$ 35,000	$ 70,000
Income Taxes Before			
Pension Credits and Age Credits	$ 5,402	$ 5,402	$ 10,804
Pension Credits	$ 373	$ 373	$ 746
Age Credits	$ 938	$ 938	$ 1,876
Net Tax Owing - After	**$ 4,091**	**$ 4,091**	**$ 8,182**
Net Benefit From Pension Income Splitting			**$ 4,250**

Before any pension income splitting is considered, Peter is eligible for the pension credit, but Diane is not, because she doesn't have any pension income of her own in this example. Also, Peter is not eligible for much of an age credit because his income is high enough that the credit is clawed back. Similarly, Diane is entitled to the age credit, but not much of one since her income is quite low. After splitting income, Peter and Diane end up with greater pension and age credits overall on a combined basis.

Now, every couple's situation is different. You may benefit as much as Peter and Diane—or not. The only way to know for sure the value of pension income splitting in your situation is to use tax software to run the numbers and compare different scenarios. A tax professional can help with this.

Some Common Questions

Canadians have had plenty of questions about this new income-splitting opportunity. Let's take a look at some of the most common questions.

What is pension income splitting?

Beginning with your 2007 tax return, you may be able to allocate up to one half of your eligible pension income to your spouse or common-law partner. This could save you tax as a couple. The amount allocated is deducted when calculating your net income and is included in the income of your spouse or partner. Both of you have to agree to the allocation for each year.

Who qualifies for pension income splitting?

Any pension recipient and his or her spouse or common-law partner can elect to split his or her eligible pension income if:

- they are married or in a common-law partnership with each other in the year and are not, because of a breakdown in their marriage or common-law partnership, living separate and apart from each other at the end of the year and for a period of 90 days commencing in the year; and
- they are both resident in Canada on December 31; or
  - if deceased in the year, resident in Canada on the date of death; or
  - if bankrupt in the year, resident in Canada on December 31 of the calendar year in which the tax year (pre- or post-bankruptcy) ends.

You and your spouse or common-law partner will still be able to split pension income if you were living apart at the end of the year for medical, educational, or business reasons (rather than a breakdown in your marriage or common-law partnership).

What is eligible pension income?

Eligible pension income is generally the total of the following amounts received by you in the year (these amounts also qualify for the pension income tax credit):

- the taxable part of annuity payments from a superannuation or pension fund or plan; and
- if received as a result of the death of a spouse or common-law partner, or if the pensioner is age 65 or older at the end of the year:
  - annuity and registered retirement income fund (including life income fund) payments; and
  - Registered Retirement Savings Plan annuity payments.

Sorry, but Old Age Security and Canada or Quebec Pension Plan payments don't qualify.

How do you elect to split pension income?

You and your spouse or common-law partner will have to make a joint election with your tax return for each year you want to split income. To do this, you'll use Form T1032, *Joint Election to Split Pension Income.*

The form will be due on or before your filing deadline for each year—so filing your tax return on time will be critical. There is also a line on your tax return (line 210) for claiming a deduction for the amount allocated to your spouse or partner, and a line for your spouse or partner to report that allocated income (line 116).

Will pension income splitting affect the pension income amount?

If you're a pensioner, you'll be able to claim whichever amount is less: $2,000, or the amount of your eligible pension income after excluding amounts allocated to your spouse or common-law partner. Your spouse or common-law partner will be able to claim whichever amount is less: $2,000, or the amount of his or her pension income that is eligible for the pension income amount, including the pension income allocated by you to him or her. Keep in mind that a pension that qualifies for the pension income amount in the hands of the pensioner does not necessarily qualify for the pension income amount in the spouse or common-law partner's hands because eligibility can depend on age.

Who will claim the tax deducted at source?

The tax deducted from your pension payments will have to be allocated between you and your spouse or common-law partner based on the proportion of the pension income allocated between the two of you.

Is it necessary to contact the payer of the pension?

No. Splitting eligible pension income doesn't involve the payer of the pension, or to whom the pension income is paid. Information slips will be prepared and sent to the recipient of the pension income, no differently than in prior years.

TO MAKE A LONG STORY SHORT:

- Pension income splitting is available to those receiving eligible pension income, starting in 2007.

- This will allow you to transfer up to one half of that eligible pension income to your spouse or common-law partner.

- To figure out whether you'll actually benefit from this transfer of income, you'll need to use tax software, or work with a tax pro to do the math for you.

Understanding Registered Pension Plans

Registered Pension Plans (RPPs) are declining in popularity. More and more employers are letting employees fend for themselves in the world of retirement savings. Nevertheless, thousands of Canadians are still members of RPPs, or will become members, and there are strategies to consider here. But first, let's look at the two basic types of RPPs:

- With a defined benefit plan, you can expect to receive pension benefits based on a formula—often a percentage of your last few years' salary. Your employer bears some risk in this type of plan since a promise is being made to you that a certain level of benefits will be paid out when you retire.
- With a defined contribution plan (also called a *money purchase* plan), both you and your employer may make contributions, but there's no guarantee about how much will be sitting there for you at retirement. The contributions will be paid to you, plus accumulated growth on those assets, but no promises are made beyond that.

If you're a member of an RPP, you've no doubt noticed that the tax collector is not going to let you contribute as much to your RRSP as your neighbour who is not a member of a pension plan. Enter the *pension adjustment* (PA). Your PA is an amount that, in a nutshell, equals the total of your contributions plus your employer's contributions to an RPP each year. The amount of your RRSP contribution room will be reduced by the amount of this PA each year. This keeps all Canadians on a level playing field when saving for retirement. That is, in theory, pension plan members will not have an advantage over those saving for retirement through an RRSP alone.

Tim's Tip 87: Consider opting out of your company pension plan if you have the choice.

I know this sounds radical, but if you have a choice of taking part in the pension plan or not, you should give serious thought to opting out. Let me explain. One thing that can really hurt your retirement savings is to move from one employer with a pension plan to another without a plan. You see, if you stop your member-ship in a company pension plan, the chances are very high that you will not walk away from that pension plan with all the money that you and your employer contributed to that plan for you. This is particularly true if you've only been in the plan a short time—say three years or less.

Now, let me ask you this. What is the probability that you'll change employers between today and the time you retire? There's a darn high probability of that, I would say. In fact, it's not unusual today to find employees who have worked for five or more employers by age 45. If you take part in a pension plan and move to another employer who may or may not have a pension plan, my bet is that you'll walk away with much less than you figured you would.

Thanks to changes introduced in the 1997 federal budget, you may be entitled to a *pension adjustment reversal* that effectively gives you back some of that lost RRSP contribution room that arose from the pension adjustment over the years while you were in the plan. But this is a far cry from actually giving you all the cash that was earmarked for you in the RPP. You'll still have to find the cash somewhere to make a contribution to use up that room.

Consider this also: If you leave a company pension plan and move to an employer without a plan, you could lose the ability to contribute to any kind of retirement plan for a full year. For example, if you were a member of an RPP in 2008 and $19,000 of contributions were made to that plan on your behalf in 2008, then you'd have a pension adjustment reported on your 2008 T4 slip that would prevent you from making meaningful contributions to your RRSP in the following year—2009. If you were to leave your employer on January 1, 2009, and join another employer without a pension plan, you would be in a tough spot. You would not be able to make contributions to an RPP since you're no longer a member of one, nor could you make RRSP contributions because of your PA from 2008. Talk about a rip-off— a full year without contributions to a tax-deferred retirement savings plan.

The bottom line is this: An RRSP is portable, meaning that you can change employers and not worry about losing a beat in your retirement savings. The same cannot be said for RPPs in every situation. You have to weigh this fact against the benefits of a pension plan, which could include a guaranteed income in retirement (under a defined benefit plan) and significant contributions by your employer to the plan. If you're quite sure you'll be with your employer for a significant period of time, then a company pension plan can make sense.

TO MAKE A LONG STORY SHORT:

- When you leave a company pension plan you could very likely be short-changed on the benefits you take with you, particularly when you haven't been a member of the pension plan for long.

- When you leave a pension plan and don't join another one, you could lose the ability to use a tax-deferred retirement savings plan for a full year.

- An RRSP is much more portable than a pension plan, but each situation should be evaluated separately.

Tim's Tip 88: Look into an Individual Pension Plan (IPP) to avoid a big tax hit when leaving your company pension plan.

This tip may not apply to everyone, but it's great when it works—as it did in Greer's case. She came to my office very recently to talk about her pension options.

Greer is a teacher and has chosen to take an early retirement. The RPP that she's a member of sent her a statement explaining her options. Option 1: She can take a pension starting the month she leaves the school board. Since she's only 55, this pension is significantly reduced compared to the amount she would receive if she retired at age 65. Option 2: She can take her pension starting at age 65. Option 3: She can take the value of her pension benefits in one lump-sum amount (called her commuted value) and transfer most of this commuted value to a locked-in RRSP, with the balance being taxable in her hands. What's her best bet?

The Most Common Option

Greer wanted to take the commuted value of her pension—option 3. I don't blame her. It's a popular option. You see, in Greer's case, this commuted value amounts to $450,000. If she's able to invest this money properly, she could provide herself with a better retirement income than the RPP was promising her. Her biggest concern is that, of the $450,000, just $350,000 can be transferred to a locked-in RRSP for her. Under our tax law, there will always be a limit to how much can be rolled tax-free from your RPP to a locked-in RRSP. The remaining $100,000 in Greer's case will face tax in her hands. That's no small tax bill.

The IPP Solution

When I asked Greer what she planned to do after leaving the school board, she told me that she wants to start a business working with children with learning disabilities. "Terrific," I said. I suggested to Greer that it might make sense for her to become the shareholder and employee of a corporation set up to provide these services. The corporation could then sponsor a pension plan specifically for Greer—called an Individual Pension Plan (IPP). An IPP is really a type of RPP. With an IPP set up, it may be possible in Greer's case to transfer the full $450,000 commuted value from her school board pension to her new company pension plan. She'll manage to defer tax on the $100,000 she otherwise would have paid tax on. She was thrilled.

TO MAKE A LONG STORY SHORT:

- You might have two or three options available when you leave a pension plan. It's quite common to take the commuted value of the plan when this is an option.

- Consider setting up an IPP if you will be running a business. This may allow a tax-free transfer of your commuted value to the new plan.

- Speak to a tax pro who is experienced in IPPs to set this plan in motion.

Getting into the Game

With careful planning, you can look forward to a golden future. And the sooner you start your plan in motion, the brighter your financial picture will be. Turn now to the Tax Planning Tip Sheet at the front of the book and review the strategies that you read about in Chapter 6. Check *Yes* or *Not Sure* for each strategy that you are willing to consider implementing. When you're finished this book, take your Tip Sheet to a tax professional for more information or help in implementing the strategies.

AMERICAN LEAGUE RULES: UNITED STATES' CONNECTIONS

In the United States you might get away with murder, but never tax evasion. Just ask Al Capone.

7

S tepping up to the plate when it comes to dealing with the U.S. tax system is going to take a keen eye. And, like Canadian tax law, the U.S. tax system can throw you a wicked knuckle ball when you least expect it. With some helpful tips from this chapter, and a little planning and preparation, you'll have the tools needed to beat the tax collector in the U.S. This chapter will speak to Canadians who invest in the U.S., as well as snowbirds, part-time U.S. residents, and others with U.S. connections. If you're a citizen of the U.S., these rules may not apply to you—a visit to a tax pro is important.

Reporting Your U.S. Income

Tim's Tip 89: Claim a foreign tax credit when you've paid withholding taxes to Uncle Sam.

The fact is, certain types of income received from U.S. sources are subject to taxes in the U.S. If you live in Canada, these taxes usually take the form of withholding taxes of 5 to 30 percent, payable to the Internal Revenue Service (IRS). For the most part, Canadian residents won't find any advantage to earning U.S. source income from a tax point of view. Here's why: You'll have to report the full amount of your U.S. income on your Canadian tax return since Canadian residents are taxed in Canada on worldwide income.

But the story's not over. You'll be entitled to claim a foreign tax credit on Schedule 1 of your Canadian tax return for any U.S. or other foreign taxes paid. This credit prevents a double-tax problem where you're paying tax on the same income in more than one country. Seems fair, doesn't it?

Here's the bottom line: You'll end up paying tax at Canadian tax rates, but you'll send a portion of the tax to the IRS (the withholding tax) and the rest to CRA. A variety of income types give rise to a foreign tax credit. Let's take a look at the most common sources.

Interest Income

Interest income earned on bonds or other debt instruments will attract a 10-percent withholding tax that will be collected by the company that pays the interest. The major exception to this rule is interest earned on deposits in U.S. banks. This interest is generally tax-free if paid to a non-resident. If your U.S. bank has been withholding tax at source, give them a completed Certificate of Foreign Status (which they should be able to provide) to avoid those withholdings. There's no need to file a U.S. tax return to pay taxes on interest income when the correct amount of withholding tax was applied.

By the way, the Canada-U.S. treaty was amended in 2007 (although the changes were not in force at the time of writing) to eliminate the 10-percent withholding tax on interest. The change should be effective sometime in early 2009, and this change will be phased-in for certain related party loans.

Dividends

The withholding rate applied to dividends is currently 15 percent under the Canada–U.S. tax treaty. Again, you don't have to file a U.S. tax return to report U.S. dividend income when the correct amount of withholding tax was deducted at the source.

Pension Payments

Periodic payments from a U.S. source pension will be subject to withholding taxes at 15 percent. If the payment is in the form of a lump sum, it will attract a withholding tax of 30 percent, which approximates the regular U.S. tax rate. Again, no need to file a U.S. tax return when the proper withholding taxes were applied.

Capital Gains

There's good news for those of you investing in U.S. securities. A sale of U.S. stocks and bonds that generates a capital gain will not normally be taxed in the U.S. as long as you're a resident of Canada—the tax treaty will protect you. The exception is the rare circumstance where you own a U.S. real property holding corporation. This is a corporation whose majority of assets are U.S. real estate. The sale of these shares will be treated the same way as the sale of U.S. real estate by an individual—and I'll talk more about real estate in a minute.

Social Security

The rules around social security have flip-flopped twice in the last few years. Here's how the current rules work: A Canadian resident who receives U.S. social security reports the income in Canada only, and just 85 percent of the benefits are taxable in

> **Caution!**
> If you're a U.S. citizen living in Canada, you'll be treated differently for U.S. tax purposes than Canadian citizens are. All U.S. citizens, regardless of where they live, must file a full-blown tax return in the U.S. And this means you'll have to report your worldwide income to Uncle Sam. As a result, you won't be subject to withholding taxes in the U.S. If you're a U.S. citizen who has been neglecting to file in the U.S., be warned that you could face civil and criminal penalties.

Did You Know?

Provided you've been resident in Canada for at least 40 years after you reached the age of 18, you'll be entitled to full Old Age Security (OAS) benefits at age 65, even if you leave Canada. If you were resident in Canada for less than 20 years after you reached 18, and you leave Canada, your OAS benefits will cease after six months.

Canada. The U.S. no longer withholds any tax. These new rules were made retroactive to 1996. By the way, the rules work the same for Canada Pension Plan (CPP) recipients resident in the U.S. That is, tax will be paid in the U.S. alone, and not in Canada. Don't forget, U.S. citizens should get the advice of a tax pro since the rules are different for you.

Other Payments

Alimony and maintenance are exempt from U.S. with-holding taxes. And if you happen to earn employment income in the U.S., that income will not be subject to withholding or other taxes in the U.S. as long as the income amounts to $10,000 (U.S.) or less in the year. Even if the income is over $10,000 (U.S.), it will still be tax-free in the U.S. if you were present in the U.S. for fewer than 184 days, and if you were paid by a Canadian-resident employer (but not a U.S.-resident employer or a permanent establishment in the U.S. that your Canadian-resident employer operates).

TO MAKE A LONG STORY SHORT:

- Certain types of income from the U.S. will be subject to withholding taxes down south.

- As a Canadian resident you'll be entitled to a foreign tax credit in Canada for U.S. or other foreign taxes you pay.

- Be sure to claim the tax credit to ensure that you're not double-taxed on the same income in different countries. The calculation is done on Schedule 1 of your tax return.

Profiting from U.S. Real Estate

Last summer, Carolyn and I spent a week visiting her brother and his family in Alabama. We spent a good part of the week at the family's cottage (they call them "lake houses" down south), not far from Birmingham. It was beautiful. While we were there, we met some fellow Canadians at the lake. Turns out they own a lake house and rent it out most of the year. I had a good talk with them about the tax rules affecting their U.S. property.

Tim's Tip 90: Use the net rental income method on your U.S. rental property in most cases.

The U.S. will normally impose a 30-percent withholding tax on your gross rental revenue. You can avoid this by filing IRS Form 4224 with the individual collecting and remitting the tax (the person renting the property from you) and electing to use the net rental income method.

---

*L*ucy and Silvio own a rental property in Alabama, and they rented it to Nadia for six months at $1,000 per month. Unless Nadia is given Form 4224, she is obliged to withhold 30 percent of the rent ($300 each month) and remit it to the IRS. If the election is made and the form is filed, then Lucy and Silvio will escape the 30-percent withholding tax, but they will be obliged to file a U.S. tax return each year to report the actual income and expenses from the rental property. Turns out that Lucy and Silvio's tax bill is much lower using this method—the net rental income method—than remitting a full 30 percent of the gross rents.

Under the net rental income method, you'll deduct from income all the property taxes, interest, maintenance, insurance, and other costs associated with the property—including depreciation, which is mandatory in the U.S.

Before deciding on the net rental income method, keep these points in mind:

- Not all expenses will be deductible under this method. Generally, you'll need to allocate your expenses between the personal-use portion and the rental portion based on days the property was rented.

- When a property is used personally for less than 15 days each year or 10 percent of the time available (whichever is greater), you won't need to allocate expenses as personal use.
- When a property is rented out for less than 15 days each year, there's no need to report any rental income and no expenses are deductible.
- When you elect to use the net rental income method, the election is generally irrevocable, and this method will apply to all your U.S. rental properties if you have more than one.
- If you want to use the net rental income method, the deadline for the 2008 year is October 15, 2010 (an 18-month deadline is imposed on "foreign nationals" by the IRS). Meet this deadline or the IRS won't allow any deductions!

TO MAKE A LONG STORY SHORT:

- When you own a rental property in the U.S., there are two ways of paying tax on the rents you earn: a withholding tax, or the net rental income method of reporting.

- The net rental income method will generally provide the greatest tax savings.

Tim's Tip 91: Take two steps to minimize the tax hit on the sale of your U.S. real estate.

Let's hope that the U.S. real estate you bought turns out to be a good investment. And if it does, this could mean some tax to pay to the IRS later when you sell the property at a profit. You can minimize your tax hit in a couple of ways.

Minimize Withholding Tax

Normally, the sale of your U.S. real estate is going to attract a 10-percent withholding tax that is remitted by the buyer or the buyer's agent to the IRS. The tax is calculated as 10 percent of the actual sale price of the property and not the gain on the sale. Keep in mind that this withholding tax doesn't remove your obligation to file a U.S. tax return to report the sale of your property. No sir. You'll have to report that sale—normally on IRS Form 1040NR if you're a Canadian citizen and resident—and you may have to hand over more tax to the IRS. The 10-percent withholding tax is simply treated as an installment on the taxes owing. If you sell the property for little or no profit, then you might actually recover some or all of that 10-percent tax withheld.

You can apply to the IRS for a "withholding certificate" based on your expectation that the U.S. tax owed will be less than 10 percent of the sale price. This certificate will tell the buyer how much money to withhold, if any. But remember, this exception applies only to the withholding tax. The gain on the sale will still attract tax, and you will still need to file a tax return reporting the gain or loss to the U.S. government.

> **Action Step**
>
> If you want to avoid the 10-percent withholding tax that is normally due when a Canadian citizen and resident sells U.S. real estate, sell the property to an individual who plans to occupy it as a principal residence, and keep the selling price below $300,000 (U.S.). In this case, the IRS will waive the requirement for the buyer to withhold that 10 percent.

Minimize Your Taxable Gain

Calculating your gain or loss on the sale of your U.S. property is not rocket science, but you'll want to do it right to minimize the tax bill you could face. In a nutshell, here's the formula to calculate your gain or loss:

	Net proceeds on sale
Minus	Cost base
Equals	Gain or loss on sale

Seems simple enough, right? Well, hold on. You need to make some adjustments to these figures to make sure you're not paying too much tax. Consider this: The net proceeds are calculated by taking the selling price minus all selling expenses—including commissions, fees, and similar expenses (most of these appear on your closing statement). If you forget these additional costs, you could be paying too much tax.

As for your cost base, be sure to take the original cost and add the cost of any major improvements—also called capital improvements. If the property is a rental,

Make sure you visit a tax pro if you owned your U.S. property before September 27, 1980, and it has been exclusively for personal use. You see, special rules exist for Canadian residents in this boat. Under the Canada–U.S. tax treaty, only the gain since January 1, 1985, might be taxed. To take advantage of this provision, you'll need a valuation of the property at January 1, 1985.

then these capital improvements would not have been deductible; rather, they increase your cost base when selling the property. Further, on a rental property, you've got to deduct from the cost base the amount of any depreciation on the property—whether you previously claimed that depreciation or not. This is going to increase your capital gain. If you owned the property solely for personal use, then no depreciation need be taken and your cost base is not adjusted.

Make sense so far? Once the gain has been determined, you can now deduct all the accumulated rental losses that you've been claiming over the years, if any.

Grace owns a home in Florida, which she rents out for half the year. She has owned the house for three years and has had rental losses averaging $3,000 (U.S.) each year. The house originally cost $100,000 (U.S.) and Grace has spent $25,000 (U.S.) over the years renovating the house. All the required tax returns have been filed over the three years. This year, Grace sold the house for $150,000 (U.S.) to a person who intends to use the house as his principal residence. What do you suppose Grace's gain on the sale is, if her real estate commissions were $6,000 (U.S.), and depreciation on the home was $13,000 (U.S.) over the three years? Time to crunch a few numbers. Here is Grace's gain:

Net proceeds on sale ($150,000 − $6,000)	$ 144,000
Cost base ($100,000 + $25,000 − $13,000)	($ 112,000)
Gain on sale	$ 32,000
Net rental losses from prior years (3 years × $3,000)	($ 9,000)
Net gain on sale	$ 23,000

Don't forget that any gain or loss on the sale of your U.S. property will also have to be reported on your Canadian tax return if you are resident in Canada. The calculation of the gain or loss in Canada may differ from the calculation in the U.S., particularly since depreciation is not a mandatory deduction in Canada. Don't worry about paying tax on the same gains in both Canada and the U.S.—the foreign tax credit I talked about earlier will protect you from this. Alternatively, you might be able to call your U.S. property your principal residence, which could save you a bundle in Canadian tax.

TO MAKE A LONG STORY SHORT:

- When you sell your U.S. real estate, you'll be subject to a 10-percent withholding tax that the buyer will have to remit to the IRS.

- Minimize this tax by selling to someone who plans to use the property as a principal residence or by applying to the U.S. for a withholding certificate.

- Minimize your taxable gain on the sale by making appropriate adjustments to your sale proceeds and your cost base.

Cutting Your Gambling Losses

Tax is definitely a game I can help you to win. As for roulette, blackjack, craps, the ponies, and the rest—you're on your own, I'm afraid. There's not much I can do to help you win in games of chance! But if you walk away from the casino or race track poorer than when you arrived, there may be some consolation.

Tim's Tip 92: Register at a casino or hotel to track gambling losses for tax savings.

The Canada–U.S. tax treaty will treat Canadian residents in the same way as U.S. citizens and residents with regard to gambling. Specifically, Canadian residents can now deduct gambling losses from gambling winnings in the same year.

Gambling and lottery winnings will be subject to a 30-percent withholding tax at the time of winning, although winnings from blackjack, baccarat, craps, roulette, and the Big-6 wheel are exempt from tax. If you're hoping to carry your losses back to previous years, or ahead to future years, don't get your hopes up. Winnings and losses cannot be carried back and forth and offset against other years. If you've received winnings that have had tax withheld and you can substantiate losses, you should consider filing a tax return—Form 1040NR—to claim some of these losses back. Keep in mind, you cannot claim a refund for tax withheld on gambling winnings prior to 1996. Also, if you've received tax-exempt winnings or you have no substantiated losses, don't bother filing a 1040NR tax return—you're not going to get any tax back.

The easiest way to provide the IRS with the information required to substantiate gambling losses is to register at one of the hotels or casinos and establish an account. As money is withdrawn from the account, a record is produced showing all your cash withdrawals. In the past, this has been accepted by the IRS as proof of gambling losses.

When filing your return, include the W-2G withholding slip the casino gave you, showing your winnings and the amount withheld plus the official record indicating your withdrawals from the casino account. This return should be filed by the regular deadline for Form 1040NR, which is June 15 for the previous year.

TO MAKE A LONG STORY SHORT:

- Canadian residents can claim U.S. gambling losses to offset winnings.

- Register at a casino or hotel and establish an account to substantiate your gambling losses.

- File a tax return, Form 1040NR, to claim your losses and recover any withholding tax.

Staying Canadian

If you're planning to spend time in the U.S. each year, there are some things you should keep in mind to avoid the long arm of Uncle Sam.

Tim's Tip 93: Understand the implications of becoming a resident of the U.S.

Becoming a resident of the U.S. for tax purposes can add a whole world of complexity to your tax affairs. If you inadvertently become a resident south of the border, you'll be required to file a U.S. tax return and pay U.S. tax on your worldwide income.

The IRS will consider you to be a U.S. resident for tax purposes if you hold a green card or if you meet the *substantial presence test*. How does it work? If the following formula adds up to 183 days or more, then you've met the substantial presence test and you'll be deemed a U.S. resident.

As a general rule, if you were physically present in the U.S. for 122 days (four months) a year over the last three years, you'll meet this test and be deemed a U.S. resident.

THE SUBSTANTIAL PRESENCE TEST	
Add	The total days you are present in the U.S. in the current year. (It must be at least 31 days or you will not be caught by this test.)
Plus	One-third of the days you were present in the U.S. in the prior year.
Plus	One-sixth of the days you were present in the U.S. in the second prior year.

If the total of these is 183 days or more, then you have met the substantial presence test.

How Do You Spell Relief?

If you meet the substantial presence test, there are still three avenues of relief that could allow you to escape having to file a full-blown tax return in the U.S.

1. **Closer Connection.** If you truly have a closer connection to Canada than the U.S., despite meeting the dreaded substantial presence test, then you can file a Closer Connection Statement with the IRS, Form 8840, telling the IRS about this closer connection. Filing this form will get you out of the obligation to report your worldwide income to Uncle Sam. To claim a closer connection to Canada, you must be present in the U.S. fewer than 183 days in the current year and file Form 8840 by June 15 of the following year (that is, file by June 15, 2009, for the year 2008).

2. **Exempt Person.** Generally, you won't be treated as being present in the U.S. on any day in which you're temporarily present in the U.S. as a foreign government–related individual, a teacher or trainee who holds a J visa, a student holding either an F, J, or M visa, or a professional athlete temporarily in the U.S. to compete in a charitable sporting event. If you're an exempt individual, you're required to file a form with the IRS stating why you're exempt from U.S. taxation.

3. **Tie-Breaker Rules.** It's possible you might be considered a resident of both Canada and the U.S. at the same time under the tax laws in each country. In this case, the Canada–U.S. tax treaty provides relief from being considered a resident of both countries by applying some "tie-breaker" rules. Now, if you hold a U.S. permanent resident visa (a green card) you should be careful about claiming to be a non-resident of the U.S. under the treaty. This could jeopardize your ability to maintain that U.S. residency permit. You should get advice from an immigration lawyer before claiming non-resident status in this case.

Caution!

Don't assume, just because you're considered a resident of Canada for Canadian tax purposes, that the IRS will agree with you. You might also be considered a U.S. resident for U.S. tax purposes! Being a resident of both Canada and the U.S. at the same time will do nothing but complicate your tax affairs.

TO MAKE A LONG STORY SHORT:

- Avoid becoming a U.S. resident for tax purposes if you hope to keep your tax affairs from becoming a complex quagmire.

- If you spend, on average, more than 122 days each year in the U.S., you might meet the substantial presence test, which will deem you to be a resident of the U.S.

- If you meet the substantial presence test and are deemed to be a resident of the U.S., filing Form 8840 could solve your problem. You may also avoid filing a full-blown U.S. tax return if you're an "exempt person," or you claim protection under the tax treaty's "tie-breaker" rules.

Considering U.S. Estate Taxes

Tim's Tip 94: Determine whether you're a candidate for U.S. estate taxes.

While Canada does not levy estate taxes upon death, the U.S. does. And if you're a Canadian citizen or resident living in Canada, but you own U.S. property, you could be hit with a U.S. estate tax bill upon your death. The kinds of U.S. properties that I'm talking about include: U.S. real estate; shares of U.S. public or private corporations; debt obligations issued by U.S. residents; personal property in the U.S.; and more. The tax bill you can expect is based on the fair market value of those U.S. assets on the date of your death.

> If you don't calculate carefully, you might just count too many days of presence in the U.S., which could cause you to meet the substantial presence test. In your calculations, be sure to exclude any days in which you were in the U.S. as a student, teacher or trainee, professional athlete temporarily in the U.S. to compete in a charitable event, or diplomat with full-time diplomatic or consular status. If these exceptions apply to you, they also automatically apply to your immediate family.
>
> **Caution!**

By the way, I should mention that, even if you're considered a resident of Canada for Canadian tax purposes, you might still be considered to be domiciled in the United States. I know it may sound confusing, but domicile in the U.S. is something different than residency in either Canada or the U.S. And if you're considered to be domiciled in the U.S., you'll be liable for U.S. estate tax on all your assets—not simply on those U.S. assets that I talked about in the preceding paragraph. In most cases, a little planning will let you avoid being considered domiciled in the U.S., and you'll have nothing to worry about. I won't go into the definition of U.S. domicile here, but you should check with your tax pro if you're spending lots of time in the U.S., just to make sure you won't be caught.

Once you recognize that you're a candidate for a U.S. estate tax bill, you should consider a number of planning strategies to minimize these taxes. See Tip 106 in Chapter 9 for all the details.

TO MAKE A LONG STORY SHORT:

- You could be liable to pay U.S. estate tax if you own U.S. assets or are considered domiciled in the U.S.

- If you think you're a candidate for U.S. estate taxes, refer to Tip 106 in Chapter 9 for details on how to minimize this tax bill.

Getting into the Game

You could be well on your way to tax savings on both sides of the border. Turn now to the Tax Planning Tip Sheet at the front of the book and review the strategies introduced in Chapter 7. Check *Yes* or *Not Sure* if you are willing to consider implementing a tip. When you've finished this book, take your Tip Sheet to a tax pro if you want more information or help in implementing your plan.

A LEAGUE OF THEIR OWN: PROVINCIAL TAX ISSUES

If a man does not keep pace with his companions, perhaps it is because he hears a different drummer.

8

A few years ago, the taxes levied by your province or territory were easy to understand. It used to be that each jurisdiction (with the exception of Quebec) simply calculated your tax bill by multiplying your federal tax by a certain percentage. This was a "tax on tax" type of system, and it was straightforward. Today, each province and territory calculates its own tax based on your taxable income figure. So far, the provinces and territories have agreed to use the same taxable income figure that the federal government uses, but don't expect this simplicity to last long. In this chapter, I want to detail the tax brackets and rates that apply in each province and territory, and talk about the specific tax changes that each jurisdiction introduced in 2008. So, let's get to it!

Walking to a Different Drummer

Tim's Tip 95: Understand the various tax changes that apply specifically to your province.

I've got news to share with you about each of the provinces and territories, so let's start from the west and work our way east, shall we?

British Columbia

2008	Tax Bracket	$0	$35,016	$70,033	$80,406	$97,636
	Tax Rate	5.24%	7.98%	10.5%	12.29%	14.7%
	Top Marginal Rate	Regular income: 43.70%		Capital gains: 21.85%		Canadian dividends: Eligible 18.47% | Ineligible 31.58%

Here are the highlights of tax changes in British Columbia in 2008:

Indexing of tax brackets and credits: Income tax brackets and tax credits in B.C. were increased by 1.8 percent for 2008 as a result of indexing.

Change in income tax rates: B.C. income tax rates were reduced for 2008 and now appear as noted in the table above. In 2007, the graduated rates appeared as follows: 5.7 percent (now 5.24 percent), 8.65 percent (now 7.98 percent), 11.1 percent (now 10.5 percent), 13 percent (now 12.29 percent), and the top rate remains unchanged at 14.7 percent.

Canadian dividends: B.C.'s dividend tax credit (on grossed-up dividends) for eligible dividends is 12 percent, which began in 2006. This rate is scheduled to fall to 11 percent in 2009, 10.83 percent in 2010, 10.31 percent in 2011, and 9.76 for 2012 and subsequent years. The rate for non-eligible dividends is 5.1 percent in 2008, to be reduced to 4.2 percent in 2009.

Low income climate action tax credit: B.C. introduced an annual tax credit of up to $100 per adult and $30 per child ($100 for the first child in single-parent families) starting in July 2008.

Climate action dividend payment: B.C. will make a one-time payment of $100 to each individual resident in the province on December 31, 2007.

Alberta

2008	Tax Bracket	$0	Alberta is the only province with a single tax rate.		
	Tax Rate	10%			
	Top Marginal Rate	Regular income: 39.00%	Capital gains: 19.50%	Canadian dividends: Eligible 16%	Ineligible 26.46%

Here are the highlights of tax changes in Alberta in 2008:

Indexing of tax brackets and credits: Income tax brackets and tax credits in Alberta were increased by 4.7 percent for 2008 as a result of indexing. The following tax credit amounts are an exception to this, and were increased by a higher percentage: disability tax credit (from $7,131 in 2007 to $12,466 in 2008); disability supplement, infirm dependant and caregiver amounts ($4,160 in 2007 to $9,355 in 2008).

Canadian dividends: Alberta's dividend tax credit (on grossed-up dividends) for 2008 is 9 percent for eligible dividends (up from 8 percent in 2007; to be increased to 10 percent in 2009). On non-eligible dividends, the dividend tax credit (on grossed-up dividends) for 2008 is 4.5 percent (down from 5.5 percent in 2007; to decline to 3.5 percent in 2009).

Health care premiums: These premiums will be eliminated on January 1, 2009.

Family employment tax credit: Alberta increased the maximum benefit and income threshold starting July 1, 2008.

Did You Know?

The federal and provincial governments entered into Tax Collection Agreements back in 1962 that saw the feds collect the taxes for each province and territory. In December 1997 at a meeting of Canada's finance ministers, the federal government agreed to change the system to allow each province to calculate its taxes based on taxable income, rather than as a percentage of basic federal tax. The system still maintains a common definition of taxable income both federally and provincially, along with a number of other common definitions.

Saskatchewan

2008	Tax Bracket	$0	$39,135	$111,814		
	Tax Rate	11%	13%	15%		
	Top Marginal Rate	Regular income: 44.00%		Capital gains: 22.00%	Canadian dividends: Eligible 20.35	Ineligible 30.83%

Here are the highlights of tax changes in Saskatchewan in 2008:

Indexing of tax brackets and credits: Income tax brackets and tax credits in Saskatchewan were increased by 1.9 percent for 2008 as a result of indexing. The following tax credit amounts are an exception to this, and were increased by a higher percentage: disability tax credit (from $6,890 in 2007 to $8,190 in 2008); disability supplement, infirm dependant and caregiver amounts ($4,019 in 2007 to $8,190 in 2008).

Canadian dividends: Saskatchewan's dividend tax credit (on grossed-up dividends) for eligible dividends is 11 percent, which began in 2006. This rate is scheduled to fall to 10.83 percent in 2010, 10.31 percent in 2011, and 9.76 for 2012 and subsequent years.

Active family benefit: A refundable income tax credit will provide up to $150 per child aged 6 to 14 for cultural, recreational, and sports activities fees. This credit begins in 2009.

Graduate retention program: Post-secondary students who graduate after 2005 can receive a refundable income tax credit that will rebate up to $20,000 of tuition fees over seven years. This tax credit begins in 2008. Last year I mentioned the introduction of the Graduate Tax Exemption, which is discontinued after 2007 due to this new tax credit.

Mineral exploration tax credit: This credit has been reinstated for flow-through share agreements entered into after March 31, 2008, and is a 10 percent credit.

Manitoba

2008	Tax Bracket	$0	$30,544	$66,000		
	Tax Rate	10.9%	12.75%	17.4%		
	Top Marginal Rate	Regular income: 46.40%		Capital gains: 23.20%	Canadian dividends: Eligible 23.83%	Ineligible 37.40%

Here are the highlights of tax changes in Manitoba in 2008:

Tax brackets and rates: Manitoba changed its tax brackets and rates to those noted in the table above. The tax rates in 2007 were as follows: Lowest – 10.9 percent, middle – 13 percent, and highest – 17.4 percent.

Canadian dividends: Manitoba's dividend tax credit on eligible dividends (grossed-up dividends) is 11 percent, which started in 2006. The rate on non-eligible dividends is 3.15 percent (3.67 percent in 2007), due to fall to 2.5 percent in 2009.

Primary caregiver tax credit: Manitoba introduced a new refundable tax credit available to the primary caregiver of a "Manitoba Home Care Client." The credit is worth $85 per month.

Community enterprise tax credits: This credit is extended to December 31, 2011. The maximum annual limit for the credit increased to $450,000 (from $150,000). This is effective January 1, 2008.

Mineral exploration tax credit: This 10-percent tax credit has been extended by one year to agreements entered into before April 1, 2009.

Ontario

2008	Tax Bracket	$0	$36,020	$72,041	
	Tax Rate	6.05%	9.15%	11.16%	
	Ontario surtax	20% of Ontario tax over $4,162, plus 36% over $5,249 (starts at income of $63,430)			
	Top Marginal Rate	Regular income: 46.41%	Capital gains: 23.20%	Canadian dividends: Eligible 23.96%	Ineligible 31.34%

Here are the highlights of tax changes in Ontario in 2008:

Indexing of tax brackets and credits: Income tax brackets and tax credits in Ontario were increased by 1.5 percent for 2008 as a result of indexing.

Canadian dividends: Ontario's dividend tax credit (on grossed-up dividends) for 2008 is 7 percent (6.7 percent in 2007) for eligible dividends (to be increased to 7.4 percent in 2009, and 7.7 percent in 2010 and subsequent years).

Property and sales tax credits and grants for seniors: Ontario will increase the income threshold at which the Ontario property and sales tax credits are clawed back for seniors. The income threshold will increase in 2008 from the former level

Did You Know?

At the time of writing, Canada's national debt stands at $454.8 billion. Our population is currently 33.4 million. This means that our country is indebted to the tune of $13,617 for every man, woman, and child in the country. Ouch. As it stands, 13 cents of every tax dollar raised goes to pay interest costs on the debt. While this is better than it was in 1992 when 42 cents of every tax dollar went to interest costs, there is room for more improvement. The more debt that is paid down, the more of each tax dollar that is freed up for uses other than paying interest charges on the debt.

of $23,820. In addition, Ontario has introduced, starting in 2009, a property tax grant of $250 ($500 for 2010 and later years).

Labour-Sponsored Investment Funds: Ontario increased the maximum investment that qualifies for the LSIF tax credit, to $7,500 (from $5,000), effective January 1, 2007. In addition, the province extended the phase-out of the tax credit as follows: 15 percent in 2008 and 2009 (previously 10 percent in 2009), 10 percent in 2010 (previously 5 percent), 5 percent in 2011 (previously NIL in 2011), and NIL starting in 2012.

Land transfer taxes: A few changes to land transfer tax legislation were made in 2008, including the following: expansion of the LTT refund program for first-time home buyers to include purchases of resale homes, for agreements entered into in 2008 or later years; exempt from LTT certain transfers of farmland from family farm corporations to individual family members after March 25, 2008; and, impose a LTT within the city of Toronto (with a rebate of up to $3,725 for first-time homebuyers).

Quebec

		$0	$37,500	$75,000		
2008	Tax Bracket	$0	$37,500	$75,000		
	Tax Rate	16%	20%	24%		
	Top Marginal Rate	Regular income: 48.22%		Capital gains: 24.11%	Canadian dividends: Eligible 29.69%	Ineligible 36.35%

Here are the highlights of tax changes in Quebec in 2008:

Indexing of tax brackets and credits: Most income tax credits in Quebec were increased by 1.21 percent for 2008 as a result of indexing. On January 1, 2008, Quebec tax brackets increased from $29,290 to $37,500, and from $58,595 to

$75,000, and the basic amount increased to $10,215 from $9,750.

Canadian dividends: Quebec's dividend tax credit (on grossed-up dividends) for 2008 is 11.9 percent for eligible dividends. The province's rate on ineligible dividends is 8 percent.

Stock option deduction: This deduction was increased to 50 percent of the stock option benefit, up from 25 percent, for employees of innovative small and medium-sized businesses, for stock options granted after March 13, 2008.

Child care expenses: Starting in 2009, the province has enhanced the income threshold and tax credit rates that apply to child care expenses. This will benefit families with incomes in excess of $46,755.

Age credit: The age credit, which is $2,200 in 2008, will be indexed beginning in 2009.

Pension income credit: This tax credit is due to increase from $1,500 to $1,750 in 2009, and to $2,000 for 2010. After 2010, the credit will be indexed.

Home support for seniors tax credit: This tax credit was increased from 25 percent to 30 percent of eligible expenses, beginning in 2008.

Tax credit for respite expenses: Informal caregivers will be able to claim a refundable tax credit for respite expenses paid for the care of a person who resides with the caregiver and has a significant disability. This credit is available for 2008 and later years.

Tax credits for infertility and adoption: The rate applicable to these credits increased from 30 percent to 50 percent for 2008 and later years. The maximum credit is $10,000 per infertility treatment and/or adoption.

U.S. social security: Payments by Quebec residents under the U.S. Federal Insurance Contributions Act (FICA payments, for social security and medicare) will be considered as income taxes paid and will qualify for a foreign tax credit. This change will be retroactive to 2004.

Harmonization with federal changes: Quebec will harmonize with many federal tax changes, including those related to Tax-Free Savings Accounts, donations of exchangeable securities, excessive business holdings in private foundations, RESPs, the medical expense tax credit, RDSPs, housing allowances, among other changes.

New Brunswick

2008	Tax Bracket	$0	$34,836	$69,673	$113,273	
	Tax Rate	10.12%	15.48%	16.8%	17.95%	
	Top Marginal Rate	Regular income: 46.95%		Capital gains: 23.48%	Canadian dividends:	
					Eligible 23.18	Ineligible 35.4%

Here are the highlights of tax changes in New Brunswick in 2008:

Indexing of tax brackets and credits: Tax brackets and credits in New Brunswick increased by 1.9 percent as the result of indexing for 2008.

Canadian dividends: New Brunswick's dividend tax credit on eligible dividends (grossed-up dividends) is 12 percent, which started in 2006. The non-eligible rate is 5.3 percent. The rate for eligible dividends is due to fall to 11.81 percent in 2010, 11.24 percent in 2011, and 10.65 percent for 2012 and later years.

Labour-Sponsored Venture Capital funds: RRSPs are now able to acquire LSVC funds directly, and investments in LSVC funds within an RRSP can be rolled over and will qualify for the LSVC tax credit, without cashing in the RRSP, provided the eight-year holding period requirement has been met. These changes are effective for 2008 and later years.

Nova Scotia

2008	Tax Bracket	$0	$29,590	$59,180	$93,000	
	Tax Rate	8.79%	14.95%	16.67%	17.5%	
	Nova Scotia surtax	10% of Nova Scotia tax over $10,000 (starts at income of $81,105)				
	Top Marginal Rate	Regular income: 48.25%		Capital gains: 24.13%	Canadian dividends:	
					Eligible 28.35%	Ineligible 33.05%

Here are the highlights of tax changes in Nova Scotia in 2008:

Indexing of tax brackets and credits: The basic personal credit increased in 2008 to $7,731 (from $7,481 in 2007). The basic personal amount is due to increase to

$7,981 in 2009, $8,231 in 2010, and indexed at 2 percent annually thereafter. Other tax credits (spouse or common-law partner, dependant, pension income, disability, caregiver, age and infirm dependants amounts) have been increased. In total, the increase amounts to 13.8 percent.

Canadian dividends: Nova Scotia's eligible dividend tax credit rate is 8.85 percent, which started in 2006. This rate is due to decline to 8.71 percent in 2010, 8.29 percent in 2011, and 7.85 percent in 2012 and later years.

Transit tax credit: The province will provide a tax credit that parallels the federal transit pass tax credit, beginning in 2009.

Healthy living tax credit: Eligibility for this tax credit is expanded, starting in 2009, to include all Nova Scotia residents that participate in sport and recreational activities. This non-refundable credit is worth up to $500.

Volunteer firefighters tax credit: This credit is now extended to ground search and rescue volunteers beginning in 2008.

Medical tax credit: The province has extended this credit to cover alternative medical practitioners (i.e., naturopaths), beginning in 2008.

Prince Edward Island

2008	Tax Bracket	$0	$31,984	$63,969	
	Tax Rate	9.8%	13.8%	16.7%	
	P.E.I. surtax	10% of P.E.I. tax over $12,500 (starts at income of $98,144)			
	Top Marginal Rate	Regular income: 47.37%	Capital gains: 23.69%	Canadian dividends: Eligible 24.44	Ineligible 36.63%

Here are the highlights of tax changes in Prince Edward Island in 2008:

Indexing of tax brackets and credits: Tax brackets and credits in P.E.I. were adjusted upward for 2008 by various amounts. The table above shows the new brackets. The basic personal amount was increased to $7,708 (from $7,560 in 2007).

Canadian dividends: P.E.I.'s eligible dividend tax credit rate is 10.5 percent. The ineligible rate is 4.3 percent. The eligible dividend rate is due to decline as follows: 10.34 percent in 2010, 9.84 percent in 2011, 9.32 percent in 2012 and later years. As for ineligible dividends, the rate is due to decline as follows: 3.2 percent in 2009, 2.1 percent in 2010, and 1 percent in 2011 and later years.

Newfoundland and Labrador

2008	Tax Bracket	$0	$30,215	$60,429		
	Tax Rate	8.2%	13.3%	16%		
	Top Marginal Rate	Regular income: 45%		Capital gains: 22.5%	Canadian dividends: Eligible 28.11	Ineligible 33.33%

Here are the highlights of tax changes in Newfoundland in 2008:

Indexing of tax brackets and credits: Tax brackets and most credits in Newfoundland and Labrador were adjusted upward for inflation by 1.1 percent in 2008. The table above shows the new brackets.

Surtaxes: The surtax that previously applied to provincial tax over a certain threshold has been eliminated starting in 2008.

Canadian dividends: Newfoundland and Labrador's eligible dividend tax credit rate is 6.65 percent, which started in 2006. The rate for the dividend tax credit applicable to eligible dividends is due to decline as follows: 6.55 percent in 2010, 6.23 percent in 2011, and 5.9 percent in 2012 and later years.

Senior's benefit tax credit: The income threshold at which this reduction is eliminated was increased to $31,930 from $21,920 for singles for 2008. In addition, the credit is enhanced for single seniors by increasing the maximum credit from $384 to $776 in 2008.

Resort property investment tax credit: Investors can now claim a non-refundable tax credit of 45 percent of the purchase price of qualifying resort development property units outside the North East Avalon, acquired after June 14, 2007, and before 2013. Certain conditions must be met. The maximum annual credit is $50,000, and the maximum lifetime credit is $150,000.

Northwest Territories

2008	Tax Bracket	$0	$35,986	$71,973	$117,011	
	Tax Rate	5.9%	8.6%	12.2%	14.05%	
	Top Marginal Rate	Regular income: 43.05%		Capital gains: 21.53%	Canadian dividends: Eligible 18.24%	Ineligible 29.64%

Here are the highlights of tax changes in Northwest Territories in 2008:

Indexing of tax brackets and credits: Tax brackets and credits in N.W.T. were adjusted upward for inflation by 1.9 percent in 2008. The table above shows the new brackets.

Canadian dividends: N.W.T.'s eligible dividend tax credit rate is 11.5 percent, which started in 2006. This rate is set to decline as follows: 11.32 percent in 2010, 10.78 percent in 2011, and 10.20 percent in 2012 and later years.

Nunavut

	Tax Bracket	$0	$37,885	$75,770	$123,184	
2008	Tax Rate	4%	7%	9%	11.5%	
	Top Marginal Rate	Regular income: 40.50%		Capital gains: 20.25%		Canadian dividends:
						Eligible 22.24 / Ineligible 28.96%

Here are the highlights of tax changes in Nunavut in 2008:

Indexing of tax brackets and credits: Tax brackets and credits in Nunavut were adjusted upward for inflation by 1.9 percent in 2008 so that they mirror the federal tax brackets and credits.

Canadian dividends: Nunavut's eligible dividend tax credit rate is 6.2 percent, which started in 2006. This rate is set to decline as follows: 6.11 percent in 2010, 5.82 percent in 2011, and 5.51 percent in 2012 and later years.

Pension tax credit: This tax credit has been increased from $1,000 to $2,000, starting in 2008.

Credit for young children: Parents can claim a $1,200 non-refundable tax credit for each child under age 6, retroactive to 2006 (the amount for 2006 will be $600).

Textbook tax credit: Nunavut will parallel the federal textbook tax credit starting in 2008.

Firefighters tax credit: Full- and part-time volunteer firefighters are now eligible for a $500 non-refundable tax credit, starting in 2008. The amount of the credit will be indexed after 2008.

Yukon

	Tax Bracket	$0	$37,885	$75,769	$123,184	
2008	Tax Rate	7.04%	9.68%	11.44%	12.76%	
	Yukon surtax	5% of Yukon tax over $6,000 (starts at income of $78,755)				
	Top Marginal Rate	Regular income: 42.40%		Capital gains: 21.20%		Canadian dividends:

					Eligible	Ineligible
					17.23	30.49%

Here are the highlights of tax changes in the Yukon in 2008:

Indexing of tax brackets and credits: Tax brackets and credits in the Yukon were adjusted upward for inflation by 1.9 percent in 2008 so that they mirror the federal tax brackets and credits.

Canadian dividends: Yukon's eligible dividend tax credit rate is 11 percent, and its ineligible dividend tax credit is 4.45 percent, which started in 2006. The rate for eligible dividends is due to decline as follows: 10.83 percent in 2010, 10.31 percent in 2011, and 9.76 percent in 2012 and later years.

Child and child fitness tax credits: Yukon provides these tax credits, effective for the 2007 and later tax years. These parallel the federal Child and Children's Fitness tax credits.

TO MAKE A LONG STORY SHORT:

- Be aware of the key tax changes that have taken place in your province of residence.

- You're generally resident in the province where you resided on December 31st of a particular year.

Getting into the Game

Turn now to the Tax Planning Tip Sheet at the front of the book and review the strategies you've read about in Chapter 8. For each one, ask yourself, "Can this apply to me?" Armed with the *Yes* and *Not Sure* answers, visit a tax professional for more information on each strategy, or for help implementing the ideas. *Bonne chance.*

BOTTOM OF THE NINTH: PLANNING FOR YOUR ESTATE

Live your life, play the game, then tip your hat to the crowd.

9

Brace yourself: This chapter is about both death *and* taxes. You might be feeling tempted to pass by these next few pages. In fact, when I first wrote this chapter, I handed it to my neighbour George for his opinion. He claimed that he didn't have time to read it—he was going to the dentist. "George, what about next week? Can you read it by then?" I asked.

"Uh, I don't see how, Tim. I'm hoping for a root canal," he said.

Hmm. I guess a root canal is decidedly more appealing than thinking about death any day of the week.

The only problem, of course, is that neglecting that day when you won't be here any more is tantamount to handing a blank cheque to the tax collector. And make no mistake, estate planning is not simply for those who are in a later stage of life. Let's face it, even the best pitchers can be taken out of the game early. Whether you're 30 years old or 80 years young, you need to plan for your tax bill upon death.

Knowing What to Expect

Tim's Tip 96: Understand the deemed disposition of your assets upon death.

It's no secret that when you die, the tax collector usually follows the undertaker to your door. In fact, did you know that, upon your death, you are deemed to have sold everything you own at fair market value? It's true. And if you own any assets that have appreciated in value, you could face a tax bill on death that might just be large enough to wipe out the entire national debt, give or take. And while it would certainly be generous of you to think of your nation that way, my guess is that if you've got to choose between the tax collector and your loved ones, you'd rather leave your remaining assets to family, friends, or charity.

What this means, of course, is that you're going to have to plan for your taxes upon death—today! Once you're gone, so are the opportunities to minimize the tax collector's share of your estate. The lesson is simple: Calculate what you expect your tax bill to look like upon death, then use the strategies in this chapter to bring that tax liability down. If you're not sure how to crunch the numbers, visit a tax professional who can help you with the calculations.

TO MAKE A LONG STORY SHORT:

- Upon death you're deemed to have sold everything you own, which could result in a whopping tax bill.

- Once you're gone, so are the opportunities to minimize this tax hit.

- Calculate your tax bill expected upon death, and then use the ideas in this chapter to reduce the tax bite. Visit a tax pro to help with the calculations, if necessary.

Giving It Away Today

Tim's Tip 97: Give assets away during your lifetime for tax and probate savings upon your death.

One surefire way to avoid income tax and probate fees when you die is to die broke! Don't get me wrong, I'm not suggesting that you should spend the last few years of your life living on the streets and sleeping on a park bench just to beat the tax collector. You might, however, consider giving away some of your assets during your lifetime. A fringe benefit of this idea is that you'll be able to see your children or other heirs enjoy that inheritance while you're still around.

While it's true that your death will cause a deemed disposition, or sale, of all that you own, there are other common situations that can give rise to this same deemed disposition at fair market value. Here are the two most common: (1) where you give an asset away to someone other than your spouse and (2) where you give up Canadian residency. The problem with a deemed disposition is that since you're not actually selling anything, there are no sale proceeds with which to pay the tax bill. Proper planning can help to minimize the tax burden on a deemed disposition.

If you're going to take me up on this idea, just be aware that our tax law could create a tax bill for you in the year you give an asset away. You see, when you give something away, you're deemed to have sold it at its fair market value at the time you make the gift. If the asset has gone up in value, you might just trigger a taxable capital gain when giving it away.

There are a couple of ways to minimize any tax bill that might arise. First, give away assets that won't create a significant taxable gain. I'm referring primarily to cash, your principal residence, or assets that have not appreciated in value much, if at all. However, if you're going to give away the home, be sure to get legal advice first—there are some potentially harmful side effects since you may lose control over the property and expose it to the creditors or a disgruntled spouse of a family member.

Caution!

> **Caution!**
>
> Make sure you don't cause a deemed disposition of your assets without realizing it. Canadians are notorious for doing this. For example, you may change your mutual fund account from "Jane Doe" to "Jane Doe and Sally Doe, joint with right of survivorship." Sure, this is going to avoid probate fees on your death—which is why people do this. The problem? Jane has just given away one-half of her investments to Sally. This generally results in a deemed disposition of one-half of those investments, and a potential tax bill. Count the cost of this tax hit before taking steps to avoid probate fees.

Second, if you're giving away assets that will lead to a tax bill, consider giving those assets away slowly, over a number of years, so that you don't trigger a huge tax bill in a single year. Otherwise, you could be pushed into a higher marginal tax bracket.

TO MAKE A LONG STORY SHORT:

- The tax collector can't tax you on assets you don't own at the time of your death.

- Consider giving assets away today to minimize taxes and probate fees upon death, but beware of the *deemed disposition* at fair market value that could lead to a tax bill when you make the gift.

Tim's Tip 98: Consider an estate freeze to minimize your tax bill on death.

Maybe you've heard of this thing called an estate freeze. It's a common technique used to freeze the value of certain assets today and to pass any future growth in value to your kids or other heirs.

The Benefits

Here are some of the key benefits of an estate freeze:
- By freezing the value of certain assets today, you'll be able to establish, fairly accurately, what your tax liability is going to be upon death. This will allow you to plan for payment of those taxes.
- By passing the future growth in the asset's value to the next generation, you'll manage to defer income tax on that growth until a much later time. In fact, taxes may not be due until your heirs die, or until they sell the assets, whichever comes first.

- A freeze might allow you to take advantage of the *enhanced capital gains exemption* if you own shares of a qualified small business corporation or qualified farm or fishing property. This exemption is available to all Canadian residents and can shelter up to $750,000 of capital gains from tax—see Chapter 5, Tip 59, for more.

- There's no need to give up control over the frozen assets during your lifetime.

The Methods

How do you complete an estate freeze? I'd put you to sleep for sure if I tried to detail the many steps to completing a freeze. Let me just say that there are two very common methods of freezing an estate. The first is through use of a corporation. By transferring your growing assets to a company and taking back, in return, special shares in that company that are frozen in value, you'll manage a successful estate freeze. Common shares in the company, which may appreciate in value over time, can be issued to your children or anyone else. The second method is through use of a trust—called an *inter vivos* trust. The idea is that you'd transfer certain assets to a trust today for the benefit of your children or anyone you'd like.

In either case, you can bet you'll need the help of a tax pro to look after the nitty gritty details, because you may trigger a taxable event when placing your assets in the corporation or trust, although there are generally ways to avoid this in the case of the corporation.

TO MAKE A LONG STORY SHORT:

- By completing an estate freeze, you'll manage to pass the future growth of the frozen assets to your heirs or others of your choice.

- This will, among other things, freeze your tax bill upon death, enabling you to estimate and plan for those taxes ahead of time.

- A corporation or trust is most commonly used to freeze an estate.

Giving It Away at Death

Tim's Tip 99: Leave it to your spouse to defer the tax hit longer.

Remember, when you die you will be deemed to have sold your assets at fair market value. This could give rise to a tax bill. The common exception to this rule is when you leave assets to your spouse. You see, when you leave something to your spouse, the ugly *deemed disposition* that takes place will no longer take place at fair market value. Rather, you will be deemed to have sold those assets at your cost base. The result? No tax to pay! In this case, you'll manage to defer the tax bill until the death of the surviving spouse, or until he or she sells the assets.

Bill passed away last year. His assets consisted of a home, Registered Retirement Savings Plans (RRSPs) of $400,000, non-registered investments worth $100,000 for which he had paid $60,000, and cash of $100,000. Bill left everything to Lois, his wife, with the exception of the $100,000 cash and some life insurance proceeds of $100,000, which he left to his kids. How much tax do you suppose was triggered by Bill's death? The answer is zero. Nil. He managed to escape tax on any assets that had appreciated in value by leaving those assets to Lois. Since he wanted to leave something to his kids, he left them those assets that weren't subject to income tax at the time of his death.

Do you follow what happened in Bill's situation? Bill left his wife any assets that might have given rise to a tax hit upon his death. This included his RRSPs and non-registered investments. He also left the home to Lois, not because it would have otherwise been subject to tax (since his principal residence exemption can work, even on death, to shelter any gains from tax), but because Lois still needed the home to live in.

Here's a final point worth noting. If you wish, you can transfer your assets to a spousal trust upon your death. This will have the same tax-free effect as if you had left the assets directly to your spouse. With a spousal trust, all the income earned on the assets placed in the trust will accrue to your spouse while he or she is still alive. And no one other than your surviving spouse can access the assets (the capital of the trust) while that spouse is still alive. There may be many reasons to set up a spousal trust rather than leaving the assets directly to your spouse. I'll talk about one of the key reasons in Tip 102.

Leaving assets to your spouse on your death will defer a tax hit. Leaving assets to your kids or other heirs will generally give rise to tax if the assets have appreciated in value since you bought them, or on your RRSP or Registered Retirement Income Fund (RRIF). So, if you're going to leave anything to your kids or other heirs, leave them the assets that won't be subject to much tax, if any. There are four assets in this category: cash, life insurance benefits, a principal residence, and investments that have not appreciated in value very much.

Caution!

TO MAKE A LONG STORY SHORT:

- Leaving assets to your spouse or a spousal trust upon death will allow you to avoid the effect of a deemed "sale" at fair market value of those assets when you die.

- If you're going to leave assets to the kids upon your death, leave them with those assets that will be subject to little tax, if any: cash, life insurance proceeds, a principal residence, or assets that have not appreciated much in value.

Tim's Tip 100: Minimize the tax on your RRSP or RRIF assets upon death by naming the right beneficiaries.

A common question pondered by many Canadians is this: "How can I avoid tax on my RRSP or RRIF assets when I die?" The answer isn't always easy. Your first line of defence is always to name your spouse as the beneficiary of your plan. Beyond this, the opportunities to avoid tax become slim, but if you have certain dependants, there may be other opportunities.

Your Spouse as Beneficiary

If you name your spouse as the beneficiary of your RRSP or RRIF, then your plan assets will transfer directly to your spouse's plan upon your death on a tax-free basis. If your surviving spouse is aged 71 or younger at the end of the year of your death, those assets can be transferred to his or her RRSP, otherwise they'll be transferred to your spouse's RRIF. Your spouse generally has 60 days following the year of your death to make the deposit to his or her own plan.

Your Dependants as Beneficiaries

Rather than leaving your RRSP or RRIF assets to a spouse, maybe you've decided that you're going to leave the assets to your kids or grandchildren. In the vast majority of cases, this is going to mean a tax bill. Typically, you'll face tax on these plan assets on your final tax return; then the balance is distributed to the children or grandchildren. But like many rules in tax, there are exceptions. In this case, there are two:

- **Infirm Dependants.** You'll manage to avoid the tax collector if you leave your RRSP or RRIF assets to a child or grandchild, of any age, who was financially dependent on you at the time of your death due to a physical or mental infirmity. Your dependant will be eligible to transfer your plan assets tax-free to his or her own RRSP, RRIF, or annuity. At the time of writing, a new rule had been proposed to allow RRSP and RRIF assets to be placed in a trust—known as a "lifetime benefit trust" for a mentally infirm dependant. A qualifying annuity can then be purchased by the trust to provide an income to the infirm dependant for his lifetime. This avoids the problems that can arise when a mentally infirm person attempts to open an RRSP or RRIF, or purchase an annuity on his own.

- **Minor Dependants.** If a minor child was financially dependent on you at the time of your death, the child will be eligible to buy an annuity to age 18 using your RRSP or RRIF assets. This won't defer tax for very long in most cases, but it beats paying tax on the plan assets in one year. If the minor is infirm, then the rules for infirm dependants apply.

It's always best to name the appropriate person as beneficiary of your RRSP or RRIF on the plan application form itself. However, naming the appropriate person in your will accomplishes the same thing.

I should mention that, prior to the 1999 federal budget, you could take advantage of this tax-free rollover to your dependants only when you did not have a surviving spouse. Today, you can transfer your RRSP or RRIF assets to those dependants under these rules even if you have a surviving spouse (generally, however, your simplest bet will be to leave the assets to your spouse first). This change is effective for 1999 and later years, although the measure will be available for deaths after 1995 and before 1999 if the recipient of the RRSP or RRIF assets and the deceased's estate make a joint election for the rules to apply.

Charity as Beneficiary

The 2000 federal budget changed the rules so that it is now possible to designate a registered charity directly as the beneficiary of your RRSP or RRIF. In this case, you'll receive a donation credit in the year of your death that could offset all the tax owing as a result of your RRSP or RRIF.

Action Step

I've met many Canadians who have been divorced and are remarried, and who have decided to leave their RRSP or RRIF to the kids rather than the new spouse. If you plan to leave your new spouse anything on your death, leave all or a portion of those RRSP or RRIF assets—it's generally the only way to avoid tax on those assets. Leave the kids with other assets—perhaps even a principal residence (with instructions that the house is to be occupied by your new spouse until his or her death). Leaving the kids with the full RRSP or RRIF will create a tax bill that could wipe out half of those assets—a high price to pay.

TO MAKE A LONG STORY SHORT:

- You'll always manage to avoid tax on your RRSP or RRIF assets upon death by naming your spouse as the beneficiary of your plan.

- You may also manage to defer tax on your plan assets by transferring your RRSP or RRIF to a person who is financially dependent on you at the time of your death.

- Designating a charity as beneficiary could eliminate all tax owing on your RRSP or RRIF upon your death.

Tim's Tip 101: Instruct your executor to make a final contribution to your RRSP after your death.

The final tax return for a deceased taxpayer is due six months after the date of death, or April 30 of the year following the year of death, whichever is later. If, for example, you died on November 30, 2008, your executor would have until May 30, 2009, to file your final tax return. By the way, your executor may file up to four separate tax returns for you, depending on the type of income you earned in your last year.

Believe it or not, the tax collector won't mind one bit if the executor of your estate makes RRSP contributions on your behalf once you're gone. But keep some things in mind here:

- After your death, no contributions can be made to your own RRSP. Rather, contributions will have to be made to a spousal RRSP on your behalf. You'll receive the deduction, but your surviving spouse will pay the tax on any withdrawals.
- Your spouse must be under age 71 on December 31 of the year you die in order for a contribution to be made to a spousal RRSP—otherwise no contribution can be made.
- You must have RRSP contribution room available at the time of your death to enable your executor to make a spousal RRSP contribution on your behalf.
- Any contribution to a spousal RRSP after your death will provide a deduction on your final tax return. This can help to minimize the taxes that would otherwise arise on your death.

The tax savings that will be passed to your heirs from an RRSP contribution after your death will range from about 25 percent to 45 percent of the contribution, depending on your province and the level of income reported on your final tax return.

TO MAKE A LONG STORY SHORT:

- The executor of your estate may be able to make final RRSP contributions on your behalf after you're gone.

- The contributions must be made to a spousal RRSP, within your contribution limits.

- A deduction may be claimed on your final tax return for these contributions.

Tim's Tip 102: Save your heirs tax by setting up a testamentary trust in your will.

A testamentary trust is a terrific tool for splitting income. It works this way: A trust can be created upon your death through instructions in your will. All or a portion of your assets would be transferred to the trust upon your death, and your intended heirs would be the beneficiaries of the trust.

Any investment income earned on the inheritance each year may now be taxed in the trust, rather than in the hands of your beneficiaries. You see, the trust is considered to be a separate person for tax purposes and will be taxed at the same graduated tax rates as any individual. Rather than adding any investment income directly to the beneficiary's income where it will be taxed at his or her marginal tax rate—very likely between 35 and 45 percent—simply split income with the trust by having the trust pay tax on the income instead, at graduated rates.

*R*ic died last year and left assets directly to his wife Shirley, now living in Kelowna, BC. Ric's assets generate $60,000 annually in investment income for Shirley. Since Shirley already has income of $60,000 annually from other sources, she now has $120,000 of income to report on her tax return each year. The tax bill to Shirley is going to total $34,719 in 2008. Ric could have done things differently. He could have set up a testamentary trust for Shirley through his will upon his death, and Shirley would be enjoying the benefits of splitting income with the trust. In this case, the trust would now be paying tax on the $60,000 earned on the inheritance each year, while Shirley would continue to pay tax on her other income. But the combined total tax bill between Shirley and the trust would be just $25,392—a full $9,327 less than without the trust! By the way, that's $9,327 in tax savings each year. Now that's something worth writing home about!

When setting up a testamentary trust, the option exists to have the income of the trust taxed in the hands of the beneficiary in any given year. This is done by *paying* the income to the beneficiary or by making it *payable* to the beneficiary. And this may be a good idea if, for example, the beneficiary has little or no other income and will enjoy the first $9,600 (in 2008) of income tax-free due to the basic personal amount.

The reason for the tax savings with the testamentary trust is simple: Both Shirley and the trust are entitled to low marginal tax rates on the first $37,885 of income. By having both Shirley and the trust paying tax, the number of dollars taxed in the lowest tax bracket is multiplied. Your tax savings may not be as high as in the example I've given here, but savings of up to about $15,990 (a Canada-wide average) each year are possible. The actual amount will depend on your income and province of residence.

Here are some last thoughts: You may want to set up a separate trust for each beneficiary, to maximize the number of dollars that can be taxed in the lowest bracket. The trusts would provide that income may accumulate in the trusts, and that tax-free capital distributions could be made to beneficiaries.

TO MAKE A LONG STORY SHORT:

- A testamentary trust provides an opportunity for your heirs to split income with the trust, maximizing the number of dollars that will be taxed in the lowest tax bracket.

- Setting up a testamentary trust must be done in your will.

- The tax savings can be up to about $15,990 (a Canada-wide average) annually, depending on your income level and your province of residence.

Tim's Tip 103: Consider an alter ego trust for probate savings and other benefits.

I've often wondered what life would be like if I could clone myself. I could do all those things I'm not crazy about doing—like mowing the lawn, painting the fence, and massaging my wife's feet—while simultaneously spending the day on the golf course. The "other me"—my alter ego—could do the dirty work (not that Carolyn's feet are offensive) while I continue a schedule of rest and relaxation.

Now, what may take hundreds of years to accomplish genetically, our Department of Finance has accomplished with one stroke of the pen from a tax perspective. That's right—it's now possible to "clone" yourself under our tax law. I'm referring to an "alter ego trust," and with it, there are some definite estate planning benefits to be had.

Legislation containing this gem known as an alter ego trust received royal assent in June 2001. It's a trust that can be set up by an individual after 1999 provided he or she has reached age 65. The terms of the trust have got to provide that the individual establishing the trust (the settlor) is alone entitled to all of the income of the trust earned before his or her death. And there's more. The trust must also provide that no one other than the individual is entitled to receive any of the capital of the trust before the individual's death. When the trust agreement is prepared, the contingent beneficiaries to receive the income and/or the capital of the trust after the settlor dies, are named.

Generally, when you transfer legal and beneficial ownership of assets to a trust (or to anyone other than a spouse, for that matter), you're deemed to have sold those assets at fair market value. This can give rise to a taxable capital gain, and a tax hit, where the assets have appreciated in value. In the case of an alter ego trust, transferring property to the trust won't give rise to a taxable disposition (unless you elect that the disposition should take place at fair market value). In addition, the clock for the 21-year rule (which deems the property of a trust to have been disposed of on the trust's twenty-first anniversary) won't start ticking until your death in the case of an alter ego trust.

At the time of your death, there will also be a deemed disposition at fair market value of the property of the trust—just as there would have been if you had continued to own the property directly.

There are at least four potential estate planning benefits to an alter ego trust:

- **Probate fee savings.** Transferring assets to an alter ego trust results in a change in legal and beneficial ownership of those assets. The bottom line? The assets fall outside of your estate and you'll avoid probate fees on those assets upon your death.

- **Compulsory succession avoided.** It may be possible for your will to be contested after your death if you leave behind an unhappy family member or two. An alter ego trust can avoid this problem by passing assets outside of your will. The trust cannot be challenged nearly as easily.
- **Power of attorney replacement.** An alter ego trust can name a successor trustee and/or provide other direction in the event of your mental incapacity. In this way, your property in the trust will be looked after if you can't handle it.
- **Privacy preserved.** When your will is probated, it becomes a public document, along with the value of your estate. The alter ego trust offers privacy both before and after your death.

By the way, it's also possible to set up the same type of trust for you and your spouse or common-law partner jointly. The same rules apply, except that both of you will be named beneficiaries of the trust and the deemed disposition at death will not take place until the second of you dies. This type of trust is referred to as a *joint partner trust* rather than an alter ego trust—but they're basically the same thing.

TO MAKE A LONG STORY SHORT:

- An alter ego or joint partner trust can be created after 1999 by those 65 or older.
- There is no taxable disposition when transferring assets to the trust.
- These trusts have four key benefits: minimizing probate fees; avoiding compulsory succession; replacing a power of attorney; and protecting privacy.

Tim's Tip 104: **Give to charity and save a bundle. But do it properly!**

Let's face it, one of the joys of giving to charity is seeing your donations put to good use, so you may want to consider giving to charity during your lifetime. And if you want to avoid probate fees, giving to charity today is going to help, since you'll no longer own those assets on the date of your death. Having said this, making a donation upon your death could go a long way toward reducing any tax bill you might face at that time. Regardless of whether you plan to make your donations during your lifetime, after your death, or a bit of both, why not give in a manner that's going to save the most tax? There are three out-of-the-ordinary methods of giving to charity that I want to talk about.

Donating Securities

The tax collector changed the rules in the 2006 federal budget to make it even easier to donate publicly traded securities to charity (including private foundations as of 2007). In fact, it now makes more sense to donate securities than cash in almost every situation when you have securities that have appreciated in value. Our tax law will allow donations for up to 75 percent of your net income annually. This increases to 100 percent in the year of death. And if your donations exceed this amount in the year of death, the excess can be carried back and claimed in the year before your death—up to 100 percent of your income in that year as well. Now, consider an example to show how donating securities (stocks, bonds, mutual funds, exchangeable securities, and other securities) can work to your advantage.

*B*ernadette owned shares in XYZ Corporation on the date of her death. XYZ is traded on the Toronto Stock Exchange, and the shares were worth $25,000 on the date she died, but she had paid just $10,000 for the shares a few years earlier. These shares were deemed to have been disposed of upon Bernadette's death, which would have triggered a $15,000 capital gain and a tax bill of about $3,375 if she had not left the shares to charity. Bernadette, however, left instructions in her will for her executor to donate these shares to her favourite charity after her death. The result is that the $15,000 gain is not taxable at all! That's right, the $15,000 gain will not be subject to tax. Normally, one-half of the gain would have been taxable under the usual capital gains rules. To top it off, a donation credit will be provided based on the $25,000 fair market value of the shares. This credit will be claimed on Bernadette's final tax return and will amount to about $10,000 in tax savings (varying slightly by province and income level).

Caution!

There are two things to remember if you're going to set up a charitable remainder trust. First, the trust will be irrevocable—once it's set up, there's no turning back. Second, transferring investments to a charitable remainder trust could trigger a taxable capital gain if those investments have appreciated in value. The donation credit received from the gift, however, will soften the blow of any taxable gain.

You'll notice that Bernadette paid no tax on her capital gain, but received a donation credit of $10,000 to more than offset these taxes. The net benefit to Bernadette's estate is $10,000.

So here's the game plan: Instead of cash, consider leaving securities that have appreciated in value to your favourite charity. This can be done by leaving instructions in your will for your executor to donate specific securities to a charity of your choice. Your heirs will thank you, since the tax savings could be significant.

Establishing a Charitable Remainder Trust

With a charitable remainder trust (CRT), you can donate certain investments to a trust during your lifetime. Your favourite charity is named as the capital beneficiary of the trust so that, upon your death, or upon the death of a surviving spouse, the investments pass to the charity. During your lifetime, you're entitled to all income generated by the investments in the trust. You get tax relief right away for the investments you have transferred to the trust. The value of the donation credit is determined by an actuarial calculation based on your age and interest rates. The older you are, the greater the tax credit when setting up a CRT.

Giving Life Insurance

There are generally three ways to help your favourite charity with life insurance: (1) make the charity the beneficiary of your policy; (2) transfer ownership of a policy to the charity and make the charity the beneficiary; or (3) make your estate the beneficiary and leave instructions in your will for a donation to be made to charity.

In the first scenario, you'll be entitled to claim a donation credit on your final tax return as a result of designating the charity as beneficiary of the policy you own. This was not the case prior to the 2000 federal budget, but this change has made things better for all deaths after 1998. This credit could go a long way to reducing your tax bill in the year of your death. I like this option most of the three listed here.

In scenario two, transferring ownership of a policy will provide you with a donation credit for any cash value that exists at the time of transfer, plus a credit for any premiums paid by you after that date. Sorry, you won't receive a credit for the death benefit when it's paid to the charity upon your death. There may be a tax hit on any cash surrender value that exceeds the cost base of the policy in this scenario, but the donation credit should outweigh this.

Scenario three used to be my favourite because it provided the most tax relief—but not any more. The drawbacks of naming your estate as beneficiary and then leaving instructions in your will to donate the cash to charity are these: (1) probate fees will be due on the amount of the life insurance, and (2) if your will is contested, the charity may never get the money you intend it to receive. Now that a credit is provided for directly designating a charity as the beneficiary of a life insurance policy you own (the first scenario), it makes much more sense to simply make this designation in the policy.

TO MAKE A LONG STORY SHORT:

- Giving to charity during your lifetime or upon death can provide significant tax savings. Making donations during your lifetime will also save probate fees.

- Consider donating securities instead of cash.

- Consider a charitable remainder trust or life insurance as tax-efficient ways to help your favourite charity.

Providing Tax-Free Death Benefits

Tim's Tip 105: Use life insurance to soften the blow of a tax bill at the time of your death.

Sometimes, avoiding a tax hit on death is impossible. In this event, life insurance may be your answer if you're hoping to leave a little more behind.

The Role of Life Insurance

The deemed disposition that I talked about in Tip 96 can leave your estate with a large enough tax bill to wipe out nearly half the assets you were hoping to leave to your heirs. Consider also the result when the second spouse in a family dies and leaves any remaining RRSP or RRIF assets to the kids: Virtually half the assets of the plan will disappear when the tax collector comes knocking.

Further, some assets can create a hefty tax bill upon your death without providing the cash for those taxes to be paid. For example, private company shares that have appreciated in value, or a vacation or rental property, can give rise to taxes, and yet it can be difficult to sell these assets in order to provide the necessary cash to pay the taxes owing.

This is where life insurance can be your friend. If you're able to estimate today your taxes upon death, you may be able to buy enough life insurance to cover the taxes owing. Remember our talk on estate freezes (Tip 98)? A freeze can help you to establish your tax bill ahead of time, which is going to make it easier for you to buy the appropriate amount of insurance.

Paying for the Insurance

Obviously your age and health will be important considerations in deciding whether this idea is for you. Life insurance may not be an option if you're in poor health or you're elderly (generally, over age 80). But even where the premiums are high, these may still cost you less than the tax bill at the time of your death. Hey, why not approach your kids or other heirs to see if they are able and willing to help cover the cost of these premiums? After all, they're the ones who stand to benefit from a reduced tax burden when you die.

People usually get a good laugh out of my suggesting that the kids pay for the life insurance. But let me tell you how to sell it to them. Your kids should think of these premiums as an investment that will lead to tax-free investment returns down the road. Suppose, for example, it's going to cost $8,000 each year in premiums for $400,000 of insurance on your life. If you've got four kids, that's $2,000 each per year. If you live for another 20 years, that's a total investment by each child of

$40,000 ($2,000 times 20 years) at which time each child would receive $100,000 tax-free ($400,000 for four children). That works out to an annual return of 8.8 percent for each child—tax-free! Of course, the sooner you die, the higher the return for your beneficiaries. Not to scare you, but you might want to check the brakes on your car on a regular basis! (Yes, I'm kidding.)

Here's one last point: There are actually many reasons to buy life insurance and covering a tax bill on death is just one of them. Other reasons to purchase life insurance might include: providing for dependants, paying off debts upon death, covering final expenses (your funeral, professional fees, etc.), equalizing an estate when you want to leave each heir an equal amount, and accomplishing certain business objectives (such as funding a buy-sell agreement, or providing funds to the business in the event that a key person dies).

TO MAKE A LONG STORY SHORT:

- Sometimes it's impossible to avoid a tax bill on death. If you want to minimize the impact of this, life insurance may be your best bet.

- Life insurance will be particularly important when you expect a tax bill on death with little cash available to pay those taxes.

- Consider asking your heirs to pick up the tab for the insurance; after all, they're the ones who will ultimately benefit.

- There are many reasons to buy life insurance and covering a tax bill on death is just one of them.

Action Step

When buying life insurance to cover your taxes owing on death, consider joint, second-to-die insurance. This is a policy that will pay out benefits upon the death of the second spouse. This insurance is easier to get since only one spouse needs to be insurable, and the premiums are generally cheaper since two events have to take place before the insurance proceeds are paid: both you and your spouse must die. This type of policy makes sense because you won't generally need the insurance until the second spouse has died. After all, there will be little tax to pay on the death of the first spouse if most assets are left to the surviving spouse.

Planning for U.S. Estate Taxes

Tim's Tip 106: Forecast your U.S. estate tax and apply nine strategies to minimize the tax bill.

Prior to changes introduced in 1995 to the Canada–U.S. tax treaty, Canadians who owned U.S. assets were subject to U.S. estate taxes on the value of those assets as figured on the date of death. A meagre $60,000 deduction from the value of those assets was provided when making the estate tax calculation. The U.S. estate tax was levied in addition to the taxes paid in Canada, if any, upon death. The result? Double taxation.

The Rules Today

Today, you could still face a tax bill, but you'll now find greater relief. Which assets are subject to U.S. estate tax? Anything considered a *U.S. situs* property, including:

- real estate (a vacation property, rental property, private home, or business property)
- shares of a U.S. corporation (public and private companies)
- debt obligations issued by U.S. residents (individuals or government)
- personal property located in the U.S. (cars, boats, jewellery, furnishings, club memberships, and more)

The tax is levied on the fair market value of these assets on the date of your death, and the tax rate for U.S. estate taxes ranges from 18 to 45 percent (in 2008 and 2009) of your U.S. assets, with most people facing a tax bill between 25 and 35 percent.

Now for the tax breaks offered: Canadian citizens residing outside of the U.S. who have worldwide estates of $1.2 million (U.S.) or less will only be subject to U.S. estate taxes on certain U.S. property. For the most part, this property will include real estate, business assets when a permanent establishment is maintained in the U.S., and resource properties. But that's not all. Canadians will be entitled to a unified credit of up to $780,800 in 2008. This credit can be used to offset, dollar for dollar, the U.S. estate tax bill otherwise owing and effectively shelter from estate tax the first $2 million of U.S. assets in 2008. In actual fact, Canadians won't generally receive the full credit of $780,800 since it's prorated based on the percentage of total assets located in the United States.

---

*L*ynda owned a condominium in Colorado worth $300,000 (U.S.) on the date of her death in 2008. Her total assets upon death were valued at $3,000,000 (U.S.). Lynda's U.S. estate taxes were calculated to be $87,800 (U.S.) before the unified credit. The unified credit that she was able to claim was $78,080, calculated as follows: $780,800 × $300,000/3,000,000. Lynda's total estate tax bill was $9,720 (U.S.) ($87,800 minus $78,080).

The unified credit is reduced when only some of your assets are located in the U.S., and this will be the case for most Canadians. You'll be glad to know that an additional marital property credit of up to $780,800 is available in 2008 if you leave your U.S. assets to your spouse upon your death. Further, you generally won't have to worry about the double-taxation problem any more, since any U.S. estate taxes paid will typically be eligible for a foreign tax credit in Canada (that is, the U.S. estate taxes paid can be used to reduce your Canadian tax bill in the year of death). You should note that the rules for a U.S. citizen who happens to be living in Canada are slightly different, but if you're in this boat you'll be eligible for similar tax relief.

Minimizing U.S. Estate Taxes

Try these nine ideas on for size to minimize the impact of U.S. estate taxes:

- Keep your U.S. assets below $1.2 million to avoid estate tax on all but your U.S. real estate and a couple of other uncommon U.S. assets.
- Consider holding your U.S. assets (other than real estate) inside a Canadian corporation.

Action Step

Okay, here's some advice for those of you who have a sense of humour and are likely to pay U.S. estate taxes in the year of your death. Given that the current law in the U.S. has scrapped the U.S. estate tax for the year 2010 only, you could save yourself a bundle by dying in that year! Apart from this strategy, the next best way to completely avoid U.S. estate taxes is by never dying at all!

- Give property to your spouse and children over time, since each person is entitled to his or her own unified credit.
- Share ownership of U.S. assets with someone else.
- Buy life insurance to cover any U.S. estate tax liability.
- Restructure your debt so that non-recourse loans are secured by your U.S. assets, since this debt will reduce the value of your taxable estate.
- Move your U.S. assets back to Canada.
- Leave your U.S. property to a qualified domestic trust (QDOT). This type of trust does not eliminate U.S. estate tax but can defer it until the death of the second spouse.
- Rent instead of owning. You're not going to pay estate tax on assets you don't own, so consider renting a place in your favourite location down south rather than buying.

U.S. Estate Tax Repeal

You might have heard that estate taxes in the U.S. have now been scrapped. While it's true that on June 7, 2001, President George W. Bush did sign the *Economic Growth and Tax Relief Reconciliation Act of 2001*, this won't mean much estate tax relief for most. You see, the estate tax will be reduced slightly between now and the year 2010. In 2010, the tax will be scrapped altogether—but only for that one year. The legislation that scraps the estate tax is itself repealed in 2011, so that the estate tax will apply again in 2011 and later years. In order for the estate tax to be repealed permanently after 2010, new legislation will have to be enacted before that time. The U.S. senate is currently debating about final changes to the estate tax, so speak to a tax professional for more details about the current status of the tax.

TO MAKE A LONG STORY SHORT:

- U.S. estate taxes will apply to any *U.S. situs* property you own on the date of your death.

- Recent changes in the Canada–U.S. tax treaty make this estate tax blow easier to take, but you still need to plan.

- Apply one or more of the nine most common strategies to minimize U.S. estate tax.

- New legislation has scrapped the U.S. estate tax—but only for the year 2010 at this point. Plan your affairs as though the estate tax may still apply.

Getting into the Game

Maybe you can't take it with you, but you can certainly have a say in where it goes after you're gone. Start now by turning to the Tax Planning Tip Sheet at the front of the book and reviewing the tips for Chapter 9. Ask yourself, "Can this tip apply to me?" Your *Yes* and *Not Sure* answers could lead to big tax savings for your estate—and that's good news for you, your heirs, and your favourite charitable causes.

Glossary of Abbreviations

ABIL	allowable business investment loss		**IPP**	Individual Pension Plan
ACB	adjusted cost base		**IRA**	Individual Retirement Account
CCA	capital cost allowance		**LSVCC**	Labour-sponsored venture capital corporation
CCPC	Canadian-controlled private corporation		**OAS**	Old Age Security
CESG	Canada Education Savings Grant		**PA**	Pension adjustment
CGRM	Capital gains refund mechanism		**QDOT**	Qualified domestic trust
CICA	The Canadian Institute of Chartered Accountants		**QPP**	Quebec Pension Plan
CNIL	cumulative net investment loss		**QSBC**	Qualified small business corporation
CPP	Canada Pension Plan		**QST**	Quebec Sales Tax
CRA	Canada Revenue Agency		**RDSP**	Registered Disability Savings Plan
DPSP	Deferred Profit Sharing Plan		**RESP**	Registered Education Savings Plan
EI	Employment Insurance		**RPP**	Registered Pension Plan
GAAR	general anti-avoidance rule		**RRIF**	Registered Retirement Income Fund
GIC	Guaranteed Investment Certificate		**RRSP**	Registered Retirement Savings Plan
GST	Goods and Services Tax		**SAR**	Stock appreciation right
HBP	Home Buyer's Plan		**SIN**	Social Insurance Number
HST	Harmonized Sales Tax		**TFSA**	Tax-free savings account
			TONI	Tax-on-income system

TAX FACTS

Marginal Tax Rates for 2008

These tables will help you determine your 2008 marginal tax rate and the amount of tax you will owe for 2008.

Your Marginal Tax Rate

When it comes to tax planning, this is probably the most important number for you to understand. It will help you to calculate both your tax savings from a deduction and your after-tax investment returns. It will also tell you how much tax you will pay on your last dollar of income. For example, if you live in Alberta and your taxable income is between $37,885 and $75,769, you'll pay tax of 32 percent on your next dollar of regular or interest income, 16 percent on your next dollar of capital gains, and 17.70 percent on your next dollar of Canadian ineligible dividends. Eligible dividends will face tax at 5.85 percent. Foreign dividends are taxed at the same rate as regular income.

Your Tax Balance Owing

These tables will also help you to calculate how much tax you'll have to pay in 2008. All you have to do find the table for your province, then look in the left column of the table and find the figure that comes closest to your taxable income without going over your actual taxable income. This is your tax bracket. Now it's easy to calculate your actual tax bill. Consider Glenda's example.

Glenda lives in British Columbia and had taxable income of $47,885 in 2008. How much tax will Glenda have to pay for 2008? First, she will find the tax table for B.C. Next, she'll find her tax bracket by looking at the column on the left for the figure that comes closest to her taxable income without going over her income. Her tax bracket starts at $37,885 in B.C. in 2008. Her marginal tax rate on regular income is 29.98 percent (second column in the table). Glenda will pay taxes of $5,825 on her first $37,885 (the column on the far right). On her next $10,000 ($47,885 minus $37,885), she will pay taxes of $2,998 ($10,000 times 29.98 percent). Glenda's total tax bill for 2008 will be $8,823 ($5,825 plus $2,998). This tax balance takes into account the basic personal credit and all provincial surtaxes and tax reductions, but no other credits.

Marginal Tax Rates for 2008

BRITISH COLUMBIA 2008

Marginal Tax Rates (%)

Taxable Income Bracket[1]	Interest and Regular Income[2]	Capital Gains[3]	Canadian Eligible Dividends[4]	Canadian Ineligible Dividends[4]	Tax Owing Up to Bracket[5]
$ —	—	—	—	—	—
9,600	15.00	7.50	(5.75)	2.08	—
16,035	23.84	11.92	(10.33)	6.75	965
26,000	20.24	10.12	(15.55)	2.25	3,341
35,016	22.98	11.49	(11.58)	5.68	5,166
37,885	29.98	14.99	(1.43)	14.43	5,825
70,033	32.50	16.25	2.22	17.58	15,463
75,769	36.50	18.25	8.03	22.58	17,327
80,406	38.29	19.15	10.62	24.81	19,020
97,636	40.70	20.35	14.11	27.83	25,617
123,184	43.70	21.85	18.47	31.58	36,015

ALBERTA 2008

Marginal Tax Rates (%)

Taxable Income Bracket[1]	Interest and Regular Income[2]	Capital Gains[3]	Canadian Eligible Dividends[4]	Canadian Ineligible Dividends[4]	Tax Owing Up to Bracket[5]
$ —	—	—	—	—	—
9,600	15.00	7.50	(5.75)	2.08	—
16,161	25.00	12.50	(4.30)	8.95	984
37,885	32.00	16.00	5.85	17.70	6,415
75,769	36.00	18.00	11.65	22.70	18,538
123,184	39.00	19.50	16.00	26.46	35,607

SASKATCHEWAN 2008

Marginal Tax Rates (%)

Taxable Income Bracket[1]	Interest and Regular Income[2]	Capital Gains[3]	Canadian Eligible Dividends[4]	Canadian Ineligible Dividends[4]	Tax Owing Up to Bracket[5]
$ —	—	—	—	—	—
8,945	11.00	5.50	—	6.25	—
9,600	26.00	13.00	(5.75)	8.33	72
37,885	33.00	16.50	4.40	17.08	7,426

Continued...

SASKATCHEWAN 2008

(Cont'd)

Marginal Tax Rates (%)

Taxable Income Bracket[1]	Interest and Regular Income[2]	Capital Gains[3]	Canadian Eligible Dividends[4]	Canadian Ineligible Dividends[4]	Tax Owing Up to Bracket[5]
39,135	35.00	17.50	7.30	19.58	7,839
75,769	39.00	19.50	13.10	24.58	20,661
111,814	41.00	20.50	16.00	27.08	34,718
123,184	44.00	22.00	20.35	30.83	39,380

MANITOBA 2008

Marginal Tax Rates (%)

Taxable Income Bracket[1]	Interest and Regular Income[2]	Capital Gains[3]	Canadian Eligible Dividends[4]	Canadian Ineligible Dividends[4]	Tax Owing Up to Bracket[5]
$ —	—	—	—	—	—
9,250	11.90	5.95	1.31	10.94	—
9,600	26.90	13.45	(4.44)	13.02	42
22,500	25.90	12.95	(5.89)	11.77	3,512
30,544	27.75	13.88	(3.21)	14.08	5,595
37,885	34.75	17.37	6.94	22.83	7,632
66,000	39.40	19.70	13.68	28.64	17,402
75,769	43.40	21.70	19.48	33.64	21,251
123,184	46.40	23.20	23.83	37.40	41,829

ONTARIO 2008

Marginal Tax Rates (%)

Taxable Income Bracket[1]	Interest and Regular Income[2]	Capital Gains[3]	Canadian Eligible Dividends[4]	Canadian Ineligible Dividends[4]	Tax Owing Up to Bracket[5]
$ —	—	—	—	—	—
9,600	15.00	7.50	(5.75)	2.08	—
11,820	27.10	13.55	(8.51)	4.38	333
14,960	21.05	10.53	(7.13)	3.23	1,184
36,020	24.15	12.08	(2.63)	7.11	5,617
37,885	31.15	15.58	7.52	15.86	6,067
63,430	32.98	16.49	8.14	16.87	14,025
72,041	35.39	17.70	11.64	19.88	16,865
74,720	39.41	19.70	13.81	22.59	17,813
75,769	43.41	21.70	19.61	27.59	18,226
123,184	46.41	23.20	23.96	31.34	38,809

QUEBEC 2008

Marginal Tax Rates (%)

Taxable Income Bracket[1]	Interest and Regular Income[2]	Capital Gains[3]	Canadian Eligible Dividends[4]	Canadian Ineligible Dividends[4]	Tax Owing Up to Bracket[5]
$ —	—	—	—	—	—
9,600	12.53	6.26	(4.80)	1.74	—
12,769	28.53	14.27	1.14	11.74	397
37,500	32.53	16.27	6.94	16.74	7,451
37,885	38.37	19.18	15.42	24.05	7,577
75,000	42.37	21.19	29.05	21.22	21,818
75,769	45.71	22.85	26.06	33.22	22,144
123,184	48.22	24.11	29.69	36.35	43,817

NEW BRUNSWICK 2008

Marginal Tax Rates (%)

Taxable Income Bracket[1]	Interest and Regular Income[2]	Capital Gains[3]	Canadian Eligible Dividends[4]	Canadian Ineligible Dividends[4]	Tax Owing Up to Bracket[5]
$ —	—	—	—	—	—
8,817	15.12	7.56	4.52	12.27	—
9,600	30.12	15.06	(1.23)	14.35	119
9,660	25.12	12.56	(8.48)	8.10	137
34,836	30.48	15.24	(0.70)	15.24	6,461
37,885	37.48	18.74	9.45	23.55	7,391
69,673	38.80	19.40	25.20	11.36	19,305
75,769	42.80	21.40	17.16	30.20	21,670
113,273	43.95	21.98	18.83	31.64	37,722
123,184	46.95	23.48	23.18	35.40	42,078

NOVA SCOTIA 2008

Marginal Tax Rates (%)

Taxable Income Bracket[1]	Interest and Regular Income[2]	Capital Gains[3]	Canadian Eligible Dividends[4]	Canadian Ineligible Dividends[4]	Tax Owing Up to Bracket[5]
$ —	—	—	—	—	—
9,600	15.00	7.50	(5.75)	2.08	—
11,150	23.79	11.90	(5.83)	3.44	233
15,000	28.79	14.40	1.42	9.69	1,149

Continued...

NOVA SCOTIA 2008

(Cont'd)

Marginal Tax Rates (%)

Taxable Income Bracket[1]	Interest and Regular Income[2]	Capital Gains[3]	Canadian Eligible Dividends[4]	Canadian Ineligible Dividends[4]	Tax Owing Up to Bracket[5]
21,000	23.79	11.90	(5.83)	3.44	2,898
29,590	29.95	14.97	3.10	11.14	4,941
37,178	36.95	18.48	13.25	19.89	7,214
59,180	38.67	19.33	15.74	22.04	15,344
74,357	42.67	21.34	21.54	27.04	21,213
80,972	44.34	22.17	22.67	28.16	24,036
93,000	45.25	22.63	23.99	29.31	29,369
123,184	48.25	24.13	28.35	33.06	42,897

PRINCE EDWARD ISLAND 2008

Marginal Tax Rates (%)

Taxable Income Bracket[1]	Interest and Regular Income[2]	Capital Gains[3]	Canadian Eligible Dividends[4]	Canadian Ineligible Dividends[4]	Tax Owing Up to Bracket[5]
$ —	—	—	—	—	—
9,600	15.00	7.50	(5.75)	2.08	—
10,260	24.80	12.40	(6.77)	8.95	99
31,984	28.80	14.40	(0.97)	13.95	5,737
37,885	35.80	17.90	9.18	22.70	7,436
63,969	38.70	19.35	13.38	26.33	16,774
75,769	42.70	21.35	19.19	31.33	21,341
98,143	44.37	22.19	20.09	32.88	30,895
123,184	47.37	23.69	24.44	36.63	42,005

NEWFOUNDLAND AND LABRADOR 2008

Marginal Tax Rates (%)

Taxable Income Bracket[1]	Interest and Regular Income[2]	Capital Gains[3]	Canadian Eligible Dividends[4]	Canadian Ineligible Dividends[4]	Tax Owing Up to Bracket[5]
$ —	—	—	—	—	—
7,566	8.20	4.10	2.25	4.00	—
9,600	23.20	11.60	(3.50)	6.08	167
30,215	28.30	14.15	3.90	12.46	4,949
37,885	35.30	17.65	14.05	21.21	7,120

NEWFOUNDLAND AND LABRADOR 2008

Marginal Tax Rates (%)

Taxable Income Bracket[1]	Interest and Regular Income[2]	Capital Gains[3]	Canadian Eligible Dividends[4]	Canadian Ineligible Dividends[4]	Tax Owing Up to Bracket[5]
60,429	38.00	19.00	17.96	24.58	15,078
75,769	42.00	21.00	23.76	29.58	20,907
123,184	45.00	22.50	28.11	33.33	40,822

NORTHWEST TERRITORIES 2008

Marginal Tax Rates (%)

Taxable Income Bracket[1]	Interest and Regular Income[2]	Capital Gains[3]	Canadian Eligible Dividends[4]	Canadian Ineligible Dividends[4]	Tax Owing Up to Bracket[5]
$ —	—	—	—	—	—
9,600	15.00	7.50	(5.75)	2.08	—
12,355	20.90	10.45	(13.87)	1.96	413
35,986	23.60	11.80	(9.96)	5.33	5,352
37,885	30.60	15.30	0.19	14.08	5,800
71,973	34.20	17.10	5.41	18.58	16,231
75,769	38.20	19.10	11.21	23.58	17,529
117,011	40.05	20.02	13.89	25.89	33,284
123,184	43.05	21.53	18.24	29.65	35,756

NUNAVUT 2008

Marginal Tax Rates (%)

Taxable Income Bracket[1]	Interest and Regular Income[2]	Capital Gains[3]	Canadian Eligible Dividends[4]	Canadian Ineligible Dividends[4]	Tax Owing Up to Bracket[5]
$ —	—	—	—	—	—
9,600	15.00	7.50	(5.75)	2.08	—
11,360	19.00	9.50	(8.94)	2.08	264
37,885	29.00	14.50	5.56	14.58	5,304
75,769	35.00	17.50	14.26	22.08	16,290
123,184	40.50	20.25	22.24	28.96	32,885

YUKON 2008					
	Marginal Tax Rates (%)				
Taxable Income Bracket[1]	**Interest and Regular Income[2]**	**Capital Gains[3]**	**Canadian Eligible Dividends[4]**	**Canadian Ineligible Dividends[4]**	**Tax Owing Up to Bracket[5]**
$ —	—	—	—	—	—
9,600	16.41	8.20	(6.90)	2.73	9
14,927	22.04	11.02	(11.49)	5.32	874
15,000	25.04	12.52	(7.14)	9.07	890
25,000	22.04	11.02	(11.49)	5.32	3,394
37,885	31.68	15.84	2.49	17.37	6,234
75,769	37.44	18.72	10.84	24.57	18,236
78,755	38.01	19.01	10.87	25.01	19,354
123,184	42.40	21.20	17.23	30.49	36,242

Notes:

1. This column indicates the amount of taxable income at which particular tax rates apply.

2. This column shows the marginal tax rates that apply to interest and regular income (which includes most other types of income such as net rental, net business, pension income, and more).

3. This column shows the marginal tax rate on capital gains, and already takes into account the 50-percent inclusion rate for capital gains.

4. This column shows the marginal tax rate on actual dividends, both eligible and ineligible, from taxable Canadian corporations. Dividends from foreign corporations are taxed at regular income rates.

5. This column shows the amount of tax owing for interest and regular income up to the beginning of the tax bracket indicated. The calculation takes into account the basic personal credit and all provincial surtaxes and tax reductions, but no other credits.

Federal Personal Tax Rates for 2008

Your total tax bill is made up of both federal and provincial taxes. The following table shows the federal component only. For the provincial personal tax rates, see the next section. Your federal tax rate is applied to the taxable income figure on line 260 of your tax return.

FEDERAL PERSONAL TAX RATES FOR 2008

Taxable Income			Tax Payable
$ —	to	$37,885	15% of income
$37,886	to	$75,769	$5,683 plus 22% on income over $37,885
$75,770	to	$123,184	$14,017 plus 26% on income over $75,769
$123,185	and	over	$26,345 plus 29% on income over $123,184

Note:

1. The tax amounts shown are before any credits, which will reduce taxes owing. In particular, the basic personal credit will eliminate taxes on the first $9,600 of income and will reduce taxes owing by $1,440. There is no federal surtax.

Provincial Personal Tax Rates for 2008

By the year 2001, all provinces and territories had moved to the new tax-on-income (TONI) system. Provinces and territories used to calculate tax based on a percentage of federal tax (a tax-on-tax system). Today, all jurisdictions calculate tax based on taxable income (tax-on-income, or TONI system).

I discussed in Chapter 8 the key tax changes introduced in each province and territory, and detailed the tax brackets and highest marginal tax rates in each jurisdiction. Turn to Chapter 8 for those details.

Federal Personal Tax Credits for 2008

The following represent the most common personal tax credits available. The base amount is the amount on which the federal credit is calculated. Each province generally offers similar tax credits.

FEDERAL PERSONAL TAX CREDITS FOR 2008		
	Federal Base Amount	Federal Credit (15%)
Basic personal credit	$9,600	$1,440
Married or equivalent[1]	$9,600	$1,440
Dependants over 18 and infirm[2]	$4,095	$614
Age credit[3]	$5,276	$791
Disability credit	$7,021	$1,053
Caregiver credit[4]	$4,095	$614

Notes:

1. Reduced by every $1 of dependant's net income.
2. Reduced by dependant's net income in excess of $5,811.
3. Reduced by an amount equal to 15 percent of net income exceeding $31,524.
4. Reduced by dependant's net income in excess of $13,986.

Additional Federal Tax Credits

The following represent additional non-refundable federal tax credits that may be available. The amount of the credits is based on actual income received or expenditures incurred, as the case may be.

ADDITIONAL FEDERAL TAX CREDITS	
Pension income credit	15 percent of up to $2,000 for a maximum credit of $300
Medical expense credit	15 percent of amount in excess of: lesser of a) 3 percent of net income and b) $1,962
Tuition fee credit	15 percent of amount paid in respect to attendance at a post-secondary institution
Education amount	15 percent of $400/month of full-time ($120/month of part-time) attendance at a post-secondary institution
Textbook tax credit	15 percent of $65/month of full-time ($20/month of part-time) attendance at a post-secondary institution.
Charitable donation credit	15 percent for first $200, 29 percent of the balance; donations limited to 75 percent of net income[1]
Canada Pension Plan credit	15 percent of employee contributions
Employment insurance credit	15 percent of premiums paid
Public transit credit	15 percent of public transit costs (at least weekly passes only will qualify).
Children's fitness credit	15 percent of eligible amounts, up to $500 per child for registration in an eligible program.
Child tax credit	15 percent of $2,000 per child under 18 at the end of the year.

Note:

1. 100 percent in the year of death and the year prior to death.

Canada Pension Plan Contributions 2008

CANADA PENSION PLAN CONTRIBUTIONS 2008	
CPP maximum pensionable earnings	$44,900
Basic exemption	$3,500
Maximum contributory earnings	$41,400
Maximum contributions:	
Employees (4.95 percent)	$2,049.30
Self-employed (9.9 percent)	$4,098.60

Employment Insurance Premiums 2008

EMPLOYMENT INSURANCE PREMIUMS 2008		
Maximum insurable earnings	$41,100	
Employee maximum premium[1]:	1.73 percent x $41,100	$711
Employer maximum premium[2]:	2.42 percent x $41,100	$995

Note:

1. Maximum annual premium of $571 for Quebec (1.39 percent)
2. Equals 1.4 times the employee rate.

Dividends

The following actual amount of Canadian ineligible dividends can be received by a Canadian resident in 2008 with no tax payable, assuming no income or deductions other than the basic personal credit and dividend tax credit. For federal tax purposes, the gross-up rate for ineligible dividends is 25 percent. The federal dividend tax credit is 13.33 percent of the grossed-up dividend.

DIVIDENDS			
British Columbia	$37,770	New Brunswick	$14,110
Alberta	$23,520	Nova Scotia	$27,620
Saskatchewan	$15,750	Prince Edward Island	$13,380
Manitoba	$10,070	Newfoundland and Labrador	$15,530
Ontario	$36,460	NWT	$37,780
Quebec	$20,440	Nunavut	$37,780
		Yukon	$20,900

Old Age Security Benefits

The following amounts represent the maximum benefits available under the OAS program:

OLD AGE SECURITY BENEFITS		
2007	January to March	$491.93
	April to June	$491.93
	July to September	$497.83
	October to December	$502.31
2008	January to March	$502.31
	April to June	$502.31
	July to September	$505.83
	October to December	$516.96

For 2008, benefits are repayable if net income exceeds $64,718. The repayment is 15 percent of excess income to a maximum of the OAS received. OAS is eliminated once income reaches $104,903. A tax-free Guaranteed Income Supplement (GIS) of up to approximately $634 monthly is available for low-income individuals.

Canada Pension Plan Benefits

The following amounts represent the maximum benefits available under the CPP program:

CANADA PENSION PLAN BENEFITS 2008

	Annual Total	2008 (monthly)
Death benefit (lump sum)	$2,500.00	—
Retirement benefit	$10,614.96	$884.58
Disability benefit	$12,930.24	$1,077.52
Survivor's benefit — under 65	$5,919.36	$493.28
— over 65	$6,369.00	$530.75
Children of disabled person	$2,505.24	$208.77
Children of deceased person	$2,505.24	$208.77

RRSP Contribution Limits

The following contribution limits reflect the most recent changes announced.

RRSP CONTRIBUTION LIMITS

Year	18 percent of earned income from the prior year to a maximum of:
2008	$20,000
2009	$21,000
2010	$22,000
2011	indexed

Minimum Annual RRIF Withdrawals

Minimum annual withdrawals from a registered retirement income fund (RRIF) are based on the value of the assets inside the RRIF on January 1 each year. Simply find the appropriate percentage in the table below and multiply it by the value in the RRIF on January 1. RRIFs established before 1993 are generally *qualifying RRIFs* and annuitants should use the right-hand column, below.

The appropriate age for this calculation is your age at the start of January 1 each year. If you are under age 65, the formula to calculate your minimum withdrawal percentage is 1 *divided by* (90 *minus* your age).

MINIMUM ANNUAL RRIF WITHDRAWALS (%)					
Age	General	Pre-1993 Qualifying RRIFs	Age	General	Pre-1993 Qualifying RRIFs
65	4.00	4.00	81	8.99	8.99
66	4.17	4.17	82	9.27	9.27
67	4.35	4.35	83	9.58	9.58
68	4.55	4.55	84	9.93	9.93
69	4.76	4.76	85	10.33	10.33
70	5.00	5.00	86	10.79	10.79
71	7.38	5.26	87	11.33	11.33
72	7.48	5.56	88	11.96	11.96
73	7.59	5.88	89	12.71	12.71
74	7.71	6.25	90	13.62	13.62
75	7.85	6.67	91	14.73	14.73
76	7.99	7.14	92	16.12	16.12
77	8.15	7.69	93	17.92	17.92
78	8.33	8.33	94 or older	20.00	20.00
79	8.53	8.53			
80	8.75	8.75			

Index

A

ABIL (allowable business investment loss), 171–172

accident insurance, 74

active family benefit, 260

Adamson v. The Queen, 53

addictions, 73

adoption tax credit, 263

adult children

    income splitting strategies, 24–25, 26

    principal residence exemption, 50

advertising, 127

age and infirm dependants amounts, 265

age credit

    2008 federal amounts, xx, 302

    pension income splitting and, 236

    in Quebec, 263

    transfer of, 29

aircraft expenses, 90

air miles, 76, 79

Alberta

    2008 tax changes, 259

    health care, 134

    ineligible dividends limits, 304

    marginal tax rates, 295

alimony, 246

allowable business investment loss (ABIL), 171–172

allowances

    for automobiles, 98–99

    to children, 25

alter ego trusts, 39, 280–282

alternative medicine practitioners, 265

Alternative Minimum Tax (AMT), 211

annuities

    prescribed, 177–179

    RRSP purchase of, 230–231

artists, 92

assessments

    disputing, 12–14

    promises of CRA, xxxii

assets

    capital cost allowance claims, 123–124

    disposition upon death, 270

    in divorce, 60–61, 63

    estate freeze, 272–273

    giving away, 271–272

    non-compete provision, xxx–xxxi

    purchase from employer, 73

    swapping, 23

    transfer of, 20–21, 33

    in U.S., 255–256, 288–291

    when leaving Canada, 26–27

    See also non-registered assets

assistant's salary, 90, 92

attendant care deduction, 58

attribution rules, 20–21

    automobiles

    2008 expense limit changes, xxii

    2008 logbook changes, xxvii

    allowances for self-employed, 127

    expenses, 90, 98–101

    loans as employer benefit, 82

    provided by employer, 94–97

    purchase from employer, 73

    self-employment deductions,

HST, 134
ineligible dividends limits, 304
marginal tax rates, 297–298
Nunavut
2008 tax changes, 267
automobile allowance, xxii, 98, 127
ineligible dividends limits, 304
marginal tax rates, 299
payroll taxes, 134

O

OAS (Old Age Security)
claiming RRSP contributions, 215
clawback minimization, 168, 169
clawbacks, 31, 157, 163
dividend transfer and, 31
leaving Canada, 246
maximum benefits, 304
office rent, 91
Ontario
2008 tax changes, 261–262
health care, 134
ineligible dividends limits, 304
marginal tax rates, 296
payroll taxes, 134
Opco, xxxi
open money. See non-registered assets
operating cost benefits, 95–96
option strategies, 156
Overs v. The Queen, 131–132

P

partnerships
about, 113–114
income splitting and, 32
incorporating, 116
Specified Investment Flow-Through,

xxv
year-ends, 117–119
payroll taxes, 134
penalties, 14–15
pension adjustment (PA), 102, 239
pension adjustment reversals, 240
pension income
splitting with spouse, 234–238
transfer of, 30
from U.S., 245
pension tax credit
income splitting and, 236
in Nova Scotia, 265
in Nunavut, 267
pension transfer and, 30
in Quebec, 263
transfer of, 29
personal counselling, 73
personal expenses, 126
personal services business expenses,
126–127
personal tax credits. See tax credits
phantom stock plans, 88
phone monthly charges, 90
PHSPs (private health services plans),
74–75, 127
pipelines, xxix
portfolios. See assets; investments; non-
registered assets
preferred shares, 139
prepaid expenses, 126
prescribed areas, xxii, 72–73
prescription drug plans, 74–75
Prévost Car (2008 TCC 231), xxxi
PriceWaterhouseCooper, xxv
primary caregiver tax credit, 261
Prince Edward Island

WaterStreet
FAMILY WEALTH COUNSEL

THE FIRM

The WaterStreet Group Inc. is one of Canada's most prominent Family Office firms. We provide a broad array of services to some of the wealthiest families in the country. Our real value comes from providing independent, objective advice in a multi-disciplined approach. Our Family Office practice is carried on under the name of WaterStreet Family Wealth Counsel. The core capabilities that we possess fall in the areas of investment consulting, risk management, integrated planning, strategic philanthropy, family continuity, and family administration.

Tel: 905-332-4455
Toll-free: 1-877-974-7687
Fax: 905-332-5955
www.waterstreet.ca

ABOUT THE AUTHOR

Tim Cestnick, FCA, CPA, CFP, TEP, is the best-selling author of *The Tax Freedom Zone, Winning the Tax Game, Winning the Estate Planning Game,* and *Winning the Education Savings Game,* and is co-author of *Death & Taxes* and *Your Family's Money.* Tim is a frequent guest in the national media. He writes a weekly column in the *Globe and Mail* and regularly appears on *Canada AM, BNN, CBC Newsworld,* and many investment programs on both television and radio across the country.

   Tim is experienced in all areas of personal taxation, particularly those related to families, owners/managers, and U.S. personal tax. He has completed the CICA's In-Depth Tax Course and the Canadian Securities Course and is a member of the Canadian Tax Foundation and the teaching faculty of the Institute of Chartered Accountants of Ontario. Tim has also been inducted as a fellow of the Institute of Chartered Accountants of Ontario for raising the profile of, and bringing distinction to, his profession.

   After obtaining his CA designation with Deloitte & Touche, Tim became a partner at a local accounting firm, and then was managing director of national tax services at one of Canada's largest investment managers. Most recently, Tim co-founded WaterStreet Family Wealth Counsel, Canada's first and largest Multi-Family Office advisory firm.

www.waterstreet.ca
www.timcestnick.com